POVERTY CHILDREN AND THEIR LANGUAGE

POVERTY CHILDREN AND THEIR LANGUAGE:
Implications for Teaching and Treating

SOL ADLER, Ph.D.
Professor and Director
Pediatric Language Programs
Department of Audiology and Speech Pathology
University of Tennessee
Knoxville, Tennessee

Grune & Stratton, Inc.
A Subsidiary of Harcourt Brace Jovanovich, Publishers
New York   London   Toronto   Sydney   San Francisco

Grune & Stratton, Inc.
111 Fifth Avenue
New York, New York 10003

Distributed in the United Kingdom by
Academic Press, Inc. (London) Ltd.
24/48 Oval Road, London NW 1

Library of Congress Catalog Number 79-5091
International Standard Book Number 0-8089-1194-5

Printed in the United States of America

I wish to dedicate this book, with love, to my wife, Betty Tunnell Adler

Contents

Part IV: The Emerging Roles of the Speech Clinician with the Culturally Different Child

Appendices

Preface

This book, which is designed to be an introductory textbook, is addressed to a broad spectrum of professional workers, including speech/language clinicians, special educators, teachers (including preschool, Head Start, early elementary, secondary, remedial reading, and bilingual teachers).

The intent of *Poverty Children and Their Language* is to alter the attitude of the middle-class professional worker toward the lower-class or poor child. The author hopes to precipitate an attitudinal change in the worker—trained conventionally to cope with the varied problems of his cultural peer—to readjust to the valid demands of the culturally different client or student. In general, the book is concerned with the language processes of the racially, ethnically, and culturally different children who speak a variant language or dialect and who possess different mores, values, and behaviors. In particular, the text is designed to introduce professional workers to the concepts undergirding a cultural parity model and the beneficial effect of this model upon teaching and treating strategies. Furthermore, it points out that the conventional ethnocentric, compensatory, cultural disparity model generates much teacher–clinician prejudice, an attitude which has a pervading detrimental effect upon teaching and treating programs.

The fundamental premise inherent in this book is that conventional programming for the underprivileged child has failed in its mission to lead the child to the "American dream"—a better life. The poor child is still poor, and he remains undereducated. Therefore, a different strategy is apparently required. The author suggests that a bidialectal and bicultural approach be utilized *in conjunction with* the conventional "enrichment" programs; such an approach insists upon cultural parity in all educational and habilitative interactions with the child. Specifically, the philosophic goals discussed pertain to the enhanced understanding and use of the child's native mores, values, and dialect, while at the same time enriching the child's understanding of and ability to function in establishment culture.

The suggestions in this book, it should immediately be noted, *are recommended for all children*—not just culturally different and poor children. Thus, those children from all sociocultural, socioeconomic, and racial groups who are integrated into school classrooms deserve the opportunity to learn the cultural mores of their peers. Mere physical integration does not provide the vehicle; rather, it can only be achieved through instruction in relevant subject manner.

The basic thrust of the book, though, is that subject matter and acculturation will not be ingested or accomplished until effective communications occur among members, including the teacher, of different cultural groups. And to communicate effectively requires an ability to encode and decode in the same language or dialect. To do otherwise, as is generally the case today, does not permit for proper understanding of cultural differences. As pointed out in the sections dealing with verbal and nonverbal systems of communication, cultural differences between speaker and listener may create a variety of problems. Succinctly, language systems employ codes comprised of interacting linguistic symbols, suprasegmentals (mainly intonation), and gestures or movement patterns. Unless speaker and auditor mutually comprehend these codes, a communication breakdown may occur.

Nevertheless, professional workers continue to employ their own middle-class language system to communicate with children who possess different systems. Furthermore, these workers often test these children in a nonnative tongue and sometimes manifest certain behaviors during the testing which undoubtedly create a cultural "shock" that interferes significantly with test reliability. The noxious effects of such interactions have created an adverse and unhealthy relationship to the point that extremely negative concepts concerning these children (the genetic concepts of Jensen, Shockley, Herrnstein, etc.) are in danger of being institutionalized in the establishment value system.

Finally, some general comments are in order. We have unabashedly presented a political statement in our vigorous position in support of cultural pluralism. We do not believe such a position is inconsistent with our political heritage. It is, however, in conflict with much of our educational and habilitative programming; as such, we considered our discussion of this position to be essential to the acceptance of our suggested teaching-treating concepts.

Also, we have deliberately presented a one-sided view of the problem; we have not included any significant amount of information relevant to the compensatory or unicultural approach to teaching and treating programs. In our previous text, *The Health and Education of the Economically Deprived Child,* we presented such information in much detail.

As will be obvious to the reader, material from many of our articles written in past years has been incorporated in the text. In general, much has been altered to eliminate redundancy, achieve cohesiveness, and enhance the impact of the subject matter.

Previous to its publication, the material in this book was used for many years as class lecture notes in a course the author teaches at the University of Tennessee, Knoxville. Although the major student enrollment was from the department of audiology and speech pathology, undergraduate and graduate students from the disciplines of rehabilitation counseling, psychology, educational psychology (school counselors), remedial reading, special education, and education also enrolled. This multidisciplinary interaction has resulted in a unique and stimulating experience for both teacher and student.

To these students I owe a vast debt of gratitude for their comments, their criticisms, and their positive reinforcements. In particular, I would like to acknowledge the significant contributions of Michael Smith and Guy Bailey; others who have contributed are Ken Clayton, Carol Curtis, Diane File, Collette Edwards, Beth Kell, Wanda Means, Kathy Meeks, and my secretary, Debbie Blazier.

To my wife, Betty Tunnell Adler, a special thanks is tendered for her help in editing this volume, as well as my other works, and for her constant support and encouragement.

Sol Adler, Ph.D.
University of Tennessee, Knoxville

Introduction

THE POPULATION ABOUT WHOM THE BOOK IS WRITTEN

Our major concern is with poor and dialectally different black or Appalachian children; however, it should be apparent that much of what we say is equally appropriate for all poor children. Thus, we believe the lower-class Spanish- and Indian-speaking minorities as well as other linguistically different speakers (i.e., bilingual speakers) will find this volume helpful.

All poor children possess inordinate numbers and types of different speech and language disorders in addition to their dialectal or linguistic differences. It is incumbent upon educators and clinicians to distinguish between these communicative deficits or differences and to treat and/or teach properly these speech patterns.

It is not our intention to present inclusive and definitive examples of the black and Appalachian dialects since alteration in each dialect occurs as a function of the sociocultural heritage of the speakers. Thus, each clinician must address himself to the problem of determining which utterances are deficit and which are different for *his unique population of clients.* *

Our vigorous support of the bidialectal method of instruction is based upon our work with Head Start children and children attending our Pediatric Language Laboratory. Without exception, our work with these children *suggests* the viability of the bidialectal method developed in the text; however, it should be noted that our work is merely preliminary and that additional research needs to be generated regarding this teaching strategy.

Finally, it should be pointed out that although many of these data, opinions, and contentions of the bidialectal approach have been long recognized and understood by some linguists, linguistic anthropologists, and sociolinguists, there is unfortunately (1) much disagreement among these professionals and the disciplines they represent regarding the role of the nonlinguistic specialist and (2) much confusion regarding the utilization of these ideas by the professional workers to whom this book is addressed. That differences of opinion regarding our contentions and ideas will be generated is inevitable; it is my hope that these differences will not detract from the pluralistic message that is the basis of this text.

THE POPULATION TO WHOM THE BOOK IS DIRECTED

Clinicians

Traditionally, the speech clinician has functioned as a worker who treated children or adults in rather centralized geographic locations and whose client population was frequently comprised of rather affluent, i.e., middle-class, people. By involvement in different service systems and by broadening their focus to encompass all segments of the populations the

---

*For those readers interested in more detailed dialectal analysis, the following references are recommended:

Wolfram, Walt and Christian, Donna, *Appalachian English*. Arlington, Va.: Center for Applied Linguistics, 1976.
Dillard, J. L., *Black English: Its History and Usage in the United State*. New York: Random House, 1972.
Labov, W., *Language in the Inner City: Studies in the Black English Vernacular*. Philadelphia: University of Pennsylvania Press, 1972.

clinicians can become an effective force in (1) the education of language-different children as well as in (2) the treatment of language and learning impaired children.

Personal economics will also figure in speech clinicians (and other professional workers) seeking clients in other than their traditional "markets." Increasing numbers of people are being trained in speech pathology, remedial reading, etc.; thus professional survival will make it mandatory that those workers capable of transcending their conventional training look to unorthodox programs for jobs. To this end, we envision speech clinicians becoming involved in increasing numbers of programs for the rural and inner-city poor, and the use of mobile service programs will assume increased importance as they "reach out" to these populations. Similarly, the role of the clinician will probably be expanded in preschool programs, such as Head Start, nursery and day-care Centers, and in early intervention programs for high-risk infants and children. Also, the traditional habilitative role in the schools may be expanded to include bidialectal teaching or provision of consultative help to teachers of bidialectal and bilingual programs.

Teachers

Billions of dollars have been expended in compensatory education programs; yet, poor children still remain undereducated when compared to their middle-class peers. We believe that proper motivational models are lacking in our schools for a variety of reasons, one of the most important being the communication barrier between teacher and pupil. We urge teachers, particularly those in the preschool or early elementary grades, to interface with the clinician in promoting effective bidialectal-bicultural programs in their classrooms. Our interactions with teachers who have used these techniques have been most rewarding. We see no reason why other teachers could not expand their teaching methods to include the teaching of such skills to their children. This is particularly indicated since our research suggests that standard English is learned more effectively when taught by the bidialectal method rather than through the conventional language arts curriculum.

Finally, as we note in the text, when a child does not progress properly, it is never the child who is at fault but always the teacher or clinician. We grant that this cliché has many exceptions, but it is our belief that more progress will not be manifested by many of the poor children who remain undereducated and improperly treated in our country until the current unicultural philosophy of education and habilitation is altered to a pluralistic one.

PART I

A Theoretical Framework

1

An Introduction to Cultural Parity

. . . the idea of democracy as opposed to any conception of aristocracy is that every individual must be consulted in such a way, actively not passively, that he himself becomes a part of the process of authority, of the process of social control; that his needs and wants have a chance to be registered in a way where they count in determining social policy.

—John Dewey,
Problems of Men

THE PROBLEM: THE ECOSYSTEM OF THE POOR
AND SOCIOCULTURAL ADAPTATION

Underlying the study of man is the principle that there is a reality, or several realities, to which man must adapt if he is to survive, reproduce, and perpetuate himself. Social groups must develop adaptive mechanisms if there is to be order, regularity, and predictability in their cultural patterns. Indeed, a function of cultural development is simply the acquisition of a set or sets of patterns of conduct which allows members of that culture to deal effectively with recurring problems, i.e., to adapt successfully to the existential world surrounding them. As a result, many different behavioral patterns must emerge as different subcultural groups develop the means to adapt to their unique realities. Behaviors, then,

3

should be analyzed in these terms: How successful are they in providing the means to cope with problems? Such analysis must proceed without the imposition of artifactual conclusions—without our own institutionalized concepts of right or wrong imposing themselves onto our evaluation of these different behaviors.

When the behavioral systems of culturally different and poor children are viewed from this vantage point, it becomes inescapably clear that their patterns of conduct are successful adaptations to their unique phenomenological worlds; i.e., there is order, regularity, and predictability in their behaviors which allow them to survive. In other words, the behaviors manifested by poor children are eminently suitable and proper for them if they and their social-cultural peers are to survive in the world around them. It becomes apparent, then, that to tamper with this survival mechanism is no small thing; to alter adaptive mechanisms may result in adaptive failure. Perhaps this is the reason why so many programs designed to help "uplift" the poor have failed. Such programs are "culture-centric"; they impose "standard" cultural concepts of behavior upon the culturally different without regard for the desirability or, indeed, the necessity for maintaining the "undesired" behavior.

To design effective "uplift" programs necessitates an understanding of those forces that precipitate the adaptive mechanisms; furthermore, such programming should then attempt to alter the forces or causes rather than the behaviors or effects. Finally, the alteration should proceed in a comprehensive and multifaceted manner that is related to all of the realities of the poor child's world. Health, education, and prejudice are among the foremost of these realities; poverty, however, is the real antagonist. A science of human ecology that will attack all of these causes of man's despair is required. Attempts to change only the adaptive behaviors—such as psychologic, linguistic, or familial behaviors—are probably doomed to defeat. This is particularly true when the forces precipitating these behaviors are of little concern to mainstream society.

Cultural Pluralism

The term "cultural pluralism" was originated by Horace Kallen, a philosopher and favorite student of William James at Harvard and later a close associate of John Dewey at the New School for Social Research. Kallen provided the view that if America is to retain its democratic integrity, it must provide opportunity for all of its citizens to preserve their own ethnic traditions while enjoying equal rights and the privileges of citizenship. If deviations from the standard of the day are to be considered signs of inferiority, impossible burdens will be placed upon the culturally different.

Prevailing moods of nativism initially countered this concept as it applied to emigrant white ethnic groups, but the desire to integrate into the national matrix has been generally accomplished. Likewise, nonwhite ethnic groups are confronted also by nativistic moods and goals, but they have been unable to integrate successfully into the mainstream. Racism—that is, the exploitation of ethnic differences as a badge of social inferiority—is the major problem in this instance. Many of our institutions, particularly our schools, have become nativist and racist strongholds. The middle-class standard is considered the only proper standard, and the promulgation of its values and mores are fostered so that a single life style will be produced. The establishment of a single set of norms in our schools and other institutions means that conformity is rewarded and deviance punished. Yet established norms are nothing but ruling norms—norms defended by the mainstream society. This means that the person who will be most favorably placed in society is the person who best succeeds in adapting himself to the ruling norms.

Interestingly, for the different white ethnic groups a kind of religious pluralism is replacing the traditional ethnic pluralism. For example, it is not uncommon for one Catholic church to accommodate various ethnic Catholics, whereas each group had its own cultural and religious institutions in the past. A great deal of cultural assimilation has occurred among social-class peers of the three main religious communities in this country. They agree on standards generally; the religious middle class adheres to the rules that were and have always been its standard. New rules generated by other and less prestigious groups conflict with these established rules.

The creation of a single life style is the melting-pot hypothesis in action, a melting pot that produces a single alloyed metal; *but America is not such a melting pot.* As a result, cultural pluralism argues for social cohesion through a humane regard for various traditions and stresses local unity within national diversity. It is the antithesis of the melting pot.

Adaptation

Biological evolution, that is, the process of sequential change in the forms and behavior of living things, is the classic example of adaptation. Evolution itself demonstrates that adaptation has also taken place; if adaptation had not characterized the survival and development of living forms, evolution could not have occurred.

Among animals, adaptation takes place primarily by means of genetic mutation. For humans, adaptation is also accomplished by cultural means—that is, through behavioral changes in relation to the group's total environment, its ecosystem. According to Cohen (1968), "the purpose of life is to maintain life; adaptation is life. Like all other living forms, man constantly seeks to maintain and improve his adaptations to the habitats in which he lives" (pp. 8–9). Behavioral systems constantly seek new adaptive strategies because social change never stops, and no ecosystem, habitat, or environment in which these systems thrive remains unaltered. An adaptation is deleterious only if the environment changes so drastically that the initial adaptive mechanism is incapable of accommodating, is ineffective under the new conditions.

Our contention is simply stated: such deleterious change is currently generated by culture-centric compensatory concepts which disregard this premise. Thus, a philosophy of viable cultural pluralism must be advocated; inherent in this doctrine is an insistence that each subculture generates adaptive mechanisms which are eminently suited to the ecosystem in which it exists. Rather than through compensatory programming, we should educate the culturally different with regard to their differences. In compensatory programming an attempt is made to eliminate an adaptive mechanism; in cultural pluralism, other behavioral systems are supplied. But new systems can be utilized successfully only if the facets of a new ecosystem—i.e., health, education, and welfare, or financial aid—are also provided.

In this sense, then, the entire concept of disadvantage requires reconsideration. We must ask, disadvantaged according to what criterion? What adaptive changes must nonstandard subcultures make to function well in a different ecosystem—one that is appropriate and geared to the desires of the middle and upper classes? If we continue to apply middle-class standards to all people, and if we continue to believe that all behaviors that differ from these standards are inferior or substandard, the results are likely to be disastrous. It is only by exploring and thereby uncovering the adaptive behaviors of subcultures and learning to tolerate and, indeed, respect these behavioral differences that the philosophy of cultural pluralism becomes viable and the concept of adaptation can become a successful reality.

Currently the behavioral systems are mainly being altered, but with relatively little success. Our premise is that our mainstream society must consider both the behavioral systems and the ecosystems of the nonstandard subcultures if desirable and successful adaptations are to occur. Our hypothesis about the relationship between the philosophical-political construct of cultural pluralism and the sociocultural concept of adaptation allows for insights into the different kinds of effective adjustments which groups of people are capable of making and into the technological tools we should use to help them make these adjustments.

Cultural Pluralism and Bicultural Teaching

To treat the poor as a homogeneous class is prejudicial and detrimental to their well-being. Among the poor there are many cultural and regional differences which correlate with linguistic variants, with differences of behavioral mores and value systems. All of these differences are subject to change and acculturation through the national media and the by-products of social and racial integration. But the poor person must be considered in the context of his subculture and the forces that have shaped his life style before any changes in life style are considered desirable or even viable.

What are some of these linguistic variants and differences? What kind of life styles do people from different subcultures have? What are the forces that tend to create such subcultures? What can or should be done to create change in any of these factors? These are questions that demand rigorous answers. This book will attempt to provide preliminary answers to them.

Dialect Differences

Most of the world's languages consist of a variety of dialects which distinguish them from one another in their phonological, syntactical, and lexical systems. Nevertheless, each dialect is systematic and proper for the subcultural group using it; that is, dialectal variations follow regular rules that are determined by the linguistic and social environment of a particular culture. The speech and language utterances of English-speaking members of different cultural groups (e.g., inner-city blacks and Appalachian whites), however, have traditionally been compared to the phonology, syntax, and the lexicon of speakers of standard English. Where differences have been noted, the nonstandard utterance has been generally considered deviant, abnormal, or deficient. The presence of any of these evaluative labels necessitates the consideration of clinical concepts such as remediation, treatment, or therapy by the speech clinicians.

If nonstandard dialects are not substandard but rather are systematic and proper, then the speech clinician is obviously using an improper conceptual tool in interactions with children who speak nonstandard dialects. Perhaps the clinician should *teach* standard English as a second language rather than *treat* those children who use nonstandard dialects. Those children who possess both nonstandard speech and substandard speech should be taught and treated; in other worlds, the speech clinician must be prepared to *teach* standard English to nonstandard speakers as well as be prepared to *remediate* the defective speech of those speakers.

The Current Dilemma

Higham (1974) so appropriately points out that the essential dilemma confronting our society "is the opposition between a strategy of integration and one of pluralism. . . . The integrationist looks toward the elimination of ethnic boundaries. The pluralists believe in maintaining them. From this fundamental distinction others flow. In the United States both integrationists and pluralists claim to be the true champions of democracy; but democracy means different things to them . . . . The integrationist expects a simple majority to approximate the general will [whereas the pluralists believe in] a philosophy of minority rights. . . . [Said differently] the democracy of integration is an equality of individuals; pluralist democracy is an equality of groups." Higham concludes his essay by pointing out shortcomings inherent in both models and suggests a new model based upon both of these concepts—a "pluralistic integration." A rapproachment between individual and group needs is the basis of pluralistic integration, a model that "will uphold the validity of a common culture, to which all individuals have access, while sustaining the efforts of minorities to preserve and enhance their own integrity." We agree; we believe our educational institutions would function more effectively through a pluralistic integration model that meaningfully caters to the cultural differences existent among peoples.

THE CAUSE: CONCEPTS OF DEPRIVATION, DISADVANTAGE, AND DIFFERENCE

Labeling the Poor

The term "culture of poverty" was conceived by Oscar Lewis to describe the interplay of circumstances and attitudes of a particular segment of society. Orientation to the present, passivity, and cynicism, among other behaviors, are realistic responses to the facts of poverty and are frequently manifested by members of this culture. Admittedly, these behaviors may interfere significantly with programs designed for the benefit of the poor, but the cynicism of the poor, as well as the other related behaviors, is understandable in view of the psychological and physiological damage to which they are heir. If a certain set of values is responsible for poverty, then it is society's obligation, perhaps, to alter these values; but if the values are the result of poverty—of an ecosystem in which there is substandard housing, insufficient food, or food of inferior nutritive value, as well as poor health and educational services—then the behaviors require a different mode of attack.

The basic or foundational concept which has been utilized in this attack has been the deprivation and disadvantage idea; there are, however, other concepts which may be utilized and which may be more appropriate. The use of the term "culturally different" allows for meaningful questions, which attack the core problems, to be asked while the continued utilization of other labels leads to an insidious ethnocentrism which is self-defeating. In the book, *Perspectives on Human Deprivation* (1969), a publication of the Department of Health, Education and Welfare, describes these concepts as follows:

A. Deprived/Disadvantage/Deprivation Concept
　　1. *Malnutrition model*—e.g., child who is deprived; has received insufficient quantities of nutrients of the sort needed for appropriate growth and development; a lack of, or absence of, some desired quantity.
　　　　a. Economic deprivation—in most writings, the idea of economic deprivation, or financial poverty, is assumed to be intimately related to the problems of the "disadvantaged."
　　　　b. As a lack of exposure to beneficial stimulation.
　　　　c. As a lack of pattern (stability) in the experiential world.
　　　　d. As an absence of contingencies in the environment (improper reinforcement schedules).
　　　　e. As interaction between maturational development—milestones, and lack of proper environmental stimulation. A common point of view in the malnutrition model is that certain cognitive activities play a biologically stimulating role in the maturation of neural structures that are important for later cognitive development and learning (i.e., the critical period hypothesis and infant education programs.)
B. Difference Concept
　　1. *Cultural Disparity Model*—a number of writers, particularly anthropologists and sociologists, are concerned with cultural and societal components in psychosocial deprivation. Their views emphasize

structural features, seeing the difficulty as residing in disparaties and conflicts of values and goals between subcultures and the large sociocultural system.

a. As an outcome of cultural pluralism—our pluralistic society allows for ghettos, or conclaves, or segregation of ethnic groups, and the concommitant emergence of differences in language styles, values, and mores. Acculturation, or the Americanization of peoples from subcultures is designed to eliminate the ethos of these different communities. The use of black power and separatism are examples of the recognition that a pluralistic society does have certain advantages and that cultural differences therefore, should be retained.

b. As a learning behavior not rewarded by middle-class society. The emphasis of the proponents of this point of view is not on the inability of the child to learn, but on the lack of congruence between the behavior he has learned and the behavior valued by the middle-class, school-oriented society.

c. Due to the inadequacy of social institutions (related to the above point of view) is the perspective that the difficulty resides in the institutions of middle-class society whose representatives in the school, the police force, and other parts of the social structure fail to understand the child or the adult, to be sympathetic to his problem, to be able to communicate with him, or in other ways to permit him to learn about and relate to the central components of society.

Treating/Teaching the Deprived or Disadvantaged or Different Child

The concepts just noted cause ethnocentric prejudgments that trigger negative child or client expectations. We tend to view all children from our own perspective, and those who do not comfortably fit our preconceived notions are considered unfortunate beings in need of much help and attention. Unfortunately, we attempt to cater to these perceptions according to our own cultural standards rather than according to the standards of the particular child.

Nevertheless, it is important to note that the culturally different and poor have sometimes been treated as different peoples—different from other cultural groups—and that programs have at various times and places been successfully adapted to their needs. How this was done is described in later sections. As is pointed out by Gordon (1965), "existing programs of compensatory education vary widely in size and scope throughout the country, [but] they have in common the dual goals of remediation and prevention. . . . The principal focus of fundamental curriculum change in compensatory programs has been *reading and language development"* (author's italics) (p. 383). But the malnutrition model, implicit in the compensatory approach to language training, has failed to make adequate changes.

THE TREATMENT: COMMUNICATION COMPETENCY IN CHILDREN WHO ARE CULTURALLY DIFFERENT AND POOR

The thesis of this book is reflected simply in the term *cultural parity*—do unto other cultures as you would have them do unto you. In other words, to give and not to take of values and mores is the mark of the centrist culture; to give as well as to take of these values and mores is the mark of the pluralistic culture. America is supposed to be functioning in the latter state, but it pragmatically continues to espouse the former philosophy. Continuance of this can serve only to create greater divisions among our people by perpetuating our institutionalized prejudices.

Language is the prime vehicle by which people think and act and develop attitudes. By changing first our attitudes toward different language patterns and by accepting them as proper utterances and then by learning to use these dialectal forms in our schools in order to communicate more effectively, we can obviate much of the problem. Language is currently the tool that mars our interactions with the poor; we insist they use "our" standards (that of the middle and upper classes). As long as we do so, we shall not overcome cultual differences—differences that could and should become accepted as part of our national fabric. To this end, it is incumbent upon us to postulate that people should examine and learn all about these differences. Let us encourage our children to become bicultural—indeed, bilingual and bidialectal; at a more basic level, let us at least encourage the acceptance of culturally pluralistic behaviors in our schools.

The fact that different cultural systems employ different languages or dialects suggests that all systems should receive equal consideration; that we use "nonstandard" to describe a system different from that "standard" used by the establishment is clearly prejudicial. In point of fact, all systems are nonstandard to members of "other" communities, and that which is used by a particular community is its standard. Another point of interest is

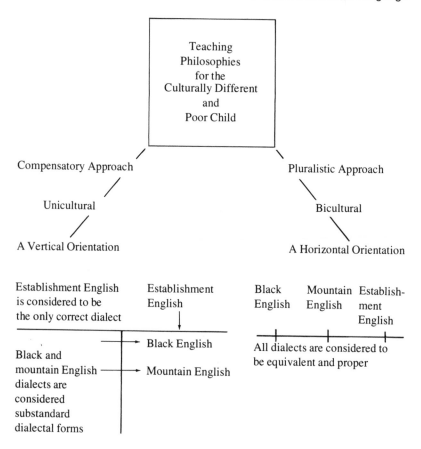

Figure 1-1.   Teaching philosophies.

that members of nonestablishment cultures are frequently able to "switch" from one dialect or language to another—certainly not as well as is desired but, on the other hand, much better than most members of the establishment culture are able to switch. As indicated above, it is our responsibility and obligation to afford equal educational opportunity to all. This responsibility certainly involves the opportunity for all children to learn about other cultural systems and different dialects and languages. Or, as Goodman (1973) says, "the goal of education must be for children to regain their free speech without class limitations" (p. 53). Figure 1–1 shows these relationships.

The Clinician and Educator

Each year children from ghettos, barrios, and hollows enter our public schools with substantial handicaps in education readiness related to their culturally different heritages. These children bring with them unique experiences and differences in standards and values. They possess a culture of their own with different learning and living styles and different speech and language patterns. The manifestations both of speech and language patterns and of other cultural styles that differ significantly from those used by members of the dominant culture, however, are frequently rejected by not only their peers but also, too frequently, by their instructors. As a by-product of this rejection, many students in the public school systems have been labeled functional retardates, and many of these are labeled solely because of linguistic conflicts and cultural differences between themselves and the teacher. Dialectal and cultural differences often result in low academic achievement in the classroom and low scores on intelligence tests. As a result, the role of the educator must also be reexamined. Children born into poverty cultures are being educated by traditional methods in which "correct" expressions of standard English patterns are required. The children are not being given the chance to *compare* and *contrast* standard English with their own native dialect or language. Instead, their dialect or language may be rejected as an inferior method of communication.

A preschool intervention program to introduce linguistically different children to the linguistic patterns of standard English before they reach the first grade would give them a "head start." In part, such an early introduction to standard English may enable more poor students to succeed academically as compared to the many who fail and drop out of school at present. Most school dropouts are fully capable of achieving in school and their withdrawal from school does not reflect a legitimate lack of ability. It should be noted that most of the school dropouts are from lower socioeconomic families and minority groups and that these children are retarded by at least two years in reading ability—a fundamental educational skill without which no student can perform adequately.

The reasons these children are doing poorly at school in reading and other academic areas may be due in part, we suspect, to the language barrier which exists between them and their teachers. The failure of the child to learn, then, is the fault of the schools—and not of the child. Heretofore the blame has been placed on the child, who supposedly was deficient in language and therefore in other abilities. Most schools have failed to develop curricula consistent with the environmental experiences of culturally different children, and many times their abilities are seen as disabilities. From the very start the child is confused and lost. In the first year of school he is being forced to build on a vocabulary which he does not possess, he is forced to learn graphic symbols for words which he has never before encountered, and he is forced to reason and express himself in a language which is somewhat foreign to him. If the child were taught basic skills in his own vernacular before he entered the primary grades, some or most of the confusion and feeling of "being lost" might be eliminated.

Despite a recently awakened interest in and implementation of numerous early childhood projects for low-income, disadvantaged bilingual children throughout the country, relatively little attention has been given to the child who enters school speaking a dialect other than that of the broader community in which he lives. Most of the current preschool intervention programs are the typical nursery school–kindergarten type, with little alteration other than providing the "deprived" child with environmental enrichment; that is, they try to bombard him with stimulating experiences that middle-class children receive but poor children supposedly lack. Again, such preschool programs are built on middle-class values and mores and ignore the different needs of the culturally different child.

Our educational programs generally lack significant emphasis on cross-cultural experiences. Even though Americans are highly exposed to other cultures through the mass media, this exposure is illusory because it is passive. Only by living in a different cultural context, going to school with children from different cultural backgrounds, and experiencing other behavior patterns and cultural traits do individuals become really aware of the cultural distinctions which are uniquely their own and gain respect for those of other people. If a goal of education is to teach people to learn to function effectively in a multicultural society, multicultural experiences are not only valid but essential. Serious attention should be given to research and demonstration projects which allow teachers and students to gain a new understanding of the nature and importance of cultural pluralism in a democratic society. If we are to be a truly democratic society, we must give each individual an equal place at the starting line. Every minority pupil should be assured that he has the freedom to express openly and with pride his own unique cultural heritage. This basic freedom is an important prerequisite to addressing the problems of poverty. Therefore, it is evident that programs are needed which are geared for the poor child, programs which will take into consideration the poor child's own special heritage and, especially, his own particular language or dialect so that he may compete with his middle-class counterpart in mainstream society.

This can most effectively be accomplished by an interface between the classroom teacher and the clinician, that is, a team approach that would allow these workers to coordinate their interactions with the children in the development of a bidialectal-bicultural program.

If we do not move with increasing vigor toward cultural pluralism, we shall continue to alienate and undereducate the minority poor in our country. According to the Zacharias (1964), "the majority of urban and rural slum schools are failures. In neighborhood after neighborhood across the country more than half of each age group fails to complete high school." We doubt that this figure has been significantly altered.

According to William L. Smith (1974):*

In the past, some weak starts have been made in the schools to introduce a multicultural approach. But often it was done for the wrong reasons—an expedient move to reduce tensions, to defuse protest, and to relieve anticipated community pressures. Since reasons for doing something subtly influence how we act, these attempts failed. They were stop-gap measures hastily decided upon and inadequately implemented. Often these programs brought kids, teachers, and materials together in a classroom in the hope that something would happen. However, no number of crossed fingers or lucky rabbits' feet or speeches at school boards can replace honest assessment of the problem and adequate program preparation.

The school's ultimate objective is the design and implementation of a culturally pluralistic curriculum which will accurately represent our diverse society. These studies in cultural heritage must emerge from introspection on the part of curriculum designers, students, and teachers. Fusing this introspection with objective historical scholarship and the results of current research about the learning processes will provide a sound formulation. Curriculum materials of excellence and innovative teacher training can then be finally screened by having them subject to confirmation by members of the racial/ethnic group to which the materials refer. . . .

We need to exert our efforts to make the school a place where differences, between and among people, are not merely tacitly accepted but are celebrated as a national blessing. (Author's italics.)

*Used with permission of the American Association of Colleges for Teacher Education.

REFERENCES

Cohen, Y. A. (Ed.). *Man in adaptation: The biosocial background.* Chicago: Aldine, 1968.

Goodman, P. Sublanguages. In J. A. DeVito (Ed.), *Language: concepts and processes.* Englewood Cliffs, N.J.: Prentice-Hall, (1973), pp. 46–55.

Gordon, E. A review of programs of compensatory special education. Cited in R. L. Jones (Ed.), *New directions in special education.* Boston: Allyn & Bacon, 1970.

Higham, J. Another American dilemma. *The Center Magazine: A Publication of the Center for the Study of Democratic Institutions.* July/August 1974, 4:67–70.

National Institute of Child Health and Human Development. *Perspectives on human deprivation: Biological, psychological and sociological.* U.S. Department of Health, Education and Welfare, Public Health Service. Washington, D.C.: U.S. Government Printing Office, 1969.

Smith, W. L. Forward. In W. A. Hunter (Ed.), Multicultural Education, Washington, D.C.: American Association of Colleges for Teacher Education, 1974, pp. III-IV.

Zacharius, J. *Innovative and experimentive education.* Washington, D.C.: U.S. Government Printing Office, 1964.

2
The Sociocultural Bases of Language

In every child who is born, under no matter what circumstances, and of no matter what parents, the potentiality of the human race is born again; and in him, too, once more, and in each of us, our responsibility towards human life; towards the utmost idea of goodness, of the human error, and of God . . . .

I believe that every human being is capable, within his limits, of fully realizing his potentialities; that this, his being cheated and choked of it, is infinitely the ghastliest, commonest, most inclusive of all the crimes of which the human world can accuse itself . . . .

—James Agee
Let Us Now Praise Famous Men

SOCIAL CLASS*

The term "social class" refers to those distinctions and differences that stratify people into different groups—e.g., socioeconomic status (SES), sociopsychological behavioral patterns, and sociolinguistic factors. Of particular interest here is the apparent increasing amount of conflict regarding these social-class categories with respect to language development and language pathology. Thus, there is a need to reexamine

*Part of this chapter is originally from Adler, S. Social class bases of language: A reexamination of socio-economic, socio-psychological, and socio-linguistic factors. *ASHA*, *15*, 1973, pp 3–9. Used with permission of the publisher.

some of the basic assumptions undergirding the relationships between social class and language.*

Such reexamination is especially relevant at this time since class stratification and subsequent class rankings appear to affect our behavioral management and habilitative relationships with children—i.e., the Hawthorne and Rosenthal effects. The Hawthorne effect involves people responding favorably to the greater attention they receive in being the object of the investigator's or teacher's interest; the Rosenthal (Pygmalion) effect involves people changing in the direction they think the investigator or teacher wants them to. In our society in general culturally-different and poor children tend to receive lesser amounts of attention and/or meet with a lower level of expectation. Thus, poor or lower-class children whose social, racial, or ethnic status differs from that of the investigator or teacher may suffer accordingly due to overt or institutionalized prejudices. Many of these prejudices are related to invalid and untenable assumptions regarding these children. One of the most apparent and damaging is that the speech and language of the lower class is an inferior verbal pattern characterized by many articulatory deficits, grammatical errors, and lexical inadequacies. As a consequence of this assumption, compensatory speech, language, and educational programs have been instituted in many schools. According to some writers, compensatory programming has failed; its failure may well be related to its invalid foundation. We accept the fact, however, that many cliches regarding culturally different children and their families, although lacking validity, nevertheless, automatically trigger drastic educational and habilitative strategies.

SOCIOECONOMIC FACTORS

Validity of the Factors

The most common factors used in judging economic social-class differences are (1) occupation, (2) education, and (3) income. Other and less frequently used criteria are rent and the value of one's home. That

---

*In an unpublished paper by Helton and Adler (1978) entitled, "The Confusing Use of Status and Class Concepts in Studies of Children's Speech and Language: Some Comments on Criteria and Concepts Commonly Used to Stratify or Label the Research Populations," it is noted that it may appear to be a simple task to rank children in terms of status or class levels. The implications of the rankings, however, have far greater significance then is generally reported. Due to the many unique operational definitions of status or class reported in our journals, there may be a number of studies which have introduced error into their design by using improper status and class designations.

these criteria allow for valid social-class distinctions is questionable (Helton, 1974); nevertheless, most researchers use them. Sarbin (1970) has also questioned the propriety if not the validity of these factors:

> Whatever system is used for assessing socio-economic status . . . two facts emerge: (1) the classification of an individual or group as lower class or middle class carries a tacit or expressed criterion of earnings . . .; (2) the classification of persons at the lower end of the dimension tends to homogenize the respectable poor and the downgraded poor, the latter being participants in the culture of poverty (p. 31).*

Earnings. That the criterion of earnings may be a particularly prejudicial factor is of concern for members of cultural minorities since a significant discrepancy has been noted to exist between occupational level (i.e., earnings) and educational achievement. For example, it is not unknown for blacks, Chicanos, or females who possess relatively high levels of education to be unable to obtain employment commensurate with their education. Earnings, furthermore, are based solely on income generated by the father in many stratification systems. This kind of chauvinism does not allow for an adequate social-class portrayal of matrifocal homes in which the mother is the "breadwinner" or, for a more common current practice, situations in which both parents contribute to the economic well-being of the family.

Education. Educational attainment is measured in our census statistics according to years of schooling completed. No distinction is made, however, for differences in the quality of training provided or received or for the quantity of education attained. Thus "years of school completed" may mean vastly different things; education, after all, is not synonomous with time spent in the classroom. That the quality of education provided for or received by nonwhite ethnic groups has been generally inferior is well recognized. Nevertheless, the quality of education as an important criterion is not considered in class rankings.

Homogenization of the poor. The homogenization of the lower-class respectable and downgraded poor, as Sarbin (1970) labels them, is particularly a problem for those who desire to measure and quantify discrete behaviors both unique and common to members of the different

---

*From Sarbin, J. R. The culture of poverty, social identity, and cognitive outcomes. In V. L. Allen (Ed.), *Psychological Factors in Poverty*. Chicago: Markham, 1970, pp. 29–46. Used with permission.

subcultures of the "culture of poverty." The better known SES stratification systems do not allow for valid characterization of the lower-lower class—the unstable and degraded poor. Those who are interested in obtaining information regarding language development and language use in children from these discrete subcultures have had difficulty in finding a valid system that allows for proper and rigorous identification of them. We have found it useful, however, to distinguish between the upper-lower and lower-lower social classes by a socioeconomic criterion involving the presence or absence of chronic welfare. Another socioeconomic criterion intimately related to duration of welfare is the presence of a father in the upper-lower-class home who is generally employed in unskilled-type work. A useful sociopsychological criterion for identification of discrete subcultures is stability or instability of the home environment; the presence of a father usually, but not necessarily, generates well-defined and coordinated behaviors among the various family members. These criteria are not sufficiently objective to allow for rigorous identification. We need quantifiable measures that would remove or attentuate much of the subjectiveness now inherent in the stratification system.

Stratification Systems

There are a variety of stratification systems utilized by the researcher in categorizing populations. Only a few will be reviewed to indicate their diversity. Warner (1960) uses an index of social characteristics involving three out of four criteria: occupation, source and amount of income, dwelling area, and house type. Reiss (1962) employs only one criterion, paternal occupation, and Hollingshead (1957) uses both parental occupation and education. Deutsch (1967) stratifies families according to a deprivation index involving six criteria. This index is derived from a questionnaire administered to a large sample of parents—usually the mothers—of black and white children from the middle and lower classes. One of the items is based on the educational aspirational level of the parent for the child. According to Labov (1969), if a child's mother says that she wants her son to go all the way through college, the child will fall into the "deprived" class on this variable. In order to be classified as less deprived, the mother would have to say she wanted her child to finish graduate or professional school (p. 31).

Birch and Gussow (1970) use the following sociodemographic data for social classification: (1) mothers premarital occupation, size of family, area of residence, degree of crowding; (2) evaluation of poverty by amount of assistance given to families by social and welfare agencies; (3)

evaluation of family disorganization by duration of unemployment, desertion of either or both parents, prison sentences, evidence of neglect of child; (4) type of parent, i.e., fatalistic, aspirational level, present or future orientation.

Golden and Burns (1968) and Bernstein (1968) utilize three different SES groupings to categorize people. The former classifies by (1) welfare families—neither father nor mother currently employed; (2) low-educational-occupational-status families—neither parent has more than a high school education or has been employed at more than unskilled or semiskilled jobs; (3) higher-educational-occupational-status families—either parent has some schooling beyond high school or has been employed at skilled or professional jobs. Bernstein has similar criteria but calls his groups (1) the nontransitional working class, (2) the transitional working class, (3) and the middle class, which is defined in terms of nonmanual occupation and education.

Gerrard (1970), interestingly, uses type of church membership and church behavior to distinguish between "upwardly mobile poor" and "stationary poor." The former are described as those who attend churches mainly identified by them with the lower-middle class (the class to which these families aspire)—Baptist, Methodist, or sometimes Presbyterian. According to Gerrard, if the need for respectability is accompanied by a nostalgic yearning for the rigid fundamentalism and for some of the fervor of "old-fashioned religion," the families may join such evangelical churches as the several Churches of God, the Adventists, Churches of Christ, various Pentecostal churches, the Church of the Nazarene, and the Assemblies of God. The latter group is described as possessing a fatalistic outlook which is expressed through their religion—i.e., "one's destiny is in God's hands." The group's adherents find ritual formalistic and unsatisfying, and they prefer to seek religious fellowship in their own unpainted one-room frame churches, in abandoned school houses, in barns, in crudely constructed tabernacles, in tents, or in each other's homes. Revivals, very fundamentalist beliefs, sometimes serpent handling, and glossolalia (speaking in tongues) accompanied by convulsive dancing and shrieking, rolling on the floor, etc. are frequently manifested during their church services.

Validity of Molar Stratification Systems

The significant differences in value system and mores within the middle and the lower classes as a result of ethnic, racial, economic, and geographic factors may not be as gross as those between classes;

nevertheless, the fact that there are differences has been well documented. Utilization of the conventional molar stratification system, i.e., middle vs. lower class, smothers these differences and may contribute to an uncontrolled bias in research studies. It follows that if a researcher has only middle-class children, per se, for his study, he may inadvertently be utilizing children from mainly the upper-middle or from the lower-middle class. To suggest, then, that the results of the study can be generalized to the middle class en toto is perhaps an unwarranted assumption. This criticism is perhaps even more relevant to the lower class, in which a more significant dichotomy may exist.

We do not suggest that such generalizations are always valid; we only suggest caution. Some of our pilot studies have suggested, for example, that upper-middle-class children may be superior to lower-middle-class children on the Peabody Picture Vocabulary Test. We have noted also the possibility that, on some tasks at least, the lower-middle-class and upper-lower-class child may be more similar to each other than to their respective class peers. As a matter of fact, there may well be three significant stratifications in terms of socioeconomic (SES) criteria: (1) the upper-middle class, (2) the lower-middle and upper-lower classes, and (3) the lower-lower class.

A Recommended Stratification System

In a study conducted by Helton (1974), it was noted that "occupational prestige scores, education as the number of school years completed, and gross wage income were in significant positive correlation with the children's PPVT scores, [those Helton tested], although the correlations were modest. The highest correlation obtained in the study was between education and the PPVT scores (rho = .44)" (p. 79). The mother's educational level was found by Helton to be the most effective predictor of language behavior, although it should be underscored that it too was a weak predictor.

There is simply no one measure or combination of measures that is a strong predictor of language behavior. In our own research we divide the social classes as follows: The maternal education level is formulated as follows:

Level 1   Upper-middle class—13 years of school and over (college)
Level 2   Lower-middle class—high school
Level 3   Lower class—0 to 9 years (elementary and junior high)
Level 4   Upper-lower class—6 to 9 years (elementary or junior high)
Level 5   Lower-lower class—0 to 5 years (only some or no elementary)

Even though education often serves as the single factor for SES position, the information regarding occupation may also be utilized; it is tabulated according to the following criteria:

Level 1   Upper-middle class (professional, managerial)
Level 2   Lower-middle class (trade)
Level 3   Upper-lower class (laborer)
Level 4   Lower-lower class (chronic welfare aid)

In addition to these formal criteria regarding socioeconomic status, a sociopsychological analysis of lower-class position is made by virtue of the home environment or life style. Thus, for level 4, upper-lower (in the education system), stable environment, father figure is present, welfare aid is nonexistent or is transient; for level 5, lower-lower; unstable and fairly disorganized environment, father figure not present or rarely present, welfare aid is fairly chronic.

SOCIOPSYCHOLOGICAL FACTORS

Verbal Factors: The Type, Quality, and Quantity of Verbal Stimulation in Culturally Different Homes

Many authors suggest that the verbal stimulation and cognitive enrichment encountered in lower-class homes is inferior to that manifested in middle-class homes. This statement is a gross oversimplification, but it is true, unfortunately, that many people have accepted its validity. For example, according to Hubbard and Zarate (1967), middle-class homes, which are for the most part culturally advantaged, are essentially verbal homes. They maintain also that because of the value system of middle-class culture, parents play a major role in teaching their young so that, by the time they reach school age, these children have achieved a relatively high level of language ability. That is, their parents talk to them, read to them, and, in general, foster a verbal give and take which helps the children develop their potentialities.

The child in many middle-class homes is given a great deal of instruction about the world in which he lives, to use language to fix aspects of this world in his memory, and to think about similarities, differences, and relationships in this very complex environment. Such instruction is individual and is timed in relation to the experiences, actions, and questions of the child. Parents make great efforts to motivate the child, to reward him, and to reinforce desired responses. The child is read to, spoken to, and is constantly subjected to a stimulating set of experiences in a very complex environment. In short, he "learns to learn" very early. He comes to view the world as something he can master through a relatively enjoyable type of activity, a sort of game, which is learning. In fact, much of the approval he gets is because of this rapid and accurate response to this informal instruction in the home . . . While all of this is not absent in the culturally deprived home, it does not play such a central role in child rearing in such homes. (Bloom, Davis, and Hess, 1965, p. 15)

Numerous articles can be cited to support the contention that the verbal environment of the middle-class child is superior to that of the lower-class child's environment. Labov (1969), however, has pointed out:

In the literature we find very little direct observation of verbal interaction in the Negro home [or any other subcultural member's home]; most typically, the investigators ask the child if he has dinner with his parents, and if he engages in dinner-table conversations with them. He is also asked whether his family takes him on trips to museums, and other cultural activities. This slender thread of evidence is used to explain and interpret the large body of tests carried out in the lab and in the school [which suggests that the environment is a poor one] (p. 4).

In fact we do not know the relative benefits or disadvantages of the type, quality, and quantity of verbal stimulation in culturally different homes. To suggest that all lower-class families, regardless of subcultural membership or discrete class membership (i.e., upper-lower or lower-lower class) manifest the same pattern of verbal stimulation seems a patent absurdity. Although there are bound to be many similarities in linguistic behaviors, there are also significant differences. Furthermore, much of the information available has been obtained through retrospective-type questionnaires—and the reliability of such a data gathering technique is notoriously suspect (Yarrow, Campbell, & Burton, 1970).

More specifically, Jensen (1968) has said that the lower-class child, in comparison to his middle-class peer, has less verbal play and receives less verbal interaction and reinforcing behavior. Therefore, the lower-class child's speech and language development is retarded or deficient. Such assumptions are generally based on data obtained from retrospective questionnaires, not from field observations relevant to the nature of the verbal interactions in specific homes. For example, Young's (1970) data, as obtained from her observations of black families in a small community in Georgia, tend to negate Jensen's assumptions. Young found that during the first year of life the baby was held quite frequently by the mother (rather than being allowed to sleep isolated in a crib); furthermore, the position in which the baby was held allowed the baby and mother to see each other and thus encouraged many verbal interactions. Such enhancement of the "prelinguistic" or "babbling" period might well have significant impact upon the baby's future language development.

Young also found that the time period from 1 to 2 years—also known as the "knee-baby" period—is a time when the baby receives much less attention from the mother relative to the previous year, a period during which the baby is allowed to crawl around with much more freedom than in the typical middle-class home. Similarly, during the time period from 2 years to the schooling years the youngsters are monitored by an older child, a child known as the "nurse-child."

These latter periods, the knee-baby and the nurse-child periods, are said to be inferior in terms of the type and amount of verbal stimulation the child receives in comparison to the quality and quantity of verbal stimulation received by the typical middle-class child. It is important to note that this assumption might also be invalid since certain types of linguistic stimulation may be of more importance than others in relation to language growth and development. For example, active as opposed to passive dialogue between parent and child is accepted as an extremely important variable insofar as language growth is concerned. Conceivably, the peer group activities and the nurse-child relationship might allow for more active dialogue than occurs in the middle-class home where the mother, in contradistinction, may more frequently read to her child. Which variable is more important? Can the relative importance of the different variables be weighed? Such information is not available at this time; obviously, until such information is obtained, one should be cautious in the interpretation of the verbal environment of the lower-class child. The environment may be as good as or better than the middle-class environment. We simply do not know! There is need for much additional research before this question can be adequately answered. The paradigm in Table 2–1 suggests the kinds of information that should be obtained in order for valid cross-cultural comparisons and analyses to be made.

Stratification System(s) Based on Sociopsychological Data

It can be expected that the kind of home environment in which a child is reared is relevant to emerging speech and language skills. If life styles vary as a function of differences in home environment and familial stability, then these differences should be considered another means of stratifying children.

Table 2-1
Type, Quality, and Quantity of Verbal Interactions

Type	Quality or Kind	Quantity or Amount
Talking to child Mother Father Peers Others	May be active or passive; may differ significantly dependent upon respondent.	The amount of time spent in active or passive verbal interactions needs to be determined.
Reading to child Telling stories to child Singing to child TV watching by child	Usually passive	

Pavenstedt (1965) found important differences in the functioning of families in the stable, secure upper-lower class and in the unstable, disorganized lower-lower class. She observed, for example, that parents in the upper-lower subgroup encouraged and responded to the vocalizations of their children, whereas parents and children in the lower-lower subgroup did not communicate verbally with each other.

In her utilization of the Pavenstedt data, McCaslin (1971) made some alterations in methodology and evaluated life style according to a decreasing numerical scale of 2, 1, 0 points (i.e., typical, sometimes, not typical). It should be noted that of a possible 28 points, a cut-off score of 22 points was utilized in determining the unstable poor category. The criteria were as follows: (1) family relations (separations, divorce or frequency of desertion, parents involved in petty crimes, alcoholism, prostitution, or cohabilitation); (2) care of children (older children tend to look after younger, no supervision at play, activities determined by mother and child impulse); (3) maternal relationships (mother pays little attention to comfort and needs of children, punishment dealt indiscriminately, communication by means of words hardly exists); (4) other relationships (emotions masked, children use smiles and frowns inappropriately, child manipulates adults and other children skillfully for his own advantage, indistinct ownership of toys and clothes); (5) school (parents show distrust and fear of danger from the outside); (6) housing (disorder and chaos, dirt or urine smell present).

Miller (1965) suggested that both economic security and familial stability be factors in classifying lower-class subjects. To evaluate familial stability, he inquired as to the following: (1) Has the family moved frequently within the past 5 years due to failure to pay rent? (2) Is anyone in the family frequently in trouble with the law? (3) Do the parents engage often in loud and/or violent quarrels? (4) Does either parent drink to excess? (5) Are young children left at home without proper supervision? (6) Are the children physically abused? (7) Are the children improperly fed? (8) Are any of the members physically handicapped, emotionally disturbed, or mentally retarded? (9) Has there been a frequent change of the male head of the house? (10) Is there a lack of interest in education in the home? (11) Is there a lack of verbal interactions between mother and child? (12) Is the home overcrowded?

Whether these criteria and methods of scoring are relevant and valid for members of differing subcultures is problematical. Young's (1970), Curtis' (1972), and Vaughn's (1973) analyses of the white and black homes and life styles suggest that only some of the criteria may be appropriate for the stratification of poor children.

SOCIOLINGUISTIC FACTORS

Origins

Sociolinguistics is the newest in a series of terms that has been used to describe a relatively new field which draws from linguistics, anthropology, and sociology. Basically, it involves systematically studying the relationship between both verbal and nonverbal linguistic forms and social communications; it is concerned with attitudes and opinions and how these judgments are influenced by language transmission systems. In other words, it involves not only *what* a person says but also *how* he says it and the *effect* it has upon the speaker-listener.

The origin of sociolinguistics can be traced to the 1920s and the work of Franz Boas and Edward Sapir, two anthropologists who pioneered the field of social anthropology. Until 1952 the bulk of sociolinguistics consisted of studies of foreign and primitive languages and the characteristics that made the systems different or similar. At that time Hertzler (1965) officially merged linguistics and sociology in a paper read at a meeting of the Midwest Sociological Society, in which he called for more work in the field of the Sociology of Language. Even though attention was then focused on the sociology of language, "sociolinguistics as an activity specifically directed to an examination of the interaction of language structure and social structure and of the interimplications of speech behavior and social behavior has developed only since the beginning of the sixties" (Grimshaw, 1971, p. 93). Labov's remarks made in 1969 still pertain in 1979:

The study of language change in its social context has been described by some as a virgin field; by others, as a barren territory. A brief examination of what has been written in the past on this subject shows that it is more like an abandoned back yard, overgrown with various kinds of tangled, secondary scholarship. The subject has been so badly treated with voluminous, vacuous, and misleading essays that one can sympathize with linguists who say that it is better left alone . . . We are then left with such a limited body of fact that we are condemned to repeat the arguments of our predecessors: we find ourselves disputing endlessly about bad data instead of profiting from the rich production of new linguistic change around us (Labov, 1972, p. 260).

Sociolinguistic Methods

The crux of sociolinguistic methodology, especially in dialect observation, involves determining how people talk when they are not being systematically observed, but no convenient method has been discovered to observe and record this data without systematic observation. The aim is to record the people in their natural milieu without letting them know they are being evaluated. Failure to record responses in the natural milieu of the speaker may cause problems, for evidence now suggests that "disadvantaged" children may be nonverbal and/ or nonsensical in situations they see as threatening, while in nonthreatening situations they display an adequate verbal ability. Furthermore, it is not easy to record some important features of language. Crystal (1972) points out that observation and delineation of the nonsegmental aspects of speech "are among the most difficult to receive, transcribe, and measure . . . The distinction between a falling tone and a rising-falling tone, or between one and two degrees of stress, is sometimes extremely difficult to hear," (p. 186). Kleederman (1973) says that the question to be asked in assessing language development in these children is, "Are the linguistic structures that the child uses highly ordered rules or random utterances, and how well do these utterances approximate the ordered rules of adults in his environment?" (p. 6).

Ethnography and Dialect

The heart of sociolinguistic investigation invariably centers around and involves some description of ethnography and dialect. "Ethnography is the process of constructing, through direct personal observation of social behavior, a theory of the workings of a particular culture in terms as close as possible to the way the members of that cult review the universe and organize their behavior within it" (Bauman, 1971, pp. 335-336).* Because

*The material appearing here and on pages 29 and 31 is reprinted from Bauman, R. An ethnographic framework of the investigation of communicative behaviors, *ASHA, 13,* 1971, 334- 340. Used with permission of the author and publisher.

every culture is unique in its views and goals, ethnography attempts to determine how the members try to control or impose order on their environment, how they view their own speech and language in terms of what is good speech, bad speech, appropriate speech, inappropriate speech, defective speech, and how these views are acquired.

Dialect refers to a variety of language spoken by the members of a given speech community, either geographic or social. A dialect may vary in pronunciation, vocabulary, and grammar from other varieties of the same language. Thus, people united by dialect form a speech community. The members of such a community frequently share interests, values, ambitions, and communication systems. Malmstrom (1971) goes on to explain that the dialect is a common group of "idiolects"—each person's individual dialect. It is very hard to differentiate between where a dialect stops and another language starts, but, basically, dialects are enough like each other to be understood by other speakers of different dialects of the same language. Thus, standard or "network" or "establishment" English and its regional variants are mutually understandable.

Ethnographically, "people of different societies think differently about language, value it differently, evaluate it differently, acquire it through different social mechanisms, use it in different situations, and turn it to different ends" (Bauman, 1971, p. 335). For instance, "among the Araucanions it is an insult to be asked to repeat an answer, . . . a prompt answer from a Toba means he has no time to answer questions, . . . [and] a Wasco prefers not to answer a question on the day of its asking" (Hymes, 1971, p. 75). Bauman (1971) also makes a comparison between the Cuna Indians, who speak without interruption for hours at a time, and the Paliyans, whose communication is so limited that as they get older, they become more silent. He further adds that "it is this variability which underlies most of the so-called language problems of the culturally different in this country when it is confronted by the built-in ethnocentric assumption of our dominant educational institutions that there is one and only one way to acquire and use language" (Bauman, 1971, p. 335). That assumption is similar to some nineteenth century anthropological assumptions which, as late as 1883, still maintained a positive correlation between distinctive characteristics of a language and the mentality of its creators and users. This followed the general belief that primitive language speakers "were incapable of anything beyond a minimal generalization and abstraction" and that "primitive languages were incapable of precision and specification, because their vocabularies were extremely small and limited" (Hensen, 1971, p. 7).

Have things really changed in the last 100 years? Bernstein (1967) has said that children reared in the restricted code never learn the "why" of things because nothing is ever explained to them—the restricted code evokes authority via categorical statements with the result that children are ordered about, their natural curiosity pushed back is ultimately lost, and they soon learn not to think for themselves. Deutsch (1967) believes that poor children have inferior auditory discrimination, faulty visual discrimination, and inferior judgment concerning time, numbers, and basic concepts caused by inferior discrimination perceptions (habits) in hearing, seeing, and thinking. Bereiter and Engelmann (1966) even go so far to suggest that "culturally-deprived" children do not just think at an immature level; many of them do not think at all. That is, they do not exhibit any of the processes usually related to thinking behavior. For example, they can't retain questions while searching for an answer; they can't compare perceptions reliably; they are oblivious to the discrepancies between their statements and actions.

Dialectal Differences

Although only three major dialects are usually recognized in the United States, sociolinguists recognize at least two others in the form of Appalachian and black English dialects. Appalachian dialects are but a series of subcultural dialects that are similar enough to be included in one category. However, as Stewart (1972) points out:

Today for better or for worse and in spite of its regional seniority, mountain speech is no longer accepted by most Appalachians as a generally respectable way of talk. While many older mountaineers can undoubtedly still be found to use a more or less "pure" form of rural dialect, the younger ones have begun to reject the more rustic speech patterns in favor of standard English ones, which they learn in school or hear on T.V. and the radio (p. 111).

He further states that no dialect survives or remains unchanged forever and that "the tragedy of the growing rejection of mountain speech is not so much that it is causing rural dialects to die out . . . but rather that the form it is taking is bound to cause the mountaineer to despise his own origins" (Stewart, 1972, p. 111). Besides, the overly pessimistic picture that has been painted of Appalachia tends to promote misunderstanding, especially between these Southern Highlanders and outsiders.

The other major dialect is commonly labeled black English, or black dialect. It is also a cohesive linguistic system which is substantially yet subtly different from standard American English dialects. It is spoken by some blacks, particularly those of the lower socioeconomic classes.* In analyzing black speaking behaviors, Bauman (1971) describes several "key acts and events including rapping, capping, playing the dozens, signifying, shucking, rifting, louding, loud talking, marking, toasting, gaming and others. How many whites know what these are? Yet, to many blacks, they are the most important speech activities in which one can engage. Good talking form then means proficiency in these activities, not talking like English teachers" (p. 336).

Black dialect, according to some linguists, unlike mountain or Appalachian dialect has a different origin from standard English. Stewart, Dillard, and Bailey "have maintained that present day Negro dialects are derived, not from British dialects as dialectologists have assumed, but from a Creole variety of English which was spoken by the earliest slaves" (Shuy, 1969, p. 13). A Creole language is the permanent and primary language form of "pidgin." Since pidgin languages are developed to meet a communication emergency, Creole is then a secondary, derived language. As future generations acquire this language, it becomes their primary language. Thus, Creole is a pidgin language made permanent.

Dialect Speech Communities

It is common knowledge that there are dialects unique to subcultures, but few are aware that some commonalities are shared by the various dialectal communities. One of the commonalities involves *diglossia,* ** an ability to switch from peer language to standard language. Diglossia is most evident in grammar and vocabulary. Much less frequently can dialect

---

*In order to make a valid determination of the different varieties of black English or Applachian dialect that may be spoken by speakers of these dialects, it is important that the varied educational, occupational, income, and age groups, i.e., the different socioeconomic, socio-psychological, and other demographic factors, contribute to a language data base. It is only in this way that an accurate picture can be obtained of these varied dialects. And such data bases can best be obtained through an analysis of the speech patterns of speakers from different environments. To date many of the studies have analyzed the speech patterns of informants from restricted environments. As Williams (1976) points out in his excellent article "The Anguish of Definition: Toward a New Concept of Blackness," "the lect that one speaks has nothing to do with race but everything to do with social environment" (p. 24).

**An excellent treatment of diglossia and bidialectalism can be found in J. A. Fishman (Ed.), *Advances in the Sociology of Language,* Vol. 1 (New York: Humanities, 1971, pp. 286–299).

switching be done with phonology. Lexical and syntactic items are apparently more amenable to diglossic self-alterations than phonological ones. Yet it is these pronunciations that most clearly label the dialectal community of the speaker. It is clear, therefore, that additional stress needs to be placed on the achievement of phonological diglossia than perhaps has heretofore been suspected.

Our schools have traditionally worked to eliminate what is properly thought of as uneducated or folk speech, and, in particular, certain kinds of grammatical usage received much attention. For example, the verb agreement (e.g., they is) and the use of adjectival forms for adverbial forms (e.g., he talks good) are considered substandard speech forms in our schools. Little attention has been paid, however, to the intersections of grammar and phonology. Such relationships need to be carefully evaluated. If a speaker or writer regularly drops a final consonant in certain clusters (e.g., omission of final t in clusters), the past tense may be lost (e.g., walked becomes walk). If the final s is dropped (e.g., two pound), the traditional method of pluralizing words may be altered. Thus, the grammatical consequences of phonological differences need to receive attention, especially as they relate to articulation testing and writing.

Some grammatical differences, as well as variant uses of prepositions, are quite common in Appalachian mountain speech; note "quarter-till" rather than "quarter-to"). All but the last of these are also quite common throughout the South.) These and other grammatical forms, such as the double negative, "smack" standard English auditors (i.e., the teacher or clinician) and are socially detrimental. Unfortunately, social detriment gives rise, too frequently, to poor expectations insofar as progress is concerned (Rosenthal effect). Of particular importance is the apparent fact that these kinds of variants cause relatively less immediate damage to the communication process between speaker and auditor than do lexical differences.

As Hartman (1969) points out, "the words he uses . . . can be down-right misleading." Hartman gives an example of a man asking a clerk in a clothing store if he packed extra large shirts. The clerk replied they would box any clothes they sold. The customer irritatedly told the clerk that he did not care about boxes but that what he wanted was a white shirt in an extra large size. The matter was finally resolved, but some "heat" would have been eliminated if the clerk had known that "packed" shirts means "carry" shirts. That lexical items exist that are unique to different subcultures is well known. Unfortunately, the standard speaker tends to denigrate their importance and, as a consequence, refuses to recognize them, thus creating communication difficulties and distortions.

Phonological differences call attention to the dialect of the speaker; it labels him. Lexical differences create the communicative "breakdown" that may exist between culturally different people.

Social Implications of Dialectal Speech Patterns

Value judgments are too often the basis for ranking the differences that exist among humankind. In this country, in most cases, the values, mores, and behaviors, including linguistic behavior, of the middle-class essentially white establishment is accepted as the norm and, therefore, "that" which is desirable. Thus, this class's speech pattern is the "standard." As we have alluded to elsewhere, however, all dialects should be considered nonstandard, including the so-called "standard" dialect; to do otherwise is to perpetuate an ethnocentric value system which ranks the different dialects on a scale ranging from positive to negative.

The social problems or benefits that dialectally distinctive phonological, syntactical, and lexical features may create are not difficult to predict. If one wants to communicate effectively and, at the same time, appeal to certain subcultural groups in our country, one might indicate an awareness of the dialect difference by trying to converse with them in their own dialects. Certainly this thesis is not new; politicians and others attempt to generate such communication each time they interact with members of different cultural groups.

Thus, dialectal speech patterns can be of much benefit to their users, and to surrender such a potential advantage is clearly unwise. Yet much pressure is exerted in our schools and clinics to eliminate differences in speech and language patterns. What is good for the politician, however, may also be desirable for the teacher. To communicate effectively with students is the sine qua non of good teaching, and such communication occurs only when all parties concerned in a verbal interchange clearly understand the denotative and connotative aspects of the interchange. Rather than attempting to eliminate the various dialectal patterns by labeling them substandard, the teacher and clinician should try to learn them and to use them. Such utilization, among other gains, should foster better social acceptance of the teacher and clinician by the child. It should be clearly understood however, that we do not advocate the acceptance of dialectal patterns as the "finished product". Rather, we stress the need for the child, and when possible the teacher, to become a diglossic speaker.

THE INTERRELATION BETWEEN REGIONAL AND SOCIOCULTURAL DIALECTS

From a synchronic point of view, languages may vary both regionally and socially. Regional dialects are those varieties of a language which are distributed geographically, while cultural or social dialects are varieties which are distributed along any of a number of social-scale values—e.g., income, education, occupation, as well as subcultural membership, and perhaps racial or ethnic group. It would be a mistake to assume that regional and cultural dialects exist independent of each other, for that which is a regional feature in one area may be socially significant in another. In fact, the relationship between regional and cultural dialects are so complex that such dialects as "standard English," "mountain English," and "black English" are meaningless unless considered in relation to regional varieties of American English.

Regional Varieties and Standard English

Linguistic geography, the study of regional variation in language, has made a number of important contributions to the study of American English. Perhaps the two most important were the debunking of the notion of "general American" English and the destroying of the myth of a monolithic spoken standard English. Until the publication of Hans Kurath's *A Word Geography of the Eastern United State,* (1949) most students of American English had assumed that while people in the South and in New England spoke rather distinct and esoteric dialects, everyone else in the United States spoke "general American." Kurath demonstrated that in the East alone there were actually three major dialect areas—Northern, Midland, and Southern—each of which was made up of several subdialects. Although Kurath studied only lexical variation, later studies (Atwood, 1953; Kurath & McDavid, 1961) showed that these dialects differed systematically in grammar and pronunciation too. The dialect areas are most clearly defined along the Eastern seaboard, but they do extend into the Midwest (Allen, 1964; Marckwardt, 1957). Table 2-2 presents these dialect areas.

Because differences between dialects involved pronunciation and

Table 2-2
Dialect Areas of the Eastern United States

North	Midland	South
1. Northeastern New England	*North Midland*	14. Delmarva (Eastern Shore)
	7. Delaware Valley (Philadelphia)	
2. Southeastern New England		15. The Virginia Piedmont
	8. Susquehanna Valley	
3. Southwestern New England		16. Northeastern North Carolina (Albemarle Sound & Neus Valley)
	10. Upper Ohio Valley (Pittsburgh)	
4. Inland North (western Vermont, Upstate New York & derivatives)	11. Northern West Virginia	
		17. Cape Fear & Peedee Valley
5. The Hudson Valley	*South Midland**	18. The South Carolina Low Country (Charleston)
6. Metropolitan New York	9. Upper Potomac & Shenandoah	
	12. Southern West Virginia & Eastern Kentucky	
	13. Western Carolina & Eastern Tennessee	

*Appalachian, or mountain, dialect is simply a variety of South Midland speech.

grammar as well as vocabulary, because those differences were systematic, and because dialectal differences were prevalent among the most prestigious speakers as well as the uneducated ones, dialectologists concluded that there was no monolithic spoken standard English in the United States (McDavid, 1966). As a matter of fact, there are a number of standard Englishes in the United States. Furthermore, what is "standard" in one part of the country may be nonstandard in another. While the middle-class Midwesterner may consider "ain't" a sure sign of ignorance or carelesness, the cultivated Charlestonian will frequently use the form in conversation with intimate peers. While the absence of *r* after vowels is socially stigmatizing in New York (Labov, 1966), it is quite prestigious in many parts of the South (McDavid, 1948).

The fact that what is "standard" in one part of the country is nonstandard in another sometimes creates problems. Language differences may cast doubt on one's cultural and educational credentials. For example, McDavid (1966) notes that Southern children who spoke perfectly standard Southern English were often put in speech-correction classes when they moved to cities in the North. Usually, however, the various regional standards are accepted and respected; for that reason neither Edward Kennedy nor Jimmy Carter is hindered politically by his speech. It is because the regional standards vary for the most part in vocabulary and pronunciation that they are generally accepted and respected. There are, however, social varieties of the regional dialects which stigmatize speakers; they stigmatize the speaker because they differ grammatically. As McDavid (1966) notes, "the surest social markers in American English are grammatical forms."

Clearly, then, cultural or social dialects must be studied within their regional contexts. What is "standard" varies from region to region; so does what is "nonstandard." Just as standard English varies geographically, so do the various cultural dialects. Thus it is doubtful that there is a monolithic black English or mountain English; rather there are probably black Englishes and mountain Englishes. No account of language variation is complete unless both the horizontal and vertical dimensions are studied.

There is a direct interrelationship of (1) dialect to (2) one's social status and to (3) geographic region of residence. Thus, a speaker of black English who is lower class and lives in Watts (Los Angeles) will manifest differences in this dialect as compared to (a) a middle-class black who also lives in Watts as well as to (b) another lower-class speaker who lives in Knoxville. Similarly, the speaker of standard (network or establishment) English will speak different dialects dependent upon his social status (middle vs. lower class) and geographical residence (e.g., Boston or Atlanta).

Similarities as well as differences in dialect are found as a function of social class and race. For example, lower-lower class black and white speakers possess many similarities in their speech patterns as well as some notable differences. Similarly upper-middle-class black and white speakers may manifest some slight differences in prosody if their sociocultural environment were characterized by segregated schooling. But the similarities far outweigh the differences that may be present. The same patterns exist between middle- and lower-class black speakers or white speakers; that is, there are similarities as well as differences in their varied speech patterns. The determining factor is, as noted above, the sociocultural environment in which the children are reared. When the children are exposed to integrated communities, they learn to use dialectal forms representative of the different speech models inherent to the community.

Regional Varieties and Black English

Perhaps the most controversial issue in the study of American dialects involves the question of "racial" or "ethnic" dialects. There is a great deal of disagreement among dialectologists as to whether there is such a thing as a racial or ethnic dialect independent of regional, cultural, and class experiences. Taylor (1970), Stewart (1971), Fasold (1972), and others maintain that black English is in effect a separate language. They suggest that there are distinct differences between black and white speakers, that certain features of black English do not occur in varieties spoken by whites, and that black English has a unique origin and development. Stewart and others maintain that black English is not simply the speech of white plantation owners taken over by blacks; rather, black English is the development of a Creole language which was used by slaves to communicate both with other slaves who spoke different languages and with overseerers and slave owners. Because black English has undergone a partial decreolization, the Creolists maintain, it shares certain similarities with other varieties of American English; however, these similarities are only superficial and only serve to mask deep structural differences. There is then an African substratum to black English. Taylor (1970) lists the following as the general characteristics of black English, a language which is the development of a "creolized" language:

1. No inflection of verb stems to indicate person or tense.
2. Person typically indicated by a subject prefix or pronoun.
3. Tense indicated by a number of monosyllabic markers inserted between the subject prefix and verb stem. These markers focus on *mode* (continuative, habitual, and perspective) rather than time of action—past, present, and future.

From these general characteristics, a number of specific features result:

1. Absence of copula verb.
2. No distinction in gender for third-person plural pronoun.

3. Distinction between second-person singular and plural.
4. Prefixing or suffixing third-person plural objective case pronouns for noun pluralization.
5. No obligatory plural morpheme.
6. No obligatory third-person singular marker for verbs.
7. No obligatory possessive marker.
8. Use of specific phrases to announce beginnings of sentences.
9. Use of intonational ranges to mark meaning differences.

Not all students of American English agree with the Creolists. McDavid (1966) suggests that it is not always possible to distinguish blacks and whites by speech alone, and Juanita Williamson (1968, 1970) provides a rather large body of evidence which demonstrates that none of the features of black English are peculiar to black speech; in fact, in many cases they occur in the speech of the best educated whites. Dialectologists usually have no quarrel with the creole hypothesis, an hypothesis which is really about 50 years old (see Krapp, 1925). Dialectologists, however, find no evidence to support the claim that decreolization has not been completed. The linguistic geographer would claim that any statement suggesting that black English is a separate ethnic dialect is the result of the study of a social dialect out of its regional context. Most comparisons between black and white speakers involve only Northern whites; thus regional variables are not held constant.

Most dialectologists would support the views of Labov (1971) who contends that there exists no one speech pattern common to all blacks. Rather, their dialects are part of a regionally and culturally inherited pattern which has been extended into Northern ghettos by Southern immigrants, the majority of whom happen to be black. Most of the speech patterns found in ghettos in the North were originally regional and still may be identified in the speech of many whites in the South. These features, however, have lost their geographical significance in being transplanted and instead have taken on social significance, serving to identify blacks as a distinct ethnic group.

In his book, *Lexicon of Black English,* Dillard contends forcefully that such a difference exists; that there are qualitative as well as quantitative differences between black and white speakers of similar educational levels, social class, age, and locales. He claims that the linguistic geographers are wrong who suggest that the major differences between black and white speech are only quantitative (i.e., differences in the frequency of occurrence of certain forms). Dillard argues that qualitative differences (i.e., differences in the presence or absence of certain forms) are evident. For example, there appears to be a distinction of black speech, such as *he sick* (he is sick right now) and *he be sick* (he's been sick a great deal lately, or he's sick all the time), that whites do not make—apparently not even in the closely related varieties of Southern speech—and that are of obvious importance to language comprehension of black speakers. Similarly, the distinction between lower- and middle-class blacks seem to be related to their quantitative use of black English forms. Also most middle-class blacks, but not all, use some black English dialectal forms in their speech; the amount appears to vary considerably as a function of their sociolinguistic heritage.

Regional Varieties and Mountain English

Many of the problems in the study of black English are also present in the study of mountain English, but mountain, or Appalachian, English, unlike black English, has been virtually ignored, perhaps because of its strong regional ties. Furthermore, mountain English has been both ridiculed and stereotyped by the media. As a result, the public for the most part conceives of mountain English as a kind of monolithic substandard made up of illiteracies and deviations from "standard English." Just as the migration of blacks to cities in the North has generated a new interest in black culture and language, the migration of Appalachians to Dayton, Columbus, Detroit, and other cities in the Midwest has served to make the outside world aware of both the distinctiveness and variety of Appalachian cultural institutions—including language.

In its native setting, mountain English is a regional variety of American English. Much that distinguishes it is grammatical as well as phonological and lexical. Only when mountain English is transplanted out of its native setting does it become a social dialect. Nevertheless, even transplanted mountain English is an ordered, systematic variety of American English. Its differences are not the results of deviations from standard English but are the results of the dialects spoken by the original settlers in Appalachia and of the conservatism of mountain English. Many of the original settlers in Appalachia were Scotch and Irish, and much that is distinctive in Appalachian English can be traced to the language of these settlers. For example, a look at Joseph Wright's *English Dialect Dictionary* (1963) confirms the fact that double models are found in northern Britain and that invariant *be* is a characteristic of Irish English, both features of mountain English.

Certain other unusual features of Appalachian English are due to its conservatism. For example, the use of *hit* as a third-person singular neuter pronoun is quite old (we find the form in Chaucer), and it is *it* that is really the modern innovation. Likewise the *a* prefix attached to progressives is the result of the preservation of an older form. A list of some of the distinctive grammatical features of mountain English follows. It is adapted from Wolfram and Christian (1975), one of the few full-scale studies of mountain English.

1. *a* verb*ing* (a-hunting)
2. double modals (might could)
3. completive done (done finished)
4. invariant *be*
5. *s* form in third plural of verbs (some people makes it)
6. irregular plural forms in nouns (waspes; waspers)
7. expletive they and it (They's catfish in the river)
8. plural possessives with *-n* (yourn)
9. irregular relative pronouns (he's the man what did it)
10. positive anymore (he lives here anymore)

A word of caution is in order for the student of mountain English. First, the various Appalachian dialects have been largely ignored; further study may alter the descriptions given here. Secondly, as has been shown in this section, the study of regional dialects without consideration of their social implications or the study of cultural-social dialects out of their regional context is meaningless.

REFERENCES

Allen, H. B. The primary dialect areas of the upper Midwest. In *Readings in applied English linguistics*. New York: Appleton-Century-Crofts, 1964, pp. 231–241.

Atwood, E. B. *A survey of verb forms in the Eastern United States*. Ann Arbor: University of Michigan Press, 1953.

Bauman, R. An ethnographic framework of the investigation of communicative behaviors. *ASHA, 13* 1971, 334–340.

Bereiter, C. and Engelmann, S. *Teaching disadvantaged children in the preschool*. Englewood Cliffs, N.J.: Prentice-Hall, 1966.

Bernstein, B. Social class and linguistic development: A theory of social learning. Cited in D. Lawton (Ed.), *Social class, language and education*. London: Routledge & Kegan-Paul, 1968.

Birch, J. G., & Gussow, J. D. *Disadvantaged child: Health, nutrition and school failure*. New York: Harcourt Brace Jovanovich, 1970.

Bloom, B. S., Davis. A., & Hess, R. *Compensatory education for cultural deprivation*. New York: Holt, Rinehart & Winston, 1965.

Chomsky, N. *Language and mind*. New York: Harcourt Brace Jovanovich, 1968.

Curtis, C. *A study of the grammatical patterns of two groups of white children from different life styles*. Unpublished master's thesis, University of Tennessee, Knoxville, 1972.

Crystal, D. Prosodic and paralinguistic correlates of social categories. In E. Ardener (Ed.), *Social anthropology and language*. London: Travistock, 1971 pp. 185–209.

Deutsch, M., et al. *The disadvantaged child: Selected papers of Martin Deutsch and associates*. New York: Basic Books, 1967.

Dillard, J. L. *Lexicon of black English*. New York: Seabury, 1977.

Fasold, R. W. *Tense marking in black English: A linguistic and social analysis*. Arlington; Center for Applied Linguistics, 1972.

Gerrard, N. Churches of the stationary poor in southern Appalachia. In J. Photiadis & H. Schwarzweller (Eds.), *Change in rural Appalachia*. Philadelphia: University of Pennsylvania Press, 1970.

Golden, M., & Burns, B. Social class and cognitive development in infancy. *Merrill-Palmer Quarterly*, 1968, *14*, 139–149.

Gordon, E. Compensatory education: Evaluation in perspective. *IRCD Bulletin* 1970, *6* (5), 139–149.

Grimshaw, A. *Sociolinguistics: Advances in the sociology of language*. The Hague: Mouton, 1971.

Hartman, J. The language of southeastern Ohio: The social implications of history. In R. Williams & R. Ham (Eds.), *Speech and language of urban and rural poor*. Athens: Ohio University, 1969.

Helton, J. *Some comments on social-class stratification: The use of occupation, education, and income to predict PPVT scores of preschool-aged children*. Unpublished master's thesis, University of Tennessee, Knoxville, 1974.

Helton, J. & Adler, S. "The Confusing Use of Status & Class Concepts in Studies of Children's Speech and Language." Unpublished Paper, Knoxville, Tn., (1978)

Henson, H. Early British anthropologists and language. In E. Ardener (Ed.), *Social anthropology and language*. London: Tavistock, 1971, pp. 3–33.

Hertzler, J. O. *A sociology of language*. New York: Random House, 1965.

Hollingshead, A. *Two-factor index of social position*. New Haven: Yale University Press, 1967.

Hubbard, J. L., & Zarate, L. T. An exploratory study of oral language development among culturally different children, section IV. *Final Report on Headstart Evaluation and Research: 1966–67*. Austin, Texas: Child Development and Evaluation Research Center, 1967.

Hymes, D. Sociolinguistics and the ethnography of speaking. In E. Ardenar (Ed.), *Social Anthropology and Language*. London: Tavistock, 1971 1973, pp. 49–93.

Jensen, A. R. Social class and verbal learning. In M. Deutsch, I. Katz, & A. Jensen (Eds.), *Social class race, and psychological development.* New York: Holt, Rinehart & Winston, 1968, pp. 115–174.

Kleederman, F. *Black English and reading problems: Sociolinguistic considerations.* A paper presented to the Seventeenth Annual Meeting of the College Reading Association, Silver Springs, Maryland, November 1973.

Krapp, G. P. *The English language in America.* New York: Frederick Ungar Publishing Company 1925.

Kurath, H., & McDavid, R. *The pronunciation of English in the Atlantic States.* Ann Arbor: University of Michigan Press, 1961.

Labov, W. *The social stratification of English in New York City.* Arlington, Va.: Center for Applied Linguistics, 1966.

Labov, W. The logic of nonstandard English. In James E. Alatis (Ed.), *Twentieth Annual Round Table: Linguistics and the teaching of standard English to speakers of other languages or dialects.* Monograph Series on Language and Linguistics. Washington, D.C.: Georgetown University, 1969.

Labov, W. The non-standard vernacular of the Negro community: Some practical suggestions. In E. M. Kerr & R. M. Adlerman (Eds.), *Aspects of American English.* New York: Harcourt Brace Jovanavich, 1971, pp. 336–342.

Labov, W. *Sociolinguistic patterns.* Philadelphia: University of Pennsylvania Press, 1972.

Malmstrom, J. *Language in Junior college: A sociolinguistic approach.* A paper presented at the annual meeting of the National Council of Teachers of English, Las Vegas, Nevada, November 1971.

Marckwardt, A. H. Principal and subsidiary dialect areas in the north central states. *Publications of the American Dialect Society,* 1957 *25,* 3–15.

McCaslin, L. *A study of the relationships between hematocrit and grammatical competence for children of selected heights from unstable poor and lower-class life styles.* Unpublished master's thesis, University of Tennessee, Knoxville, 1971.

McDavid, R. I. Postvocalic /-r/ in South Carolina: A social analysis. *American Speech,* 1948 *23,* 194–203.

McDavid, R. I. Sense and nonsense about American dialects. *Publications of the Modern Language Association,* 1966 *81,* 2, 7–17.

Miller, S. M. The American lower classes: A typological approach. In A. Schostak & W. Gomberg (Eds.), *New Perspective in Poverty.* Englewood Cliffs, N. J.: Prentice-Hall, 1965, pp. 22–39.

Pavenstedt, E. A comparison of the child-rearing environment of upper-lower and very low lower-class families. *American Journal of Orthopsychiatry,* 1965, *35,* 89–98.

Reiss, A. *Occupations and social status.* New York: Free Press, 1961.

Sarbin, J. R. The culture of poverty, social identity, and cognitive outcomes. In V. L. Allen (Ed.), *Psychological Factors in Poverty.* Chicago: Markham, 1970, pp. 29–46.

Shuy, R., et al. *Sociolinguistic Factors in Speech Identification*. Arlington, Va.: Center for Applied Linguistics, 1969.

Stewart, W. A. Continuity and change in American Negro dialect. In H. B. Allen & G. N. Underwood (Eds.), *Reading in American dialectology*. New York: Appleton-Century-Crofts, 1971, pp. 454–476.

Stewart, W. A. Language and communication problems in south Appalachia. In D. L. Shores (Ed.), *Contemporary English change and variations*. Philadelphia: Lippincott, 1972.

Taylor, O. An introduction to the historial development of Black English: Some implications for American education. *ERIC Document No. 035 863*, 1970.

Vaughn, L. W. *Auditory discrimination skills of black children from stable and unstable poor families*. Unpublished master's thesis, University of Tennessee, Knoxville, 1973.

Warner, L. *Social class in America*. New York: Harper & Row, 1960.

Williams, R. The anguish of definition: Toward a new concept of Blackness. In T. Trabasso & D. S. Harrison (Eds.), *Black English: A seminar*. Hillsdale, N.J.: LEA Publishers, 1976.

Williamson, J. V. A phonological and morphological study of the speech of the Negro of Memphis, Tennessee. *Publications of the American Dialect Society*, 1968, *50*, 32–45.

Williamson, J. V. Selected features of speech: Black and white. *CLA Journal*, 1970, *13*, 420–423.

Williamson, J. V. A phonological and morphological study of the speech of the Negro of Memphis, Tennessee, 1968. Cited in C. B. Martin & C. M. Rulon (Eds.), *The English Language of yesterday and today*. Boston: Allyn & Bacon, 1973.

Wolfram, W., and Christian, D. *Sociolinguistic Variables in Appalachian Dialects*. Arlington, Virginia: Center for Applied Linguistics, 1975.

Yarrow, M. R., Campbell, J. D., & Burton, R. V. Recollections of childhood: A study of the retrospective method. *Monographs of the Society for Research in Child Development*, 1970, *35*, 1–83.

Young, V. H. Family and childhood in a southern Negro community. *American Anthropology*, 1970, *72*, 269–288.

3
Language Processes

"Everybody says words different," said Ivy. *"Arkansas folks say' em different, and Oklahomy folks says ' em different. And we seen a lady of Massachusettes, and' she sais ' em differentest of all. Couldn' s hardly make out what she was sayin!"'*

—John Steinbeck
The Grapes of Wrath

This chapter will examine both the linguistic and paralinguistic systems of culturally different and poor children. In the former, the common linquistic differences manifested by the speakers of black and Appalachian dialects* will be examined. In the latter, the body-language behaviors—a generic term covering all of the nonverbal movements—and the prosodic or suprasegmentals of language will be evaluated.

THE BLACK LINGUISTIC SYSTEM

Most Common Linguistic Variants

Deletion of plural and possessive forms of *s,* and *z* has been mentioned previously. When the *s* is used for the third-person singular form of present tense verbs, the irregular verbs change pronunciation

---

*Throughout the text the terms *black English* and *Appalachian* (or *mountain) English* are used. These are holistic terms referring to the many varieties of each dialect. The obvious fact is that not all blacks nor all residents of Appalachia (or Appalachian transplants in other sections of the country, for the most part cities in the Midwest) speak these dialects. If a particular dialect is spoken, it will stem from the sociocultural heritage of the speaker.

instead of omitting the final *s*. As Wolfram and Fasold (1974) cite, in black English, "has" is pronounced as *have* (not *ha'*); *does* becomes *do* (not *doe'*); and *says* is *say* (not *se*). Also the vowel sounds are distorted in other verbs, such as with cases of past tense and past participles; examples are *tell-told* becomes *tol'* ; *leave-left* becomes *lef'* ; and *sleep-slept* is *slep'*. In summary, the obvious phonological endings are absent in the past tense forms, yet the underlying linguistic concept of tensing is intact. This conclusion, however, is not valid for the actual omitted *s,* which constitutes an error in grammatical constructions.

Black English has the tendency to omit the medial *r*. When the omission occurs, a listener interprets it as a "lost" syllable. Examples such as *sto'y* (story), *ma'y* (marry), and *te'ific* (terrific) could lead to misunderstandings in meaning. Usually this phenomenon happens when the *r* follows a vowel and precedes another vowel in the same word (see previous examples). Frequently the deleted *r* occurs in the final position of a word, e.g., *ca'* for "car." Perhaps blending and/or balancing aspects are being enforced. (Wolfram & Fasold, 1974, pp. 140–141).

The addition of the perfect structure of "done" is found within the phonological character of black speech. "Done" is utilized as a means of emphasis or as a "completeness of the action." Today, evidence indicates the use of "done" is on the decline. (Wolfram & Fasold, 1974, p. 142). For example: "I done told you to stop that!"

One very unique characteristic of the black dialect is the deleted forms of contrasted auxiliaries. At times entire words are left out. The following examples illustrate this point:

"I done that lots of times."	(deletion and contraction of *have)*
"He go there tomorrow."	(deletion and contraction of *will)*
"They over there all the time."	(deletion and contraction of *are* or *is)*

It has been postulated that the contractions are used because the missing words (have, will, are/is) have lost their distinctiveness in the sentence structure. It is believed the difference between past tense and the past participle are not necessary to the black speaker who does not generalize these forms over to the past tense forms.

Finally, one of the most documented "nonstandard" usages found in the literature is the use of *be* to denote a temporal action or as an object or event distributed intermittently in time. (see Wolfram & Fasold, 1974, p. 161). Standard English speakers consider *be* to be a form of *am, is,* and *are,* but black English uses the form quite differently. *Be* can appear in three meaningful contexts.

1. "If somebody hit him, Darryl *be* mad."
   Explanation: future reaction to being hit with the deletion of "will" or the contracted form of "will."
2. "If somebody hit him, Darryl *be* mad."
   Explanation: probability of being hit with the deletion of "would be" or the contracted form of '*d*.
3. "If somebody hit him, Darryl *be* mad."
   Explanation: statement of Darryl's habitual reaction to being hit, with this form occurring most frequently.

Phonological Differences

Word-final consonant clusters.   Standard English words ending in a consonant cluster or blend often have the final member of the cluster absent in black English. In black English, words such as *test* and *desk* are pronounced as *tes'* and *des'*. Because of this, we find that pairs of words such as *build* and *bill* have identical pronunciations in black English. It is important to distinguish two basic types of clusters that are affected by this sort of reduction. First, clusters in which both members of the cluster belong to the same "base word" can be reduced, as in *tes'* and *des'*. Reduction also affects final *t* or *d,* which results when the suffix -*ed* is added to the "base word." In black English, when the addition of the -*ed* suffix results in either a voiced or voiceless cluster, the cluster may be reduced by removing the final member of the cluster. This affects -*ed* when it functions as a past tense marker, a participle, or an adjective, although its association with the past tense is the most frequent.

Related to the reduction of final consonant clusters in black English is a particular pattern of pluralization involving the -*s* and -*es* plural forms. In black English words ending in *s* plus *p, t,* or *k* add the -*es* plural instead of the -*s* plural. Thus, words like *desk* or *ghost* are pluralized as *deses* and *ghoses*. It is essential to understand that this is a *regular* pluralization pattern due to the status of final consonant clusters in black English.

th *sounds.*   In black English the regular pronunciation rules for the sounds represented by *th* are quite different from standard English. The particular sounds which *th* represents are mainly dependent on the context in which *th* occurs. At the beginning of a word the *th* is frequently pronounced as a *d* in black English, so words such as *the* and *that* are pronounced as *de* and *dat*. In the case of the voiceless *th* in words such as *thought* and *think, th* is sometimes pronounced as *t;* thus these words are pronounced as *tought* and *tink.* In the middle of the word there are several different pronunciations for *th* in black English. For the voiceless sound as in *nothing,* most frequently it is pronounced as *f,* thus pronounced as *nuf-n.* For the voiced sound as in *brother,* most frequently it is pronounced as *v,* thus pronounced as *bruvah.* At the end of a word *f* is the predominant pronunciation of *th* in words such as *tooth* and *south,* which are pronounced as *toof* and *souf.*

 r and 1. At the beginning of a word, *r* and *l* are always pronounced. The most important context to recognize is the so-called "loss" of *r* and *l* when they follow a vowel. In such items as *steal* and *bear* a reduction of *r* and *l* will be pronounced so that we hear *steauh* and *beauh.* Black English may also reveal no vestige of *r* following the vowels *o* and *u.* For these speakers *door* and *doe* may be pronounced alike. There is also a tendency to drop the *l;* thus *toll* and *toe* would be pronounced alike. The *r* absence is occasionally observed between two vowels within a word. Thus, it is possible to get *Ca'ol* and *sto'y* for *Carol* and *story.*

 Final b, d, g,. At the end of a syllable the voiced stops *b, d,* and *g* are often pronounced as the corresponding voiceless stops, *p, t,* and *k,* respectively. In addition to the devoicing rule, there are some speakers who may have the complete absence of the stop *d.* This results in pronunciation such as *goo'man.* The rule for the absence of *d* occurs more frequently when *d* is followed by a consonant than when followed by a vowel.

 Indefinite articles–a and an. In black English, as in some varieties of white Southern speech, the article *a* is used regardless of how the following word begins. With a selected group of words which may begin with a vowel similar to *a* (phonetically *ə*), the article may also be completely absent or at least "merge" together, thus resulting in *he had eraser.*

Grammatical Differences

 Verbs and auxiliaries. Differences in verb agreement are among the most frequently reported aspects of black English. Baratz (1969) states that the third-person singular has no obligatory morphological ending in nonstandard English, so that *she works hard* becomes *she work hard.* Subject-verb agreement may also differ in black English; thus, the black

Table 3–1

Phonological, Syntactical, and Lexical Contrasts in
Black English and Appalachian English Dialects

Phonological Differences—Black Dialect		
	Standard English	*Dialect*
Consonant Omissions		
r phoneme	car	ca
l phoneme	tool	too
s phoneme (indicating pluralization)		
Simplification of Consonant Clusters		
	past	pass
	meant	men
	hold	hole
	bowel	bo
Vowel and Diphthong Alterations		
Short and long *o* usually made without		
distinctions	caught	cot
Vowels not Distinguished		
Before *r*	bare	bar
Before *l*	all	oil
Before nasals	pin	pen
Prevalent Substitutions		
f for θ	Ruth	roof
v for $\eth$	bathe	bave

Phonological Differences—Appalachian Dialect		
	Standard English	*Dialect*
Consonant Omissions		
Initial unstressed	across	'crost
syllable sounds	account	'count
	appears	'pears
Two stop sounds	directly	d'ireckly
	exactly	exackly
d or *t*	children	chillern
	let's	less
Medial *r*	burst	bust
	horse	hoss
	first	fust
Consonant Omissions		
t after *ep*	slept	slep
	kept	kep
	crept	crep

Table 3–1 (continued)

Phonological Differences—Appalachian Dialect

	Standard English	Dialect
t after *f*	soft	sof
	loft	lof
t after *s*	just	jus
	Baptist	Baptis'
d after *n* and *l*	old	ole
	hand	han
p after *s*	clasp	clas
	wasp	wasper
Consonant Additions		
p if consonant is voiceless	comfort	compfort
l when followed by	miles	milts
consonant *t* or *d*	else	elts
Substitutions		
i/e	been	ben
i/a	bring	brang
e/i	get	git
	chest	chist
o/e	window	winder
	hollow	holler
u/i	brush	brish
	such	sich
	just	jist
t/d	salad	salat
d/t	twenty	twendy
k/t	vomit	vomick
ch/t	tune	chune
	Tuesday	Cheusday
dz/d	tedious	tejous

Syntactical Difference—Black Dialect*

Following is a list of some of the syntatic differences between standard and black dialectal English as compiled by Baratz (1969).

	Standard English	Black Dialect
Linking Verb	He is going.	He goin'.
Possessive Marker	John's cousin.	John cousin.
Plural marker	I have five cents.	I got five cent.
Subject Expression	John lives in New York.	John he live in New York.
Verb Form	I drank the milk.	I drunk the milk.

Table 3–1 (continued)

Syntactical Difference—Black Dialect*

	Standard English	Black Dialect
Past Marker	Yesterday he walked home.	Yesterday he walk home.
Verb Agreement	He runs home.	He run home.
	She has a bicycle.	She have a bicycle.
Future Form	I will go home.	I'ma go home.
"If" Construction	I asked if he did it.	I ask did he do it.
Negation	I don't have any.	I don't got none.
	He didn't go.	He ain't go.
Indefinite Article	I want an apple.	I want a apple.
Pronoun Form	We have to do it.	Us got to do it.
	His book.	He book.
Preposition	He is over at his friend's house.	He over to his friend house.
	He teaches at Francis Pool.	He teach-Francis Pool.
"Be"	Statement. He is here all the time.	Statement. He be here.
"Do"	Contradiction. No, he isn't.	Contradiction. No, he don't.

*From J. Baratz, "Teaching Reading in an Urban Negro School System. In J. C. Baratz & R. W. Shuy (Eds.), *Teaching Black Children to Read* (Arlington, Va.: Center for Applied Linguistics, 1969), pp. 99-100. Copyright 1969 by the Center for Applied Linguistics, Reprinted by permission.

Syntactical Differences—Appalachian Dialect

	Standard English	Dialect
Pronoun Usage		
Emphatic demonstrative	that	thar
	this	this'n
Disjunctive possessive	his	hisn
	your	yourn
Alteration of reflexive pronouns	himself	hisself
	themselves	thesselves
Other changes or variations	it	hit
	those boys	them boys
Noun Usage		
Noun compounds	church	church-house
	Bible	Bible-book

Table 3–1 (continued)

Syntactical Differences—Applachian Dialect

	Standard English	Dialect
Noun pluralism	posts	postes
	beasts	beastes
Collective sense	seven-years ago	seven year back
	six feet tall	six foot high
Adding "er" to noun compounds	deaf and dumb	deef and dumb
	new-born	new-born'der
Verbal Usage		
Strong preterites	drove	driv
	broke	bruk
	climbed	clum
Weak preterites	knew	knowed
	drew	drawed
	caught	ketched
Addition of "ed" to past tense	born	borned
	cost	costed
Conversion Noun to Verb		
	It won't please her.	Hit won't pleasure her.
Pleonasms–Redundancies		
	nap	nap o'sleep
	during	durin' the while
	a small fellow	a little bitty feller
Agreement of Subject and Verb	he is going	he go
Adding *er/est* form Comparative	only	onliest

Lexical Differences—Black Dialect

Dialect Word	Standard English Equivalent
*rapping	colorful rundown of a past event
jiving or shucking	speech used when talking to a representative of the establishment, the "man"
rundown	narration of a past event
*bread or cakes	money
wheels	car
headbreakers	policemen
whips	white power structure (acronym)
scuffler	one who barely gets by from day to day engageing in such nonprestigious activities as begging, working at odd jobs at minimum wages, collecting and returning pop bottles for deposit, etc.

Table 3–1 (continued)

Lexical Differences—Black Dialect	
Dialect Word	*Standard English Equivalent*
*drag	something not enjoyed
*hung-up	problem
*put-down	victimized by another person
strung out	victimized by heroin
nose open	victimized by love
broom	fast getaway

*These expressions in particular are being used by establishment speakers with increasing frequency.

Lexical Differences—Appalachia Dialect	
Dialect Word	*Standard English Equivalent*
stout	good health
pack	carry
sorry	inferior
heap	much
poke	small bag
bealed ear	running ear
larripin	very good
meetin'	church
peaked	sick-looking
'pears	seems
tuckered out	tired
wrench	rinse
spigot	faucet
carry (me to town)	take (me to town)
fetch	get
tote	carry
cher	chair
risins	boils
pert'n near	almost
sack	paper bag
look at him	talk to him
stoved up	injured
pocket book	purse
plum	very
reckon	believe
holler	shout
right smart	a considerable amount

speaker may say, *She have bike* or *They was going.* Baratz also states that the use of the copula is not obligatory in black English: *I going; he a bad boy.*

Nonstandard usage of verb tense among black speakers has also been reported. Furthermore Baratz (1969) states that the black speaker may use *drunk* for *drank* and *walk* for *walked.* Labov (1966) suggests that irregular tenses are marked by black speakers, but the regular *-ed* is not. Wolfram and Fasold (1974) state that *done* is utilized with the past tense of the verb to indicate completed action. Baratz also reports nonstandard usage of future tenses by black speakers: *I will go home* becomes *I'ma go* Bailey (1965) suggests that the black language system has an unmarked form of the verb which is noncommittal as to time orientation, although there are certain forms which are past and future respectively. It appears that *was* is reserved for events which are completely in the past, while *been* extends from the past up to, and even including, the present moment. *Be* is a simple future, with *gonna* the intentional future.

Loban (1966) states that the omission of auxiliary verbs is common among black English speakers: *He been here.* Wolfram and Fasold (1974) report that speakers of nonstandard English omit auxiliaries in questions using *what, when,* and *where: What you want?* In standard English the present progressive is marked in two ways: *He is going* contains the auxiliary *be* and affix *-ing.* In black English only the second element is necessary: *He going home.* In the so-called present perfect, *I have lived here* is the standard English form, whereas either *I have live here* or *I lived here* is permissible in black English. Black English exhibits the use of the uninflected form of *be* to indicate habitual or general state: *He be workin'* means that he generally works. In contrast, *he workin'* can simply mean that he is working at this moment.

-s suffixes. Black English indicates possessive by the order of the words. The phrase, *the boy hat* corresponds to *the boy's hat* in standard English. When the second noun is deleted, the black English form does mark the possessive with *'s: This is John's* is the possessive, whereas *This is John* has a quite different meaning. The *-s* (or *-es*) suffixes which mark most plurals in standard English are occasionally absent in black English. This results in sentences like *He took five book.* Black English speakers tend to omit the obligatory morphemes for the plural when numerical quantifiers such as *two, seven,* or *nine* are used: *nine cent, two foot.* Black English speakers may add the plural suffix *-s* to forms which in standard English have irregular forms: *mans.*

Pronouns. A well-known, but little understood, feature of non-standard English dialects, including black English, is pronominal apposition. Pronominal apposition is the construction in which a pronoun is used in apposition to the noun subject of the sentence. Usually the nominative form of the pronoun is used as in *My brother, he bigger than you.* Occasionally, the objective or possessive pronoun is used in apposition as well, as in *That girl name Wanda, I never did like her.* Where standard English uses *there* in an existential or expletive function, black English uses *it.* This results in sentences like *It's a boy in my room name Robert;* standard English would have been *There's a boy in my room named Robert.* Bailey (1965) states that the form *they* replaces the possessive pronoun *their* in black English: *Everybody look down at they feet.*

Adjectives. Loban (1966) reports the nonstandard modification of adjectives in black English: *That girl is more pretty than the other one.*

Adverbs. Loban (1966) also reports the nonstandard modification of adverbs in black English: *I guess he arrived quick.* The formal *-ly* adverb marker is not used in black English.

Prepositions. Baratz (1969) points out the substitution of the preposition *to* for *at* in black English: *He over to his friend's house.* Labov (1966) reports the use of *upside* for *in* in the speech of 17-year-old black boys: *Hit him upside the head.*

Negation Negation is a feature that is marked twice in black English and once in standard English. A standard English speaker might say *Didn't anybody see it?* and a black English speaker might say *Didn't nobody see it?* Baratz (1969) reports the use of *ain't* for *didn't: He ain't go.* Bailey(1965) reports an unusual usage of *ain't* and *don't* by American black speakers. *Ain't* is used consistently in nonverbal predications and before the tense markers; it also seems to be the form preferred before the progressive *-in* form of the verb. Whether this exhausts its limitations, and whether *don't* is used in all other cases, remains to be investigated. Examples of the use of *don't* and *ain't* are *I ain't paying that kind of bread for no iron like that. I don't know why he done it.*

MOUNTAIN (APPALACHIAN) LINGUISTIC SYSTEM

Most Common Mountain Variants

In Appalachian English the *r* is deleted in either of two cases—(1) after a vowel and (2) as a final consonant. The listener immediately picks up the *r* deletion in pronouns such as *their* and *your*, which become *they* and *you* in Appalachian speech.

A very common aspect of Appalachian English—the present progressive forms of certain American verbs and some past tense / nonpast tense verb forms—has been extensively studied by Walt Wolfram and his associates (1975). The *a* as a prefix is added to the verb + *ing* construction; however, the *g* is omitted. Thus, *a* + verb + *in'* is the final product.

Common verbs in mountain English are *come, go, take off*. They function as adverbial complements or as verbs to represent continuing or initial action, i.e., *keep, start,* and *stay, get to, pull, cry, want*.

The *a*-prefixing constructions are not used on verbs acting as gerunds. Wolfram and his colleagues did not find this unique structure following the prepositions of *on* and *at*. In other words, when two prepositions are used together, the speaker will not use the *a*-prefixing form. This, though, is true in standard English since standard grammatical construction does not allow the pronunciation of two successive prepositions. Another rule associated with *a*-prefixing deals with stressing. The form is not used before verbs initiated by an unstressed syllable. Two unstressed syllables usually do not occur in succession. As with the case of two prepositions, two unstressed syllables are rare in standard English usage. These two examples further strengthen the argument in favor of nonstandard dialects as being bona fide entities; they should not be considered any less complex or functional than standard English.

The phonological constraints on *a* prefixing can be summarized as follows.

1. Not observed when following a morpheme beginning with a vowel.
   Example: "John was a-eatin' his food."
2. Avoided by moving it to the preceding auxiliary.
   Example: "The movie was a-shockin'."
3. Appears more on stressed initial syllables.
   Example: "a-struttin' and a-draggin'." (Construction does not appear in *a*-prefixing.)

4. If the word preceding an *a*-prefixing form is a vowel, the deletion of *a* is favored,
   Example: "John is eating his food." (Wolfram & Christian, 1975, pp. 254–261.

During a lecture given at the University of Tennessee in 1977, Wolfram cited some other possible phonological constraints:

5. When more than one *a*-prefixing construction appears on a sentence, *a* + verb + *in'* is attached to all the verbs in the sentence.
   Example: "He just kep' a-beggin', and a-cryin', and a-wantin' to go out."
6. *A*-prefixing does not occur with determiners or other normalized forms.
   Example: "He watched their a-shootin'." (Construction does not appear in *a*-prefixing.)
7. Often *a*-prefixing is found preceding polysyllabic words, as long as the initial syllable is stressed.
   Example: ". . . so he kep' a-follerin' me around for a week."

Statistically, Wolfram and Christian (1975, p. 106) found *a*-prefixing was declining in use with the rural working class of their sample in Appalachia. Less that 50 percent of the people under study were using *a*-prefixing. The highest frequency of use was by speakers over 50 years of age (80 percent of the time); speakers of 30 years and under used it only 20 percent of the time.

Appalachian speakers tend to add the *s* to the third-person subject, despite the singularity or plurality of the subject. The typical Appalachian English paradigm would resemble the following:

Singular	*Plural*
I walk	we walk
you walk	you walk
the man walks	the men walks

The Appalachian English speakers do not use the *s* as many black English speakers do. The *s* is now weak in mountain English, nor is its use generalized to other verbs, such as go, goes. Appalachian speech is fairly consistent in using *s* in its commonly acceptable form on third-person singular constructions.

Pluralization and possessive irregularities are not as predominant in Appalachian English as they are in black English. Most examples linguists have found pertaining to pluralization consists of adding the plural forms to irregular nouns. Some rural mountain speakers will use *feets* for feet; *childrens* (chillerns) for children; and *peoples* for people. Omissions are frequently found on four *mile* five *apple* or three *pound*.

The possessive *s* forms are used fairly consistently with the accepted standard forms. One unique possessive form is indicated by the use of *n* on pronouns. Words such as *yourn, hisn, hern, ourn, theirn,* have been noted. Oddly enough the root of this peculiar form stems from an Old English form found in the south and midlands of England. The use of *n* or *en* was noted when the pronoun occurs in an absolute position, i.e., *It's yourn* but not when modifying a preceding noun phrase, as with *It's yourn house*. This form is dying out quickly, being replaced by the appropriate use of the possessive *s* (Wolfram & Christian, 1975).

The use of *ain't* is extremely common in the nonstandard dialects of the United States. It has been found in the dialects of the blacks along the Atlantic Coast (Labov, 1966) with Puerto Rican speakers (Wolfram & Fasold, 1971), and in Appalachia (Wolfram & Christian, 1975). *Ain't* is a form used to denote a negative function. Two rules exists for its use within the realms of nonstandard English:

> For emphasis, incorporate a *copy* of the NOT which is in the main verb phase in *all* indefinites after the main verb phrase, but leave the original NOT intact; (2) for emphasis, incorporate a *copy* of the NOT which is in the main verb phrase or the preverbal indefinite into the main verb phrase (if it is not there already) and in *all* indefinites after the main verb phrase, but leave the original NOT intact (Wolfram & Fasold, 1974, pp 163–164).

The use of double or multiple negatives such as "He don't know nothing," is a common negative construction in the Appalachian dialect. It can be used for emphasis and does not follow the convention that two negatives make a positive. Actually, the double negatives express the intended meaning of the sentence with the second negative acting as a "copy" of the first negative.

So, as with the discussion of black English, many linguistic and phonological differences exist between Appalachian English and standard English. The differences are not to be construed as the ignorant verbalizations of rural farmers. Appalachian speech has a definite place among standard English utterances and should be considered as equal, not as substandard. In Table 3-2 is presented a translation from standard English to black English dialect.

Table 3–2
A Translation From Standard to Black English Dialect

1. It was a man named Nicodemus. He was a leader of the Jews.

2. This man, he come to Jesus in the night and say, "Rabbi, we know you a teacher that come from God, cause can't nobody do the things you be doing 'cept he got God with him."

3. Jesus he tell him say, "This ain't no jive, if a man ain't born over again, ain't no way he gonna get to know God."

4. Then Nicodemus, he ask him, say "How a man gonna be born when he already old? Can't nobody go back inside his mother and get born."

5. So Jesus tell him, say, "This ain't no jive, this the truth. The onliest way a man gonna get to know God, he got to get born regular and he got to get born from the Holy Spirit."

6. The body can only make a body get born, but the spirit, he make a man so he can get God.

7. Don't be surprised just cause I tell you that you got to get born over again.

8. The wind blow where it want to blow and you can't hardly tell where it's coming from and where it's going to. That's how it go when somebody get born over again by the Spirit.

9. So Nicodemus say, "How you know that?"

10. Jesus say, "You call yourself a teacher that teach Israel and you don't know these kinds of things?"

11. I'm gonna tell you, we talking about something we know about cause we already seen it. We telling it like it is and you-all think we jiving and don't believe me, what's gonna happen when I tell you about things you can't see?

12. Ain't nobody gone up to Heaven 'cept Jesus, who come down from Heaven.

13. Just like Moses done hung up the shake in the wilderness, Jesus got to be hung up.

14. So that peoples believe in him, he can give them real life that ain't never gonna end.

15. God really did love everybody in the world. In fact, he loved the people so much that he done gave up the onliest son he had. Any man that believe in Him, he gonna have a life that ain't never gonna end. He ain't never gonna die. God, he didn't send His Son to the world to act like a judge,but He sent Him to rescue the peoples in the world.

W. A. Wolfram & Ralph W. Fasold, "Toward reading materials for speakers of black English: Three linguistically appropriate passages." In J. C. Baratz & R. W. Shuy (Eds.), *Teaching Black Children to Read* (Arlington, Va.: Center for Applied Linquistics, 1969), pp. 150–151. Copyright 1969 by the Center for Applied Linguistics, Reprinted by permission.

PARALINGUISTICS: BODY LANGUAGE
AND PROSODY

Laymen and professional workers alike often foster the gross misconception that the majority of communication transpires by verbal means. The realm of nonverbal communication, including body language and the prosody of the linguistic system, is of unquestionable importance in the interpretation of a message and its impact upon the auditor. Until recently, scant research has investigated the paralinguistic aspects even within the mainstream culture, much less among different cultures. Such differences among cultures appear to be glaring and may cause profound errors in communication due to ignorance of their significance. It is imperative that clinicians examine in detail all aspects of the communication of their culturally different clients. To understand and to utilize the total linguistic and paralinguistic systems of other cultures is the key to effective communication.

Body Language

Nonverbal communication is a silent language that everyone puts into use day after day, sometimes without awareness. People are constantly sending and receiving nonverbal messages, but very few stop to consider the possibilities that lie within this relatively uncharted field. The way the person decodes these variables dictates his interpretation of the people and situations involved. Linguistic symbols and their nonverbal components operate in a synchronized, coordinated way in human communication, and the nonverbal components may either be in accordance with or contradictory to the verbal message. Nonverbal components consist of such things as gesturing, eye contact, a certain distance between individuals, posture, and timing. From a variety of studies it becomes evident that verbal signals have little meaning apart from specific situation in which they are uttered. Nonverbal modes "fill in the gaps" of communication, especially in emotional and attitudinal communication, which is expressed primarily by kinesics and paralanguage. No language response can be separated from the contextual pattern in which it occurs.

Eye Contact   Eye-contact behavior is one component which appears to have wide cultural variance. In the white middle-class culture the speaker who does not meet and maintain acceptable eye contact is apt to have his sincerity doubted.. When others refuse to meet our eyes when we are speaking, we are likely to suspect disinterest or indifference. In Puerto Rican culture, however, children learn early that to communicate respect, one does not maintain eye contact with adults. To refuse to do so is a sign of obedience (Fast, 1970). Similarly, Indian children of various cultural tribes in the Southwest, like Puerto Rican children, lower their heads and eyes as a sign of deference when an adult encounters them face to face (Galloway, 1970). It has been demonstrated repeatedly that culturally different students who attend inner-city schools are frequently paying attention (e.g., sitting with lowered heads and eyes) when their behavior would seem to indicate otherwise.

Space and interpersonal distance: The use of space and desired interpersonal distance also varies considerably. Jews and Italians, for example, have greater preference for physical closeness and touching. Mexican Americans stand very close together when conversing. Blacks greet each other at a greater personal distance than whites. In Oriental cultures crowding together is a sign of warmth and pleasant intimacy (Fast, 1970).

Posture and body movement   The importance of posture and body movement for communicating varies among cultures. Among black males, postural stance is recognized as an important means of projecting self-image; among Appalachians a guarded and slow-moving movement pattern accompanying a cautious verbal response pattern has been described by Glenn (1970).

Facial displays   Although facial displays of the primary affects are pancultural, the rules that regulate affect displays are learned and are culture-specific. There is evidence that Eskimo and Indian children respond more than white children to an instructor's display of positive affect; that is, interaction in a nonverbal manner and conveying much personal warmth may enhance learning significantly in these children (Kleinfield, 1973). This may not hold true for blacks, however. A study of Hawkes and Middleman (1972) indicated that black children manifested no significant differences on task performance with regard to affect style of the teacher.

Prosody or the
Suprasegmentals of Language

The speech rhythm which accompanies each linguistic utterance of culturally different speakers is unique. In addition to its recognition value, speech rhythm contributes significantly to the intelligibility of the utterance* as well as to the attitudinal state of the speaker.

Intonational patterns are basic to the vocal code; that is, the variety of inflectional contours and pitch ranges contributes greatly to the differences that occur in cross-cultural communication. For example, the following intonation patterns were found to be characteristic of black English as opposed to white standard English: (1) a wider pitch range, extending with high pitch levels, (2) more level and rising final pitch contours, (3) greater use of falling final contours with general yes / no questions in formal and, perhaps, threatening situations, (4) the frequent use of falsetto or "high" pitch during greetings (Tarone, 1972). Pare (1968) noted that in a great many African languages, especially in West Africa (from which area came most of the slaves imported into the United States) the pitch level is an extremely important component in the communication process. It is thought that this African influence has been transmitted to the current users of black English.

Syllabication and stress are other components of the vocal code that may differ. Nober and Seymour (1974) mention that black speakers commonly stress the first syllable of bisyllabic words, while standard speakers will generally stress the last syllable.

It is obviously important that the teacher or clinician be familiar with the various vocal codes of his or her students; to do otherwise is to risk communication breakdowns which are potentially disastrous. For example, it would be inappropriate if a clinician thought the habitually and culturally proper soft voice of an Oriental child were pathological and so attempted to treat it. Likewise, attempting to alter a black child's use of a falling final intonation *when asking a question* may be improper. But the teacher, unaware of this pattern, might be upset when a child says "You the teacher?" with a falling inflection—such a pattern might well be considered rude or demanding. Further, if teachers or clinicians have little knowledge of the nonverbal language of students or patients, he or they are

*As a member of the Ohio State University Psycholinguistic Laboratory team that developed the international alphabet of the air: alpha, bravo, charlie, etc., the author noted that the use of emotion in one's voice contributed significantly to the intelligibility of the message being transmitted.

likely to impose and project their own code on a child, something which could cause an increasing withdrawal pattern and alienation of a child. Table 3–3 gives examples of different prosodic features as a function of cultural membership, while Table 3–4 shows the prosody inherent to black English.

The Interrelation of Linguistic Symbols, Body Language, and Prosody

Psychologist Albert Mehrabian (1969) has devised a formula which he feels reveals how much each of the three communicative components (the linguistic code and the two paralinguistic attributes) contribute to the effect the message has upon the receiver. He indicates that the verbal portion of the message is responsible for .07 of the total impact of the message, the prosodic or suprasegmental portion,.38, and facial expression, a facet of body language, .55 (see Figure 3–1). Thus, in face-to-face interactions people rely much more on prosodic and facial cues than on verbal content in determining another's attitude toward them. Ritchie (1973) came to the

Table 3–3

PARALANGUAGE: Some Examples of the Different
Prosodic Features as a Function of Cultural Membership

	Blacks	Middle-Class Whites	Appalachians
Pitch	Falsetto used often; wider pitch range	Increase of pitch in excitement	Monotonous and emotionless
Loudness	Often quite loud	Range from soft in intimate to loud in anger situations	At same level most of the time
Inflection	Falling final contours	Raise final contours in questions	Flat, monotonous; inflection usage is rare; monosyllabic responses
Timing	Pause and increased pitch to indicate continuation; rhythmic	Rapid-fire verbalization	Slow and deliberate with much pause and spacing

As with linguistic forms, these prosodic features will vary according to sociocultural and regional influences.

Table 3-4
Prosodic Features of the Black English Dialect

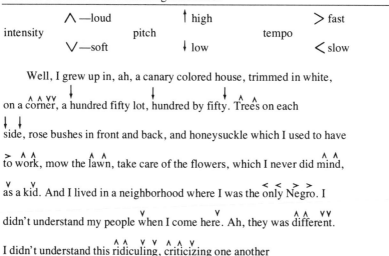

From McDavid, R. and Austin, W. *Communication barriers to the culturally deprived.* Washington: USDE Cooperative Research Project 2107, 1966.

same conclusion when defining the importance of the nonlinguistic components. Emotional and attitudinal communication is expressed primarily by means of paralanguage and not by language per se.

It is clearly incumbent upon the clinician to try to recognize and understand these paralinguistic concomitants if effective communication with the client is to occur. The average person, unschooled in cultural codes of body language, often misinterprets what he sees. Since differences between cultures appear to be pronounced in the area of nonverbal behavior, it is desirable that we learn to recognize these culture-specific differences.

Implications of Culture-Specific Behaviors for Cross-Cultural Communication

Kochman (1970) presents an intriguing analysis of communication failure. He suggests that it is the conflicting nonverbal messages that are primarily responsible when there is a breakdown of cross-cultural communication. He maintains that people fail to communicate because they do not adequately read the cultural signs that each person is sending.

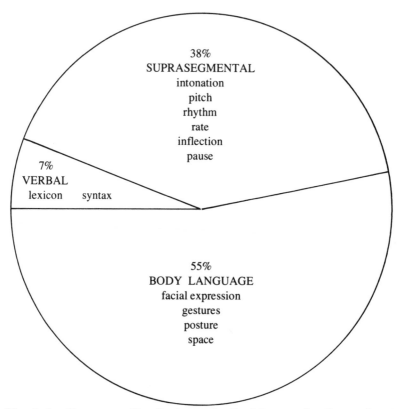

Fig. 3–1. Components Contributing to the Total Impact of a Communicated Message. (Based on findings of Mehrabian, 1969.)

This consistently produces anger, bewilderment, frustration, and pain. Communication becomes virtually impossible when people not only operate from different codes, but also are unaware that different codes are in operation! Invariably, it has been the minority or subordinate cultural groups in society which suffer when communication fails.

CULTURE-SPECIFIC BEHAVIORS AND THE CLINICIAN-CHILD INTERACTION

It is obviously desirable that the clinician be familiar with the cultural background of the client, not only to allow for correct diagnosis as to "difficiency" or "difference" in the child's linguistic patterns, but to avoid misinterpretation of the child's culturally determined paralinguistic behaviors. For example, if the clinician assumed the eye-contact behaviors of the Chicano or black child indicated inattention or disrespect, it would probably alter the clinician's relationship with the child and would definitely give the clinician a false impression regarding the child's motivation. Also, as previously noted, a lower-class black child is likely to use a falling final intonation when asking a general question. The unsophisticated teacher or clinician may consider his intonation pattern demanding or rude. Furthermore, according to Tarone, black children often "compete" verbally; this causes an element of aggressiveness and competitiveness in their communication which may be interpreted as hostility and would alter the relationship with the client.

Suggestions for Altering Possible
Detrimental Nonverbal Behaviors

Strother (1971) has developed an instructional unit in nonverbal communication for students and teachers. General goals of the unit include the following:

1. Learning to express one's own reactions more freely and accurately and recognizing how members of other cultures use nonverbal behavior to communicate.
2. Gaining an understanding of how spacing affects communication and that what constitutes negative violation of space will vary from culture to culture.
3. Understanding the effects of territory on communication. The physical environment in which therapy takes place may be communicating so much formality to the child that verbal responses are stifled.
4. Gaining an understanding of the role of posture and bodily movement in communication. The way a child sits or stands can be an important cue to his receptivity to the therapy or the activity that is being presented.

Armstrong (1972) advocates that this kind of training—as well as training in other related areas—be given to all speech and hearing majors. She states, "Indeed, the development of a whole new curriculum and even a new certificate of clinical competence should be considered for a speech specialist who wishes to work with culturally different students." We concur; we believe that students need to be able to recognize and understand these culturally specific behavior patterns.

Table 3–5 depicts some kinesic differences evident in common situations between black, particularly black lower-class speakers, and members of the middle class. Note, in particular, the style manifested during a job interview; undoubtedly such behavior "turns off" the middle-class employer; similarly, the behavior pattern manifested in school would tend to alienate most teachers who are unaware of these cultural differences.

Table 3–5
Kinesic Differences in Everyday Situations

	Black Lower Class	Middle Class
Job Interview Situation (first impressions)		
Distance	Greet people at greater distances.	
Eye contact	Reluctance to gain eye contact is a nonverbal pattern in West African cultures. This pattern is a way of communicating recognition of an authority subordinate relationship.	Direct eye contact communicates trustworthiness and sincerity.
Speaker/listener relationship	Will look away from another while listening and at him while speaking.	Opposite
Vocal activity interactions	The conversation between BLC and MC people may lack a rhythmic interactional pattern.	
Perception of space	Requires less personal space.	Requires more personal space.
Walking Situation	Slow walk with head elevated and tipped to the side. One arm swings with hand slightly cupped. The gait is slow and rhythmic almost like a walking dancer. This is called a "pimp strut."	Brisk walk, characterized by walking on the balls of one's feet with strides of presumed authority. Both arms will swing.
School Situation (teacher–pupil misunderstanding) Reprimand/lecture		
"rolling the eyes"	Communicates general disapproval and/or hostility	

Table 3–5 (continued)

	Black Lower Class	Middle Class
	to the person in the authority role. Eyes are moved from one side of eyesocket to the other side in a low arc. (This action is witnessed more often in females.)	
Greetings (to friends and to people trusted)		
Touching		Salutation and a hug or kiss.
"cutting the eyes		Eye movement toward rather than away from another persons. Immediately followed by a stare.
body stance	Assumes a "limp stance" becoming an object—no longer a person; often misread as indicating disinterest.	Assumes a stiff position—hands clamped to sides.
"walk away"	This can determine how well a reprimand has been received; for example, if "pimp strut" used in walking away from the scene, displaying discipline is usually useless.	
Distance/space	Requires more closeness from the teacher as child requires less personal space.	
Verbal greeting	Will approach another member of his culture, verbally, greet him, and then may turn his back on him. To do so requires putting oneself in a vulnerable position relative to one's physical safety and this indicates, therefore, an acceptance of the other person.	

Table 3–5 (continued)

	Black Lower Class	Middle Class
Group Gatherings (street-corners and poolhalls)		
Movement	Moving constantly in and out from the center of the circle. Assumes a starionary "pimp strut," dancing in place and practicing competitive word games. Stands with hands halfway in pockets. The free arm will swing, point, and gesture to emphasize conversation.	Remains stationary in the circle.
Conversation	"Sounding" "dozens" and "one liners" are competitive games played by adolescents. Older members of a gang participate in "toasts" or poems recited on street corners or in hang-outs. They are spoken with special voice quality and rhythym. *How* one says something is much more important than *what* one says.	
Religious Situations	In a black sermon the trials of life are cast into a rhythmic mold.	
Male–Female Relationships		
"Stances"	The "rapping stance" or stationary pimp strut is assumed when a young male talks romantically to a female.	

REFERENCES

Armstrong, A. H. Speech therapy and the culturally different student. ERIC Document 070078, 1972.

Bailey, B. L. Towards New Perspective In Negro English Dialectology *American Speech,* 1965, *40,* 171–177

Baratz, J. Teaching reading in an urban Negro school system. In J. C. Baratz & R. W. Shuy (Eds.), *Teaching black children to read.* Arlington, Va.: Center for Applied Linguistics, 1969.

Fasold, R. W. *Tense marking in black English: A linguistic and social analysis.* Arlington, Va.: Center for Applied Linguistics, 1972.

Fast, J. *Body language.* New York: Evans, 1970.

Galloway, C. *Teaching is communication: Non-verbal language in the classroom.* ERIC Document 038069, 1970.

Glenn, M. E. *Appalachia in transition.* St. Louis: Bethany, 1970.

Hawkes, T., Middleman, R. *An experimental field study of the impact of non-verbal communication of affect on children from two socio-economic backgrounds.* ERIC Document 061550, 1972.

Kleinfield, J. *Using non-verbal warmth to increase learning: A cross-cultural experiment.* ERIC Document 081568, 1973.

Kochman, T. *The kinetic element in black idiom.* A paper presented at a meeting of the American Anthropological Association at Seattle, November 1968.

Kochman, T. *Cross-cultural communication: Contrasting perspectives, conflicting sensabilities.* ERIC Document 047026, 1971.

Loban, W. Problems in oral English. *NCTE Research Reports, 5,* 1966.

Labov, W. *The social stratification of English in New York City.* Arlington, Va.: Center for Applied Linguistics, 1966.

McDavid, R., & Austin, W. *Communication barriers to the culturally deprived.* Washington, D.C.: USOE Cooperative Research 2107, 1966.

Mehrabian, A. Communication without words. In *Readings in psychology today.* Del Mar, Calif.: CMR Books, 1969.

Nober, E. H., & Seymour, H. N. *Speech recognition scores of white and black student-teacher listeners for black or white first-grade speakers.* Washington, D.C.: U.S. Office of Education, 1974.

Pare, D. *Relationship of dialect to language skill and intelligibility in a group of fourth-grade Negro children.* Unpublished master's thesis, University of Tennessee, Knoxville, 1968.

Ritchie, M. K. *Non-verbal behavior in speech acts.* ERIC Document 086005, 1973.

Strother, D. *The effects of instruction in non-verbal communication on elementary school teacher competency and student achievement.* ERIC Document 056005, 1972.

Tarone, E. *Aspects of intonation in black English.* ERIC Document 076983, 1972.

Wolfram, W. *A sociolinguistic description of Detroit Negro speech.* Arlington, Va.: Center for Applied Linguistics, 1969.

Wolfram, W. Sociolinguistic implications for educational sequencing. In R. W.
    Fasold & R. W. Shuy (Eds.), *Teaching standard English in the inner city.*
    Arlington, Va.: Center for Applied Linguistics, 1970.
Wolfram, W. & Christian, D. *Sociolinguistic variables in Appalachian dialects.*
    Arlington, Va.: Center for Applied Linguistics, 1975.
Wolfram, W. & Fasold, R. W. *The study of social dialects in American english,*
    Englewood Cliffs, N.J.: Prentice-Hall, 1974.

4
Language and Thought

Language is man's primary vehicle for thinking. Brains think with words. It is not mere verbal play to say we cannot think without speaking, or speak without thinking . . . Without properly ordered specific words, thought is vague and misty, seen dimly through the depth of "feeling" and "intuition".

—Joyce O. Hertzler,
A Sociology of Language

DEFINITIONAL ISSUES

The relationship between language and thought has probably been of interest to humankind throughout recorded history. Are language and thought interrelated so that a language difference is accompanied by a deficit in thought? This view is held generally by proponents of the compensatory approach to educating the culturally different child. Another view, not so widely held, posits that the interrelationship between language and thought has been too superficially examined. It holds that while a dialect of a language may be different from that of the standard, it is not necessarily inferior to the standard dialect; the same may be said of thought. Protagonists of this viewpoint support a system of education that vigorously respects differences in language and thought.

In order to understand better why and how these current views on the relationship between thought and language exist, we shall compare and

71

contrast the ideas presented in various disciplines. Before beginning this comparison, however, it is desirable that we first examine what is meant by the terms "thought" and "language"; these terms are quite abstract, and differing opinions are held as to their meanings.

Definitions of Language

Carrow (1972) defines language as an arbitrary system of vocal symbols that represent a conceptual system utilized for communication by man. This view is a predominant one; it regards language as a purely verbal code. The nonverbal systems are not considered language forms. Similarly, Carroll (1964) defines language as a system of vocal communication within a speech community. He, however, also states that, in theory, language can be "a system underlying any set of responses of which human beings are capable" (p. 3); thus he extends the definition to include facial expression and gestures.

These authors, and the many others who maintain this restricted view of language, have created a serious distinction between the linguistic and paralinguistic communication codes, designating only the former as "language."* This viewpoint, we posit, assumes that the paralinguistic aspects of communication are subordinate or secondary to the verbal code. The importance of the paralinguistic aspects relevant to message comprehension is, however, anything but secondary. As already pointed out, we have suggested that a much greater portion of communicative impact may be attributed to body language and prosodic elements than to the verbal symbols in a transmission. For example, Tarone (1972) reports that meaning can be changed by varying intonation, and when the verbal symbols and the intonation patterns conflict, the interpretation of the message will be determined by the intonation rather than the verbal content. Similarly, the importance of body movements in communication is discussed by Duke (1974), who states that movements can be used to modify the meaning of a verbal message. If nonverbal and prosodic aspects affect the interpretation of the message to such an extent, then it seems unreasonable and arbitrary to exclude paralinguistic elements from the definition of language. Such a division is superficial and does not convey the dependence of the communicative impact on both the linguistic and the paralinguistic components; these constituents are interrelated, and an acceptable definition of language would seem to necessitate both components.

*By linguistic symbols we refer to the phonology, grammar, and lexicon of our verbal or written language; by paralinguistic we refer to body language or prosody; the former is considered to be nonverbal, while the latter is considered to be a verbal aspect of language.

Thus, to comprehend language utterances properly, it is necessary that the auditor also understand both parameters. Yet many studies, such as those of Deutsch, Katz, and Jensen (1968), have based their evaluation of the language and logical processes of the culturally different on verbal dimensions alone, but have concluded that the culturally different are deficient in body language and thought processes as well. Deutsch et al. cite, as an example, the use of the conjunction "if" to mark dependent clauses in conditional sentences and state that a child who does not demonstrate this construction has no way of differentiating dependent and independent clauses and, therefore, will probably have difficulty conceptualizing conditionality. Tarone (1972), however, reports findings that intonation is used to mark dependent clauses by black speakers, so it cannot be said that either their language or thought processes are deficient; rather, failure to recognize intonational marking of dependent clauses is an indication of a deficiency in the tests that do not take paralinguistic elements into account.

Body language is defined by Hall and Hall (1973) as the communication of feelings and attitudes about the speaker. Its communicative power can be seen in the fact that a discrepancy between what a person says and what he actually believes can generally be sensed by others because of the body language used. Hall and Hall also indicate that there are differences in body language across class, generation, region, and culture. McCardle (1974) terms these aspects of body language "nonlexical modifiers" and states that they contribute to the communicational gestalt of the group that uses them and may be misinterpreted by outsiders. These nonverbal forms of language do not generally carry meaning apart from the verbal code, but without them the full impact of the message is not communicated.

These and other studies demonstrate the important role paralinguistic communication, along with linguistic forms of communication, plays in relaying meanings, thoughts, ideas, and attitudes. In order to define language accurately, then, it is necessary to incorporate all of these elements.

Definition of Thought

Wepman (1976) rightly points out that Albert Einstein was far from being a sophisticated verbal speaker: "He had a disability in verbal realms . . . [and was largely nonverbal]. This lack of verbal skill was contrasted by his high ability in nonverbal spheres of activity" (thought) (p. 135).*

*The material appearing here and on page 74 is reprinted from Wepman, J. M. Aphasia: Language without thought or thought without language. *ASHA, 18,* 1976, 131–135. Used with permission of the author and publisher.

Thought is defined by Carroll (1953) as "essentially a matter of how the individual handles information in central mediation processes, whether it comes to him perceptually and nonlinguistically, or already coded linguistically" (p. 103). Osgood (1953) supported this definition; he indicated that an adequate definition of thought also involved a compromise between "peripheral motor theory" and "central theory." The first of these theories holds that thinking is a set of minimal peripheral responses, the brain serving as a relay station. This is a behavioristic view espoused by Watson (1914), who felt that thoughts and ideas were implicit verbal responses. The latter theory, on the other hand, states that thought is a purely central process, with incoming stimuli being integrated and routed to various central areas and thus giving rise to thoughts, images, and ideas. These central processes are thus relevant to the person's ecosystem, to the environment in which he has been reared, to the experiences he has received. All incoming stimuli are related to these experiences. Are these emergent central processes maladaptive to the person's ecosystem? Is he unable to formulate thoughts, etc., that allow him to cope properly with the exingences of his poverty?

Language and Thought
Wepman (1976) suggests the following:

> . . . language usage is inextricably related to thought but is not identical with it; that language is the product of thought; that thought is man's highest mental process and language its maid servant; that the ability to think is innate in men while language is acquired, that Piaget (1923) stated the problem well when he said that language is not the source of logic but is on the contrary structured by logic.
> It is held to be true that without thought there would be no meaningful language; that without thought language would be merely barren repetition (p. 131).

Though most investigators will agree that linguistic coding or "internal speech" is a major mode of representation in thought, there are disagreements as to whether thought is carried out exclusively through language symbols and whether language enhances or limits the thought processes. Deutsch (1967) asserts that "language is the primary avenue for communication, absorption, and interpretation of the environment . . . it also reflects highly acculturated styles of thought and ideational modes for solving and not solving problems" (p. 215). He concludes that variables in language affect cognitive abilities and states that the lower-class poor, or what we have termed the culturally different, are therefore less sophisticated in their thought processes, or methods of handling and integrating information internally, since their language is of a restricted nature. Crow, Murray, and Smythe (1966) use Bernstein's (1962) classification system to support their view that the lower class, with its restricted language code, also has restricted thought processes. The middle class with its elaborated codes, on the other hand, is said to have a greater breadth and range of thought.

Both Deutsch and Crow and their colleagues make assumptions that need to be examined. First, they assume that Bernstein, in classifying the language codes of middle- and lower-class respondents as elaborated and restricted respectively, is judging the code of the lower-class poor to be inferior to that of the middle class. This is a misinterpretation of his findings. Bernstein suggests the language codes are different, not necessarily inferior or substandard, as has been frequently stated. Second, many psychologists and educators adopted Bernstein's postulates on differences in language styles between middle and lower class speakers and assumed that these differences implied restrictions in cognitive behavior. But Bernstein's writings pertain more to sociolinguistic stylistic differences than to cognitive functioning. Third, and most significant, they find the thought processes of the lower-class poor to be inferior, based on the fact that they are different from middle-class thought processes, as determined by language codes. But, as we note elsewhere, the behavior of a cultural group should be analyzed in terms of how successful it is in providing a way of coping with problems, and "the behaviors manifested by the poor child are eminently suitable and proper for him if he and his social-cultural peers are to survive in the world around them" (see p. 4). Also, little consideration, if any, has been given to the paralinguistic aspects of the communication. These problems are addressed in much more detail in the next section.

CURRENT APPLICATIONS

The intersection of thought and language as it relates to the culturally different child has received considerable attention from researchers since 1960. Is the language of the culturally different child indicative of his thought processes? To examine this question, to determine how it relates to substandard or normal thinking processes, we shall review the data relevant to those who support two opposite contentions.

Language Is Inferior: Therefore, Thought Is Inferior

Many researchers of varying disciplines have supported the theory that children from deprived backgrounds exhibit thought processes and oral communication skills that are in general inferior to those of middle-class children.

Educators. Hess and Shipman (1965) conducted a study emphasizing the inferiority of the culturally deprived child. They specifically evaluated interaction patterns utilizing an experimental design which included mothers from several subcultures. These subcultures were divided into four groups: Group A consisted of college-educated professional, executive, and managerial occupational levels; Group B, skilled blue-collar occupational levels, with not more than a high school education; Group C, unskilled or semiskilled occupational levels, with predominantly elementary school education; Group D, unskilled or semiskilled occupational levels, with fathers absent and families supported by public assistance.

The research plan was designed to assess mothers' teaching styles. These ultimately shape the learning styles and information-processing skills their children develop. A total of 160 mothers were interviewed, twice in the home and then at the testing situation where they were observed in structured interaction situations. The results revealed that two types of family control are present when mothers deal with their children. One type is status (position)-oriented control, in which behavior tends to be regulated in terms of role expectancy. In this situation there is little opportunity for the unique characteristics of the child to emerge in the interaction between mother and child. The other type of family control is person-oriented control. In this environment the individual characteristics of the child are taken into account in interactions between mother and child, and interactions are more individualized. Status-oriented systems were more prominent in lower-class families, whereas the person-oriented systems were more prominent in middle-class families. Hess and Shipman concluded that the homes which emphasized person-oriented control would foster a greater growth of cognitive processes since more opportunities exist in such an environment for decision making on the part of the child.

Of major importance here is the method in which the control systems were assigned to the different subcultures. Hess and Shipman revealed that their data was obtained from maternal responses to questions inquiring what the mother would do in order to deal with several different hypothetical situations. It would appear that a better indication of family control systems could be obtained from going into the homes and observing the actual mother–child interactions. As we have pointed out elsewhere in this book, retrospective interviews and hypothetical situations leave much room for misinterpretation of results.* In the home, through observance of everyday interactions, a more complete and certainly a more reliable description of family control systems might be obtained.

A second problem which may have obscured the results of the study was the exclusion of any reference to paralinguistic communication. As previously indicated, the impact of a message is determined mainly by its nonverbal and prosodic components. This could very possibly be the case when a mother is disciplining her child. The tone of her voice, her intonation patterns, and her facial features may play a very important role in this particular situation. Hess and Shipman (1965) did not mention these invaluable components of language when evaluating the type of family control. Had they considered body language and intonation, the data might have revealed results of an entirely different nature. In support of the data generated by Hess and Shipman, Olim Hess, & Shipman (1967) suggested that steps should be taken to alter the mother–child relationship in order to facilitate the child's cognitive development. A second area of concern was that of social reform. Olim and his colleagues also suggest that the entire culture must be altered: "any sizable and longer-lasting benefits from intervention must involve social reform as well as attention to the individual victims of social deprivation and cultural disadvantage."

Raph (1965) contributed to the research with her review of literature concerning language development in socially disadvantaged children. Among the studies that she cited was that of Pavenstedt (1965), who described children from lower-class families as frequently not attending to abstract instructions. More concrete demonstrations were needed to translate instructions into actions from the lower-class children. Lack of attention to abstract instructions, however, may have been a result of short attention spans rather than a lack of abstract ability. If, indeed, the language of lower-class children is "different," a short attention span would be a reasonable explanation for not attending to the more abstract tasks.

Raph also cited the work done by Anastasi and D'Angelo (1952). These researchers, in studying the effects of bilingualism on intelligence in

---

*See D. S. Harrison's Techniques for Eliciting Casual Speech Samples for the Study of the Black English Vernacular. In T. Trabasso & D. S. Harrison (Eds.), *Black English; A Seminar*. Hillsdale, N.J.: LEA Publishers, 1976, for additional information concerning this topic.

Puerto Rican children, found that a group of sixth graders of lower-class status showed a lower level of intellectual functioning. This was attributed to the very low socioeconomic level and to severe language handicaps during initial school experience. It would seem inevitable, however, that a child who was not tested in his native language would do more poorly on an intelligence test than a child who was tested in his native language.

An overview of research articles cited by Raph indicated that the lower-class children are subject to limitations in opportunities to develop mature cognitive behavior. These studies make no mention of home visits or the nonverbal components of communication—critical factors in our view.

Gordon (1965), another educator who reviewed relevant literature, cited Ausubel as one who concluded that a delay in the acquisition of certain formal language forms resulted in difficulty in the transition from concrete to abstract modes of thought, reported to occur primarily in the lower-class homes. McCandless (1952) confirmed this hypothesis. He concluded that socially disadvantaged children tended to be more concrete and inflexible in abstract thinking than did the more "privileged" child.

Gordon summarized his review by stating that the observations recorded concerning socially disadvantaged children were evaluated against a "background of experience with children from the homes of middle-class white U. S. nationals." These studies indicated that language, styles, and values of the lower-class child are "negatives" to be overcome in school. This assumption could be devastating to a child. McDavid (1972) voiced the problem quite frankly when he stated that "once a child felt that school considered his home language inferior, *nothing* could make him change" (p. 357). The particular language and culture of the child should be respected; not regarded as inferior.

Psychologists. Anastasi did much research in the field of psychology as it relates to language and thought. In her book *Differential Psychology* (1958) she supported the assumption that children from lower-class families develop intellectual and performance skills inferior to those of their middle-class counterparts. "In general, there seems to be a difference of about 20 points between the mean IQ's of the children of professional men and those of the children of unskilled laborers" (p. 517). She also concluded that lower socioeconomic groups do not contribute their proportion of intellectually productive individuals.

One of the major contributors, and frequently quoted researchers in the area of language development and cognition, has been John. In her 1963 study concerning the intellectual development of slum children an experimental design that compared three levels of language behavior was utilized. This multilevel system of language analysis, comparing labeling, relating, and categorizing, was considered to be of theoretical benefit. Her efforts suggested that middle-class children surpassed their lower-class age-mates in acquiring a larger vocabulary and a higher nonverbal IQ. Middle-class children were also considered to have an advantage over lower-class children in tasks requiring abstract thought. John further implied that cognitive learning requires specific feedback not as available to the lower-class child as to the middle-class child. Brown (1965) on the other hand, contends that one cannot draw a valid conclusion about cognitive development from the facts of vocabulary acquisition. "No one has ever proved that vocabulary builds from the concrete to the abstract more often than it builds from the abstract to the concrete. The best generalization seems to be that each thing is first given its most common name" (Brown, 1965, p. 273). There is a need for more research in more valid ways to measure cognitive development.

John and Goldstein (1964) emphasized the fact that children develop and test their tentative notions about the meanings of words and structures of sentences chiefly through verbal interactions with more verbally mature speakers. If this is the route of normal acquisition, Jensen (1967) suggested that if a child is forced to spend a great deal of his time in the company of other children who are not his verbal superiors, his language development will measureably suffer. Since it is normally accepted that lower-class children come from larger families with a number of children present in the homes, Jensen was implying that the language development of these children would be retarded and that since there was a verbal deficit in these lower-class children, their cognitive disadvantage could be attributed to this.

Deutsch (1964) supported Jensen's general philosophy in reporting that children from low socioeconomic backgrounds are less able to handle intellectual and linguistic tasks. He agreed with Hess and Shipman that maternal influences are invaluable in developing their children's cognitive skills. Class differences in maternal verbal style are credited by Deutsch for contributing heavily to the superior problem-solving performances for middle-class mothers working with their children than for mothers and children of lower-class status.

Sociologists.   Brandis and Henderson (1970) have suggested that lower-class children are very deprived because of their environment. From their research they draw several conclusions: (1) lower-class children do not show a more developed use of language, (2) lower-class children receive less stimulation than do middle-class children, and (3) the cognitive horizons of the lower class tend to be more limited. They further claim that "the relationship between measured ability and educational attainment is less direct in the case of the middle-class child, whereas the relationship between measured ability and educational attainment in the case of the working class child is more direct" (p. 119). In closer examination of this statement it would appear that little consideration was given to the fact that the educational system has been a very culturally biased institution. The middle-class standards have been inadvertently imposed upon children of lower-class environments. The effect of being continuously bombarded by educators who adhere to the assumption that lower-class children are inferior must certainly be devastating. Similarly, the children themselves begin to assume they are inferior and are incapable of doing the work required in school. The high dropout rate of lower-class children could conceivably influence the direct relationship between mental ability and educational attainment that was referred to earlier.

Other researchers. Freeberg and Payne (1967) conducted a study which specifically dealt with parental influence on cognitive development. Their results indicated that mothers play an important role in developing cognitive skills. They claimed that lower-class mothers tended to use a more restricted language code. This code ultimately affected the cognitive growth and created within their children a more concrete outlook in problem-solving activities. Freeberg and Payne also emphasized the importance of verbal stimulation by the parents. Results indicated a positive relationship between the amount of verbal stimulation and encouragement which the child receives from the parents and the child's level of cognitive development. These findings are highly consistent with those of Wachs, Uzgiria, and Hunt (1971).

From this review of the literature it becomes increasingly obvious that these researchers imply that something is indeed lacking in the environment, family, and child of the lower class—specifically the standard English language patterns and cultural system of the predominate middle class. In order for these "deprived children" to coexist with the middle class effectively in the United States educational system, they must adopt the middle-class standards.

Language Is Not Inferior; Therefore, Thought Is Not Inferior

We have pointed out that the advocators of the inferior thought and language model have developed a widely accepted doctrine in American society. Other researchers, however, are now suggesting that the language patterns and cognitive processes are *not* inferior but merely reflect the influences of the culture of which they are a part.

A speech pathologist.   Anastasiow (1972), addressing the problem of language and thought, has contended that poverty children's language was different but not deficient. He devised a sentence repetition technique based on the work of Menyuk (1968), who had shown that if children were asked to repeat a sentence, they would do so only if the sentence matched or was below their level of language development. Anastasiow's results demonstrated that black inner-city children will alter the sentences they were asked to repeat so that the sentences will conform to the regularities of their dialect: "The fact that children will change the sentence to conform to their own language appears to be strong evidence that poverty children have a different rather than deficient language" (p. 27). According to the same theory, the cognitive processes of the poverty child will also be different rather than deficient.

Psychologists.   Genshaft and Hirt (1974) conducted a study concerning the language differences between black and white children. They cited the works of Stewart (1965) as among those indicating that the language development and ultimately the cognitive development of ghetto children are merely different. Stewart emphasized the sociological factors, stating that language development and thought development are determined primarily by one's culture. Thus, different speech and cognitive systems are created as a result of different orders of relevance. Language development is interrelated with learning the requirements of one's social structure.

With these theories in mind, Genshaft and Hirt concluded that in order to evaluate effectively the language differences of black and white children, an experimental design should be developed that allows for the presentation of stimuli in more than just the standard English. They used such a design, and the results were very enlightening. On standard English sentence presentations, both black and white children performed equally well. On sentence presentations in black dialect, however, the white children performed significantly worse. Genshaft and Hirt (1974) concluded from these findings that there is bilingual language development in the black ghetto child. In view of this theory it would not be presumptious to assume that cognitive development is not deficient but that it too is influenced by the language system. One would not venture to say that the white child, because he scored lower on the black English sentence task, has inferior language and cognitive development. Yet, the advocators of the theory that adheres to the inferiority of lower-class children have used that same argument for decades.

Although a psychologist by discipline, Cole (1971) discusses language and thought from an anthropological viewpoint. Cole has performed extensive cross-cultural research, and his main emphasis has been with the cultural influences that shape cognitive processes. In applying research to the problem of subcultural differences in cognitive behavior in the United States, he stated that "cultural differences in cognition reside more in the situations to which particular cognitive processes are applied than in the existence of a process in one cultural group and its absence in another" (Cole, 1971, p. 233).

Educators must eliminate the assumption that all children living in the United States need to conform to the same thought and language patterns. Not all children have the same experiences to which to relate their cognitive processes. To evaluate all children by one standard, an American middle-class standard, is clearly improper if one is to assume, as did Cole, that intelligence is not to be viewed separately from the social context of which it is a part.

Sociolinguists.   Entwisle (1968) made most provocative statements about the language development of slum children, many of which are in direct contradiction to those of researchers who adhere to the inferiority of language and thought of the slum child. She suggested that the pressures of a young child growing up in the slums may be such that certain kinds of verbal proficiency may be more powerful than those impinging upon the suburban child. "The slum child must find his own way around and it is common to see preschool children unattended on sidewalks near busy streets. Lack of supervision could force the slum child to develop verbal skills at an early age" (Entwisle, 1968, p. 18). Therefore, the cognitive proficiency for certain types of problem-solving activities may also develop at an early age.

Entwisle cited the Hess and Shipman study (1965) in which the restricted verbal environment of the lower class was discussed in detail. Hess and Shipman surmised that the lower-class child was subjected to very simple verbal interactions, television being an example of such an uncomplicated verbal model that is available to the slum child. Entwisle suggested that television may be a help instead of a detriment to the slum child. Unlike the suburban child, who is exposed to a large variety of verbal models, the slum child may be exposed almost entirely to straightforward and redundant sets of utterances. "Such exposure could favor early development and lead to an early appreciation of form class properties, particularly for the very common words and for verbal concepts at a low level of abstraction" Entwisle, 1968 p. 19).

In her test of this hypothesis, Entwisle revealed some surprising statistics. First-grade white and black slum children are accelerated compared to first-grade white children living in the suburbs. As the slum children progress through school, however, they fall increasingly further behind the suburban child. It might be possible that as the slum child is bombarded by the middle-class biases of the school establishment, his intellectual functioning is negatively affected.

In view of these facts, Entwisle (1970) denounced the theory of genetic influences regarding inferior language and throught patterns. If, indeed, the black child performs on par with the white child at a specified age level, it certainly destroys the theory that there are genetic factors responsible for the lower intellectual attainment of the slum child. What educators must now come to grips with is the fact that the school establishment is not providing lower class children with the kind of education they need. If schools were fulfilling these needs, the slum child would always be on par with the suburban child—regardless of age level.

Baratz (1969a) addressed herself to the dispute over language and cognitive differences of "disadvantaged" black children. She attacked the statements made by those researchers (Deutsch, 1964; Hess & Shipman, 1965; Raph, 1967; Wei, Lavatelli, & Jones 1971) who support the assumptions that the ghetto child is underdeveloped in his cognitive abilities, that his language is inferior, and that his environment is impoverished in language experience. Their view disregards the fact that "different language systems may give rise to different cognitive strategies." Baratz stated emphatically that ghetto children are not verbally destitute, nor are they nonverbal. They merely have a fully developed but different system from that of standard English.

In another study Baratz (1969b) made good her criticisms of past researchers, obtaining results which indicated that there are two dialects involved in the education complex of black children, especially when these children are exposed to the middle-class standards of most educational curricula. Further implications of the findings suggest that black children are generally not sufficiently bidialectal. Although this assumption conflicts with the results of Genshaft and Hirt (1974), the point is well taken that there is evidence of dialect interference when black children attempt to use standard English. Baratz provided an excellent summary of her research in the following statement: "Using a standard English criterion for tests that ask, 'How well has standard English been developed in this child?' is excellent; however, using a standard English criterion for tests that ask, 'How well has this child developed language?' is absurd if the primary language that the child is developing is not standard English" (Baratz, 1969b, p. 899).

Labov (1973), also an advocator of the "difference" theory as opposed to the deficit (or deficient) theory, repeatedly emphasizes that previous psychologists and educators knew very little about language and thought in relation to the lower-class child, especially the black child. His research is now providing analysis of one dialect in particular, nonstandard Negro English (NNE). Labov denounced much of the findings of supporters of the assumption that the thought and language of the black child is inferior and asserted that many of their conclusions have been based upon interviews that do not reveal evidence of the child's total verbal capacity and upon intelligence tests that are irrefutably biased.

The concept of verbal deprivation has no basis in social reality. In fact, Negro children in the urban ghettos receive a great deal of verbal stimulation, hear more well-formed sentences than middle-class children, and participate fully in a highly verbal culture. They have the same basic vocabulary, possess the same capacity for conceptual learning, and use the same logic as anyone else who learns to speak and understand English (Labov, 1970, pp. 153–154).

Labov's research indicated that NNE is a separate communication system closely related to standard English but set apart from surrounding dialects by a number of very persistent, logical, and systematic differences. Fisher (1964) gave a possible explanation for these variations, stating that variants express how they feel about their relative status in comparison to other conversants. There are equal ways of expressing the same logical content. If, indeed, NNE is a logical nonstandard—but not sub-standard—language system, cognitive development would also follow logical patterns since the language spoken in a culture helps to shape the cognitive structure of the individuals speaking that language (Brown & Lenneberg, 1954). Admitting that lower-class children have no capacity for conceptual thinking would be admitting that they speak a very primitive language. The literature certainly does not support this view.

Sociologists. Bernstein is perhaps one of the most frequently quoted pioneer researchers in the area of language and its effects upon cognitive processes (1962). In his study Bernstein described two opposing language codes existing in middle-class mothers and working-class mothers. The former exhibited an "elaborated" code in which tasks were explained more completely and linguistic structures were more complex. In the lower-class environment the mothers exhibited a "restricted" code, characterized by simple linguistic structures and the explanation of tasks in a concrete manner. The restricted code ultimately influenced the cognitive development of the lower-class child, creating, according to some people, a cumulative deficiency in cognitive growth (Hess & Shipman, 1965).

Unfortunately, although Bernstein himself has repeatedly said that he was describing patterns of actual speech performance, his research has been used to support the assumption that there is a direct relationship between overt language form and concept formation (Cazden, 1970). Bernstein initially made these distinctions between the "elaborated" and "restricted" codes from observations he made with British citizens. These definitions have been severely modified in order to apply to the United States socioeconomic standards. Baratz addressed herself to this matter emphatically stating that "Bernstein's theories have been so bastardized in this country that, for example, the presence or absence of a specific word form that has a difinite structural relationship in standard English has been taken as the definition of whether or not a particular concept is present for the child" (Baratz, 1969a). Bernstein definitely found social-class differences in the degree to which meaning is expressed; however, these differences do not imply that the lower-class child is deficient in language patterns and cognitive skills.

Whiting and Hitt (1972) conducted a study in order to prove the previous statement. The sample population for this investigation consisted of 50 students between the age range of 17 and 22. The students were of Mexican-American, black, and American-Indian ancestry and were from rural, low-income (below poverty level) families in eight states. Eight middle-class white college students were randomly selected to serve as a control group. All groups participated in a puzzle-solving task. Whiting and Hitt were baffled by the outcome in that they found no significant differences among the groups. They concluded that "if restricted codes constitute a permanent bar to the learning of abstract concepts, our subjects must have been anomalies" (Whiting & Hitt, 1972, p. 73).

CONCLUSION

Unfortunately, many writers have assumed that the cognitive skills, judgmental abilities, and thought processes of the poor are inferior to those of the more affluent. Obviously, one's abilities and skills are dependent, in part, upon one's lifestyle. Since lifestyles vary considerably as a function of social class, it should not be unexpected that people from these different social classes will behave differently in response to the unique problems encountered in their environments. As long as they adequately solve these problems, their higher levels of mental functioning can not be said to be inferior.

To relate these mental functions to language patterns and to additionally suggest the existance of an interrelationship is valid if one allows for the presence of different behaviors and language patterns without the prejorative labeling of these differences.

Where thought and language have been branded as "inferior," it is noteworthy that not only the adaptive functions of thought processes, and social class, but the paralinguistic accompaniments to the linguistic code are frequently found to have been ignored. Thought, however, is inextricably related to a language system that combines both the paralinguistic and linguistic codes.

In conclusion, there are culturally different thought processes as there are also culturally different linguistic and paralinguistic processes. All are normal and appropriate in a pluralistic society.

REFERENCES

Anastasi, A., and D'Angelo, R. A comparison of Negro and white preschool children in language development and Goodenough Draw-a-Man IQ. *J. genet. Psychol.*, 1952, *81*, 147–165.
Anastasiow, N. J. Educating the culturally different child. *Viewpoints*, 1972, *48*, 21–42.
Baratz. J. C. Language and cognitive assessment of Negro children: Assumptions and research needs. ASHA, 1969 (a) *11*, 87–91.
Baratz, J. C. A bi-dialectal task for determining language proficiency in economically disadvantaged Negro children. *Child Development*, 1969 (b), *40*, 889–901.
Bernstein, B. Social class, linguistic codes and grammatical elements. *Language and Speech*, 1962, *5*, 221–40.
Brandis, W., & Henderson, D. *Social class, language and communication.* London: Routledge and Kegan Paul, 1970.
Brown, R. How shall this thing be called? In P. H. Mussen (Ed.), *Readings in child development and personality*. New York: Harper & Row, 1965.
Brown, R. & Lenneberg, A. A study in language and cognition. *Journal of Abnormal and Social Psychology*, 1954, *49*, 454–462.
Carroll, J. B. *The Study of language: A survey of linguistics and related disciplines in America*. Cambridge: Harvard University Press, 1953.
Carroll, J. B. *Language, thought and reality: Selected writings of Benjamin Lee Whorf.* New York: Wiley, 1956.
Carroll, J. B. *Language and Thought*. Englewood Cliffs, N.J.: Prentice-Hall, 1964.

Carrow, E. Assessment of speech and language in children. In J. E. McLean, et al. (Eds.), *Language intervention with the retarded*. Baltimore: University Park Press, 1972.

Cazden, C. B. The neglected situation in child language research and education. In F. Williams (Ed.), *Language and poverty*. Chicago: Markham, 1970.

Cole, M. (Ed.). *The cultural context and learning and thinking*. New York: Basic Books, 1971.

Crow, L. D., Murray, W. I. & Smythe, H. H. *Educating the culturally disadvantaged child*. New York: McKay, Inc., 1966.

Deutsch, M. Facilitating development in the pre-school child: Social and psychological perspectives. *Merrill-Palmer Quarterly*, 1964, *10*, 249–262.

Deutsch, M. The role of social class in language development and cognition. In A. H. Passow et al. (Ed.), *Education of the disadvantaged: A Book of readings*. New York: Holt, Rinehart, and Winston, 1967.

Deutsch, M., Katz, I., & Jensen, A. *Social class, race and psychological development*. New York: Holt, Rinehart and Winston, 1968.

Duke, C. R. *Nonverbal behavior and the communication process*. ERIC Document ED 088090, 1974.

Entwisle, D. R. Subcultural differences in children's language development. *International Journal of Psychology*, 1968, *3*, 14–22.

Entwisle, D. R. Semantic systems of children: Some assessments of social class and ethnic differences. In F. Williams (Ed.), *Language and poverty*. Chicago: Markham, 1970.

Fisher, J. L. Social influences on the choice of a linguistic variant. In D. Hymes (Ed.), *Language in culture and society*. New York: Harper & Row, 1964.

Freeberg, N. E., & Payne, D. T. Parental influence on cognitive development in early childhood: A review. *Child Development*, 1967, *38*, 65–87.

Genshaft, J. L., & Hirt, M. Language differences between black children and white children. *Developmental Psychology*, 1974, *10*, 451–456.

Gordon, E. W. Characteristics of socially disadvantaged children. *Review of Educational Research*, 1965, *35*, 377–387.

Hall, E., & Hall, M. Sounds of silence. In J. A. DeVito (Ed.), *Language concepts and processes*. Englewood Cliffs, N.J.: Prentice-Hall, 1973.

Hess, R. D., & Shipman, V. C. Early experience and the socialization of cognitive modes in children. *Child Development*, 1965, *36*, 869–886.

Jensen, A. R. Social class and verbal learning. In J. P. DeCecco (Ed.), *The psychology of language, thought, and instruction*. New York: Holt, Rinehart and Winston, 1967.

Jensen, A. R. How much can we boost IQ and scholastic achievement? *Harvard Educational Review*, 1969, *39*, 1–123.

Jensen, A. R. Learning ability, intelligence, and educability. In Allen (Ed.), *Psychological factors in poverty*. Chicago: Markham, 1970.

John, V. The intellectual development of slum children: Some preliminary findings. *Amer J Orthopsychiat*, 1963, *33*, 813–822.

John, V. R., & Goldstein, L. S. The social context of language acquisition. *Merrill-Palmer Quarterly,* 1964, *10,* 265–275.

Labov, W. The logic of nonstandard English. In F. Williams (Ed.), *Language and poverty.* Chicago: Markham, 1970.

McCandless, B. Environment and intelligence. *American Journal of Mental Deficiency,* 1952, *54,* 674–691.

McDavid, R. I. Sense and nonsense about American dialects. In V. Clark, P. Eschholz, & A. Rosa (Eds.), *Language: Introductory readings.* New York: St. Martin's Press, 1971.

McCardle, E. S. *Nonverbal communication.* New York: Dekker, 1974.

Menyuk, P. Children's learning and reproduction of grammatical and nongrammatical phonological sequences. *Child Development,* 1968, *39,* 849–859.

Olim, E., Hess, R., and Shipman, V. Role of mothers' language styles in mediating their preschool children's cognitive development. *The School Review,* 1967, *75,* 414–424.

Osgood, C. E. *Method and theory in experimental psychology.* New York: Oxford University Press, 1953, Chaps. 15, 16.

Pavenstedt, E. A comparison of the child-rearing environment of upper-lower and very low lower-class families. *American Journal of Orthopsychiatry,* 1965, *35,* 89–98.

Raph, J. B. Language and development in socially disadvantaged children. *Review of Educational Research,* 1965, *35,* 389–399.

Stewart, W. A. Urban Negro speech: Sociolinguistic factors affecting English teaching. In R. W. Shuy (Ed.), *Social dialects and language learning.* Champaign, Ill.: The National Council of Teachers of English, 1965.

Stewart, M. A. Toward a history of American-Negro dialect. In F. Williams (Ed.), *Language and poverty.* Chicago: Markham 1970.

Tarone, E. *Aspects of intonation in black English.* ERIC Document ED 076983, 1972.

Wachs, T. D., Uzgiria, I. C. & Hunt, J. M. Cognitive development in infants of different age levels and from different environmental backgrounds: An explanatory investigation. *Merrill-Palmer Quarterly,* 1971, *17,* 283–317.

Watson, J. B. *Behavior: An introduction to comparative psychology.* New York: Holt, Rinehart and Winston, 1914.

Wei, T., Lavatelli, C. B., & Jones, R. S. Piaget's concept of classification: A comparative study of socially disadvantaged and middle-class young children. *Child Development,* 1971, *42,* 919–927.

Whiting, G. C., & Hitt, W. C. Code-restrictedness and communication dependent problem solving: An exploratory study. *Speech Monographs,* 1972, *39,* 68–73.

Wepman, J. M. Aphasia: Language without thought or thought without language. *ASHA,* 1976, *18,* 3.

PART II

Testing and Evaluating the Culturally Different Child

5
Intelligence and the IQ Score

It is my conviction that a huge number of American children, variously called cultural-familial mental retardates, culturally deprived, school dropouts, or simply poor children, have not been given sufficient or even grossly equal opportunities to develop school-related skills and intelligences. . . .

—Burton Blatt,
The Intellectually Disfranchised

WHAT IS INTELLIGENCE?

Intelligence has been defined as the capacity to adjust to or change one's environment; the power of meeting a situation and resolving any difficulties encountered; or simply, to solve problems. The simplest definition is that that which is measured by intelligence tests is intelligence.

Perhaps it would help if we thought of two types of intelligence: the type an intelligence test measures, and the kind a person is able to utilize in life situations–one's adaptability. The first we might call theoretical intelligence, and the second we could consider as practical intelligence.

Theoretical intelligence may also be defined as genetic potentiality; it is assumed to be "fixed" by heredity. Practical intelligence develops as a function of the interaction of the organism to its environment.

What then is intelligence? There is obviously no simple answer to this question. At the present time biological intellectual capacity cannot be measured directly. It can only be inferentially derived. Specifically, the potential that the child possesses is a function of his genotype, and the genetic potential of the child is influenced by his environmental history. That is, the health of the mother previous to and during the birth of the child, as well as the health of the child postnatally, may affect the child's performance skills on certain tests. In addition, the nature of the child's experiential interactions with his environment will also influence the development of these skills. Thus a child's performance is always modified, and it is ultimately the result of an interaction among genetic, health and experiential factors overlaid by the variables inherent in the testing situation. Unfortunately, the extent and magnitude of the experiential involvement, as well as relevant information concerning the test-situation variables, are often unknown and/or neglected when inferences and interpretations regarding test performance are made.

It should be remembered that the original purpose of "intelligence" testing was to predict which children would succeed academically; unfortunately, the term "intelligence" currently possesses pejorative connotations in regard to race and genotype. Thus, a genetic inferiority theory as related to intelligence, rather than a test score's predictive value, assumes unwarranted importance. Perhaps as Mercer and Brown (1973) state, the current dialogue about ethnic differences in "intelligence" would have never developed if Binet had labeled his scale "A General Measure of Academic Readiness" rather than a measure of "intelligence." People tend to believe their own labels.

In view of these concepts, it is apparent that there is a need to reexamine the multitudinous amounts of educational, psychological, linguistic, and other kinds of test data accumulated over the years which confirm the inferiority of the poor and culturally different child. For example, Mercer and Brown (1973) found that, based upon such test results, "about four times more Mexican-Americans and three times more Blacks were being labeled as mentally retarded than would be expected from their percentage in the general population. The rate of labeling for Anglos (English-speaking Caucasians) was only about half the number that would be expected." The cultural ethnocentrism that admits to only one correct way or method or performance violates the integrity of peoples with diverse heritages.

THE GENETIC HYPOTHESIS

The current furor over IQs started in 1969 with an article by Jensen in the *Harvard Educational Review*. In his article "How Much Can We Boost I.Q. and Scholastic Achievement?" Jensen questioned the validity of compensatory educational programs, the basis of which is that differences in I.Q. are almost entirely a result of environmental differences. He began his essay with the following quotation from the U.S. Commission on Civil Rights as evidence of the failure of compensatory education: "The fact remains, however, that none of the programs appear to have raised significantly the achievement of participating pupils, as a group, within the period evaluated by the Commission" (Jensen, 1969).

Jensen believes that the verbal deprivation theorists, such as Deutsch and Bereiter, have been given every opportunity to prove their case and have failed. This leads him to say that a strictly environmental hypothesis is not consistent with the evidence. He goes on to support his assumption by saying that there are two levels of learning, which he calls Level I, or associative-type learning, and Level II, or cognitive or conceptual learning; he further argues that the middle-class white population is differentiated from the working-class white and black population in Level II learning and that this difference is genetically transmitted.

Holding socioeconomic status constant, Jensen reports that blacks test about 11 I.Q. points below the average for white populations. Since genetic pools caused by intermarriage are said to give rise to a number of phenotypic characteristics having high heritability, he questions why differences in intelligence cannot also be attributed to breeding populations or race, particularly since, "no one has yet produced any evidence based on a properly controlled study to show that representative samples of Negro and white children can be equalized in intellectual ability through statistical control of environment and education." He adds that only in cases of extreme environmental isolation is there evidence for social environmental influence.

Herrnstein, in a 1971 article published in the *Atlantic Monthly* magazine, strongly supported Jensen's thesis that IQ is largely hereditary, but restricted his arguments to social class rather than race. He stated that the correlation between IQ and social class is "undeniable, substantial, and worth noting." He made a "cautious conclusion" based on a survey of scientific literature that the upper class scores about 30 IQ points above the lower class. He then adds that the data on IQ and social-class differences show that we have been living with an inherited stratification of our society for some time. "The higher the heritability the closer will human society approach a virtual caste system, with families sustaining their position on the social ladder from generation to generation as parents and children are more nearly alike in their essential features."

Shockley (1972) describes blacks as "genetically inferior" people. With little (if any) documentation of his beliefs, he has assumed a drastic stance; for example, he has proposed a "bonus sterilization plan" under which blacks, as well as whites, with sufficiently low IQ would receive incentives if they agreed to sterilization.

In a series of articles in the December 1973 issue of *Psychology Today*, Rice gives a very interesting account of the disturbance caused by Jensen, Herrnstein, and Shockley and their disruptive beliefs about the heritability of IQ. The same issue also presents the Jensen (1969) and Deutsch (1969) controversy wherein Deutsch claimed to have found numerous errors or misinterpretations of data in Jensen's arguments, which Jensen has subsequently rebutted, but not to Deutsch's satisfaction.

An examination of these and other data reveal that the majority of the available literature supports a more dynamic interaction of heredity and environment than Jensen, Herrnstein, or Shockley are willing to accept. For example, Dobzhansky (1973) says he is convinced by Jensen's argument about IQ and race. He contends that genes determine the intelligence (or stature) of a person only in his particular environment. He believes that evidence securely establishes the fact that individual differences in scores are genetically as well as environmentally conditioned. How much of this variation is due to genetic factors, however, is unknown. Dobzhansky also supports Scarr-Salapatek's (1973) assertion that differences between humans can simply be accepted as differences and not deficits. If there are alternate ways of being successful within the society, then differences can be valued as variations on the human theme, regardless of their environment or genetic origin.

Other writers doubt that performance—intellectual, physical, or social—is developed from a genotypic or inherited base. The organism, as it evolves prenatally and postnatally, incorporates energy and information; human development, therefore, is a cumulative, active process utilizing environmental inputs, not a simplistic unfolding of a genetically given structure. What is inherited is not this or that trait, but the manner in which the developing organism responds to his environment. Humankind is capable of persuing a great variety of life styles, but it is enabled to do so by different training and education, not by acquiring different genes. Nature and nurture are so obviously necessary and inseparable that the important question is not which is more important but, rather, how they together determine our qualities. We cannot change our heredity, but, at least in some cases, we can choose an environment to which our heredity will respond most favorably.

Gordon (1969) says that developmental influences begin to

complicate research in behavioral genetics through the influence of maternal environment even before birth. He also feels there is no study, as yet, which adequately links intelligence, potential ability, educability, or even achievement to a specifiable set of genetic coordinates associated with an aggregate larger than a family line or perhaps lineage.

Many other authors have reacted, as well as overreacted, to the genetic thesis of IQ; some writers are in partial agreement, but most are in total disagreement. Jensen insists that his genetic hypothesis must be seriously considered for two reasons: (1) because the environmentalistic theory has failed in many of its most important predictions, the probability of the genetic theory is increased; (2) since genetically conditioned physical characteristics differ markedly between racial groups, there is a strong priority likelihood that genetically conditioned behavioral or mental characteristics will also differ. The crux of the matter, however, still lies in the test situation from which Jensen collects the data to make his predictions; if the data are invalid, then his generalizations are improper. We posit that such is the case.

IQ SCORES

As we have noted, the major IQ tests may generate biased test scores. Unless a particular test has been standardized on a given group of culturally different people, it is to be expected that the scores of the culturally different will be lower than "normal." Since so many poor children were receiving below normal scores, the prestigious American Association of Mental Deficiency (AAMD) has altered its definitions of mental retardation as follows.

Two criteria must be met before a child is to be considered below normal, or retarded: (1) an IQ score of 69 or below, as obtained by a state licensed psychologist on a comprehensive test such as the Stanford-Binet or the Wechsler Intelligence Scale for Children; and (2) an adaptation level not commensurate to that of the child's cultural peers. Since we have traditionally considered IQ scores between 90–110 to be within the normal range, it is of obvious importance that the new AAMD criteria be accepted by people. If not, we shall continue to mislabel people based upon their invalid IQ scores.

IQ scores, or any other scores relevant to the child's functioning, must be interpreted with caution. Frequently we meet teachers who tell us that test scores generated by school psychologists, speech clinicians, special educators, or other testers do not seem to agree with their subjective appraisal of the child. But they usually accept the information presented by the specialist as being proper and correct, and their subjective opinions as being incorrect.

A story we like to tell concerns a child who recently moved into to a new community where he attended the second grade in his neighborhood school. Since he hadn't attended the school previously, the second grade teacher had no previous information about his skills; in point of fact he had performed exceedingly well in the first grade in his former school. When the Metropolitian Achievement Test was administered to the children at the beginning of the year, this child misinterpreted the test directions on the reading sub-section. As a consequence he received a very poor grade in reading, and was then placed by the teacher in the slow (i.e., retarded) reading group. When another test was arranged for the child during the same week, and the score revealed high reading skills, he was transferred to the fast (i.e., bright) reading group. All in one week's time! Obviously, the IQ score, or any score, should be evaluated carefully by the teacher or clinician as to its reliability and validity before being accepted.

A teacher's appraisal of a child's intellectual capacity, or of a child's ability to perform various tasks, should be solicited by all professional testers. Indeed, the new Public Law 94-142, makes such input mandatory. Unfortunately teacher input is too infrequently used in planning appropriate programs for these children. In our own work, we use the teacher's opinion regarding a given child's level of competence; we have found that most teachers are very capable of making valid judgements regarding the functioning of children in their classrooms.

REFERENCES

Deutsch, M. Happenings on the way back to the forum: Social science, IQ, and race differences revisited. *Harvard Educational Review*, 1969, *39*, 523–557.

Dobzhansky, T. Differences are not deficits. *Psychology Today*, 97–101, 1973, *7*(7).

Gordon, E., & Jablonsky, A. Relevance and pluralism in curriculum development. *IRCD Bulletin*, 1969, *6*, 139–149.

Herrnstein, R. S. I.Q. *The Atlantic Monthly*, 1971, *228*(3), 43–64.

Jensen, A. How much can we boost I.Q. and scholastic achievement? *Harvard Educational Review*, 1969, *39*, 1–123.

Mercer, J. R., & Brown, W. C. Racial differences in I.Q.: Fact or artifact. In C. Senna (Ed.), *The fallacy of I.Q.* New York: Third Press, 1973, pp. 56–113.

Rice, B. The high cost of thinking the unthinkable. *Psychology Today,* 1973, 7(7), 89–93.

Scarr-Salapetek, S. (Ed.). *Socialization.* Columbus, Ohio: Merrill, 1973.

Shockley, W. Dysgenics, geneticity, raceology: A challenge to the intellectual responsibility of educators. *Phi Delta Kappan,* 1972, Jan., 297–307.

6
The Tests

Although the cultural biases in I.Q. tests have been recognized since the 1930s, they are seldom, if ever, taken into account in assessing individual performance. Socio-cultural biases are not emphasized and, usually are not even discussed in the training of psychometrists and school psychologists.

—J. R. Mercer and W. C. Brown
In *The Fallacy of I.Q.*

In the 1960s linguists, psychologists, and educators acknowledged the importance of focusing on the language competencies of the child entering the educational system for the first time. With this movement came an awareness of difference in measured performance between middle-class children and children of other ethnic and/or cultural groups. These differences were said to be characteristics of children "atypical" of a middle-class society and, thereby, language deficient. The counterpart to the deficit theory was that while differences exist among groups, these differences are not necessarily synonmous with a deficit, a concept which has been described in previous chapters.

There is a growing awareness of the legitimacy of cultural differences in the abilities of culturally different children when measured against middle-class criteria. Psychologists have known for years that ability tests are biased in favor of white, native-born Americans.

The relatively recent eruption of controversy regarding testing programs and the reliability, validity, and usefulness of information obtained from tests is apparent to all readers of professional and lay literature. Based upon test data, workers such as Jensen and Shockley are making profoundly important statements regarding the genetic inheritance of poor children—particulary poor black children. Similarly, based upon test-derived information, billions of dollars have been spent and are still being expended in educational and treatment programs designed to cope with so-called deficit patterns noted from the tests.

Psychometric and linguistic testing tools are frequently biased and researchers, teachers, or clinicians who utilize them often uncritically generate unwarranted and damaging assumptions regarding the child's skills and abilities. Furthermore, much of the standardization data upon which tests are based have been inappropriately accumulated. Thus, our current testing strategies need urgent reexamination.

The use of so called "standardized" tests is widespread. Ability tests have been powerful instruments in shaping the educational system as it exists today. In addition, test results shape teacher expectations for the child possessing a specific score. It is imperative that speech clinicians and other workers break the lock in the education system that requires the majority of culturally different children to be exposed to the same educational processes that were designed for the middle-class child. If measurement should be via instruments that are not conicident with the culturally different child's experience, then appropriate reporting of these data is required.

THE TESTS

Standardizing Tests

Most characteristics, including those measured on IQ tests, distribute themselves normally throughout the population. Abnormality, according to this concept, varies from the statistical average of a *particular* group on the characteristic being measured. To establish the "norm," then, one must specify the population of persons on whom the norms will be based and then measure a carefully selected representative sample of that population.

In general, discrete population categorizations based on ethnicity or

*Examples of culturally biased tests are presented in the Appendices.

cultural membership have not been utilized in research activities; rather, these factors have been ignored. The assumption has been that they are unimportant; as suggested previously, however, they may be quite important. It is important also to note that for test data to be valid, the sample populations being measured must compare exactly to the standardization sample. Furthermore, the so-called normal "range" will reflect generally the behavior of the most numerous ethnic-cultural group in the society and automatically, therefore, allocate to an inferior category the different behaviors of other and less prestigious groups. An examination of almost all of the commonly used intelligence, performance, language, and academic tests will reveal that such unfair and biased data have been utilized in their standardization.

The Reliability and Validity of Test Data

A plethora of data exists relevant to the different cognitive and language skills of culturally different children. There are many possible reasons for these differences; our object is to explore those factors that may influence the reliability and validity of the data. It will be apparent that present testing strategies are all too often lacking in scientific rigor insofar as cross-cultural interactions are concerned. As a consequence of this lack of rigor, much of our present-day educational and habilitative programming, which has its roots in these test data, must also be reexamined. (Adler, 1973).

One of the more conventional methods of determining the intrareliability of a specific test is to compare test results with those obtained by the same examiner but at a later time. If the scores manifest a high degree of agreement, they are said to be reliable. We have no objection to this method except we suggest that this kind of reliability measure refers to particular scores generated at particular times. If, however, exposure to and familiarity with the examiner does indeed enhance the test score, it is apparent that pre- and post-test score comparisons may be invalidated by improper reliability measures. In other words, post-test scores may improve significantly as a function of familiarity with the tester rather than with improvement in the skill being tested. To obviate such a possibility, then, it is necessary for the tester to spend a significant amount of time in practice play with the child before administering the test instrument. The practicality of this suggestion may be questioned, but the need for such a relationship seems to be a necessary one.

One of the major functions of tester–testee assessment procedures should be to determine a client's competence vis-a-vis the peer group and the standard group under optimal testing conditions. This function is not being adequately accomplished with culturally different children.

The example given with intelligence testing [referring to a series of experiments by Haggard in 1954 in which he demonstrated the influence of training periods of test-taking behavior and subsequent test scores] can be generalized to any instance in which due to differences in rapport with the examiner, understanding of instructions, level of motivation, familiarity with the measuring devices and procedure, and other similar factors, the resultant data on performance may not indicate true differences in underlying psychological structure between the poor and the non-poor, but reflect instead, artifactual differences due to the unequal weight of known and unknown situational factors. This dilemma is interestingly similar to that confronting the cross-cultural researcher who wants to be sure that his results are not due to unintended artifactual differences in response to procedure, language, etc. And, in a sense, research comparing the poor and the non-poor perhaps should be thought of as cross-cultural or cross-subcultural (Allen, 1970, p. 337).

Methods Used to Obtain the Data

There are three basic methods to evaluate children: (1) the conventional tester–testee format, (2) the tester–group format, (3) the analysis of spontaneous verbalizations and other behaviors. That differences in results can be obtained as a function of the method used to elicit the data has been suggested by Williams (1969) among others.

The first two methods can generate a number of built-in biases which could impair the validity of the test results and its utilization. These biases are related to the differences in diglossic patterns of lower-class children, in effective communications between tester and testee, and in the subjects' motivational and aspirational levels.

We have already noted that many lower-class children develop different abilities in utilizing standard English forms as well as their own "nonstandard" patterns—i.e., both "correct" English and peer-speech patterns. When a verbal test is administered to a child, or to a group of children, the middle-class examiner has no way of knowing the diglossic sophistication of the children being tested. What, in fact, he obtains from the children are samples of their diglossic abilities. He does not obtain samples of data reflective of their peer-group linguistic behavior. Such data can best be obtained by using method three—the elicitation of spontaneous verbalizations in a naturalistic setting. The use of this method may obviate the twin problems of communication and motivation that may also enter into testing arrangements.

As a function of possible biases, it is permissible only for the experimenter to claim that his data is (1) representative of a carefully defined behavior pattern, (2) exhibited by certain children and (3) is a result of the particular formal test administered to them.

Tests Used to Obtain the Data

Most researchers have utilized discrete samples of children on which to standardize their norms. Too often these samples of children are representative only of the middle-class population.* Poor children have rarely served as the base sample for standardizing our conventional tests. As a result these tests, by definition, are not culture-fair. Furthermore their continued administration to culturally different children and the subsequent attachment of labels denoting inferior performance to lower-class children are obviously unfair. When tests that have been standardized on different cultural groups are developed, one will be able to obtain clinical or educational information that is relevant to peer-group performance as well as to the middle-class, or standard, performance. Today most of our testing tools allow only for the latter comparisons. It is quite apparent, as Bauman (1971) has stated that tests do not reveal all that needs to be known about the speech and language of a cultural community.

Roberts (1971) has pointed out that there are three basic types of tests used to evaluate language: (1) IQ tests, (2) tests designed to measure particular aspects of language (e.g., Peabody Picture Vocabulary Test), and (3) readiness test (e.g., California or Metropolitan Achievement Tests). Each generates biases by virtue of the experimental differences of the children, the different verbal styles required when responding to such tests, and the linguistic and nonlinguistic factors inherent in the test.

---

*According to Mercer and Brown (1973), "Of the 128 intelligence tests listed in Buros, 58 were measures of general intelligence with no subtests. Measures of general intelligence are all highly loaded with verbal skills in the English language and knowledge about the Anglo culture. Of the 70 tests that have subtests, 77 percent have subtests entitled Vocabulary, Language, or Verbal. Fifty-one percent have subtests entitled Arithmetic (etc.), and 53 percent have subtests entitled Reasoning, Logic or Conceptual Thinking . . . To rate as intelligent in American society one must be highly verbal in the English language, and adept at mathematical manipulations. . . . One receives little official credit for musical, artistic, or mechanical abilities."

1. *Tests can be biased by being outside the experience of the testee.* Many such examples exist. On the Peabody Picture Vocabulary Test, for example, there are pictures requiring such answers as "wiener," "hydrant," etc. Either the word or the picture may be alien to many poor and/or rural children.

2. *The verbal style required by the test can be culture-specific.* For example, in one of the subtests of the Illinois Test of Psycholinguistic Abilities, the child is required to describe verbally certain items. In order to obtain full credit, the child must use a number of different verbal labels to discuss each item. The lower-class child, who may not be as verbal as his middle-class peer regarding the use of such labels, would obviously be penalized by the nature of this subtest.

3. *The non linguistic factors inherent in a test situation may bias the test score.* For example, the simple fact of being tested can intimidate a child so that his performance is inhibited. In addition, forced interaction with an adult who speaks another dialect or has a different color skin, etc., may affect test performance. It has been suggested that most middle-class children are better test takers because they have taken more tests generally administered by examiners of their own culture; if this assumption is valid, middle-class children are generally more accustomed to nonlinguistic factors and hence are not as disturbed by their presence.

4. *Various linguistic aspects of the test may contribute to a test bias.* Communication "breakdowns" may occur without the examiner being aware of them. Differing semantic denotative and connotative values, syntactic arrangements that are culturally different, or different phonological systems can perhaps unknowingly contribute to confusion regarding task expectation. Such confusion may occur more frequently than suspected, and a child who does not clearly understand what he is expected to do will probably perform at a lower than normal level.

An excellent summary of this topic is provided by Allen who says the following about intelligence tests:

> [They] show quite consistently that children from poverty backgrounds score lower than children from the middle class. These data, in themselves, have not been in dispute; but whether the data really do indicate true differences in innate intelligence . . . that is, whether the tests are valid for the poor certainly has been in dispute. Many years ago, Allison Davis [in 1948] pointed out that intelligence tests, like the institution of the school itself, have a heavily middle-class bias. Thus,

intelligence tests tend to be composed of items whose language and content are more common and familiar in the experience of middle-class children, who also tend to have more often taken tests similar in content and in emphasis on speed. In other words, middle-class children are apt to have had more practice at test taking and to have greater knowledge of the optimal strategy to follow for obtaining high scores. Also the test giver is usually a middle-class person with whom the lower-class child taking the test is likely to have less rapport and whom he would be less motivated to please, which is to say that test taking is a social situation (Allen, 1970, pp. 376–377).

SITUATIONAL VARIABLES AFFECTING TEST SCORES

The culturally different child is influenced not only by what he has learned, but also by what surrounds him at any particular time. It is particularly important for the speech clinician to remember that when a child—*any* child—uses language, it is used in a situation and for a purpose; its use has some point. To understand language in its social context requires understanding the meanings that social contexts and uses of language have for their participants. Language must be studied in its social contexts, in terms of its organization to serve social ends (Hymes, 1972).

Hertzler (1965) states that languages are both determined by and determinative of the reactions of the users to the physical, cultural, and social environmental conditions and situations in which language plays a part. Thus, the speech clinician must realize that subcultural differences in language use, such as fluency or syntactic complexity, may appear more or less pronounced depending on one or more factors of the speech situation in which the language samples are obtained. The speaker characteristics present in one situation may often represent an interaction with task, topic, or elicitation condition rather than fixed or universal characteristics of the speakers.

If a speech clinician is to appreciate the importance of situational variables to the evaluations of and interactions with culturally different children, then it is essential to be aware of what constitutes a situational variable. Many authors have devised several different categories of situational variables; however, the basic concepts remain the same. Hymes (1967) lists eight components of speech: (1) setting a scene, (2) participants or personnel, (3) ends (goals and outcomes), (4) art characteristics (message form and topic), (5) key (tone, manner, or spirit in which an act is done), (6) instrumentalities (the channel—oral, written, etc.—and code—language or dialect), (7) norms of interactions and interpretation, and (8) genres (types of speech—conversation, cursing, lecture, sales pitch, etc.). Cazden (1970) suggests five categories of situational differences: (1) topic, (2) task, (3) listener(s), (4) interactions, and (5) situations with mixed characteristics. Finally, Hopper and Noremore (1973) utilize five slightly different categories of situational context: (1) the people present (personal context), (2) what was said just before (message context), (3) the topic of conversation (content context), (4) the task that the communication is being used to accomplish (task context), and (5) the times and places in which the communication occurs (surrounding physical context). Figure 6-1 has compressed these situational variables into four factors: test variables, physical situation variables, testor–testee variables, and communication variables. As can be seen, although the number and names of various categories differ, the basic concept remains constant in the categorization systems cited above.

All of the components of the situational variables appear to be quite logical. Their validity can hardly be questioned, and it is easy to see that the various contexts must necessarily play a very important role in language usage. Surprisingly, the tendency in child-language research has been to ignore situational variables or to combine speech data from several contexts. Another grave defect in many studies has been the failure to state precisely (a) the difference and (b) the interrelationship between values pertaining to the sociolinguistic feature, on the one hand, and the values pertaining to the social context in which it can occur, on the other.

More recent research, however, has included some descriptions of how language usage varies with characteristics of speech situations. Although not all of these studies deal with lower-class children, all do

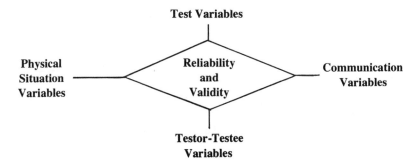

Fig. 6-1   Variables Affecting Test Reliability and Validity

provide evidence of the situational relativity of children's speech, and each gives some idea of the variables which must be considered. A more detailed examination of Hopper and Naremore's (1973) five categories of situational context follows:

Personal Contexts

It is obvious that the people involved in a situation shape that situation and have effect upon communication. Hertzler (1965) has stated that while experiencing is a personal phenomenon, individuals do not do their experiencing as isolates. Each individual's experiencing influences that of others with whom he is in contact.

When a child who is normally quite verbal and active comes into the presence of a stranger (especially an adult stranger), he, unless he is extremely outgoing, will immediately become quite silent and shy. Imagine this same child being thrust into a situation with an adult who, from physical appearances (color of the skin, clothing, etc.), looks quite unlike any of the adults with whom the child has come into contact in his environment. And, to compound the problem, when the adult begins to speak, he is using different words and in some ways a different language from the child, for example, "Come and sit down." "Look at my pictures." "Tell me what you see."

Obviously, this situation would be somewhat traumatic for almost any child. Yet, in classrooms and therapy settings teachers and speech clinicians are exposing culturally different children to this type of situation.

Teachers and clincians appear no less frightening to a culturally different child than, for example, does a dentist to most children. Although the clinician cannot change his or her own personal background, there are several ways in which the effects of personal context upon evaluations of and interactions with culturally different children can be obviated. First, when analyzing what a child says, it is important for the clinician to ask him/herself to whom the child was speaking (Hooper & Naremore, 1973). Conversely, when looking at how a child responds to someone else's speech, it is wise to ask who the speaker was—for that may be as much the cause of the child's response as what was said. Second, in attempting to elicit speech samples from a culturally different child, it is wise to remember that conversation is more likely to occur when it is initiated by the child rather than by the adult. Also, it has been found (Cazden, 1970) that adult commands to initiate action more frequently provoke verbal reply than do commands to desist an action. Finally, the clinician must be aware of the "Pygmalion (Rosenthal) effect," i.e., the attitudes which language may elicit in the listener. Certain language forms may lead to the clinician's stereotyping of children from particular ethnic groups. This stereotyping plays a key role in the process of speech rating (Williams, Whitehead, & Miller, 1971). Rather than solely evaluating the "correctness" of a child's language and speech, the clinician should weigh heavily the appropriateness of the child's speech with regard to the particular speech situation.

Message Context.

What has been said previously in a conversation can have a very definite effect upon the current conversation. For example, if someone says to you "You are a dummy," your reaction to the statement will depend upon what preceded the statement. If at the time you were sitting in a math class and happened to answer incorrectly a homework problem, your reaction to the statement would most probably be one of hurt embarassment. If, on the other hand, the statement had followed a silly joke you had just told, your reaction would likely be one of good humor and friendship.

Similarly, what a clinician says to a culturally different child will have a very definite effect upon his emotional, behavioral, and speech responses. In giving directions or in general conversation, the clinician must analyze not only what to say, but also the way in which to say it. How does it sound to the child? Does he really understand what has been said, or is he inferring something entirely different from the intent?

A wise clinician will remember that a child will respond in the manner in which he believes he is expected to respond. When a child is asked to perform, a part of his rationale for his particular behavior will be determined by whether he expects to be praised for his efforts or whether he expects to be punished for his errors.

Naturally, there are no specific rules which govern what a clinician can say to a child or the way in which it can be said. Therefore, in order to ascertain whether or not a child perceives what is said as it was intended, the clinician must observe the child's reactions. If he did not react as might have been expected, this may indicate the necessity for rephrasing the previous statement. Through this method of observation—readjustment—the clinician becomes more adept at "catering" to the needs of the particular child.

The clinician must also remember that a child must be rewarded for his efforts and not necessarily for the correctness of his responses. Punishment for errors rarely leads to correction of these errors; more often than not, punishment results in a discontinuation of responses altogether. Therefore, the way in which a therapist reacts to a child's performance will have a great effect upon the child's succeeding responses.

Content Context.

Fishman (1972) states that "topic, per se, is a regulator of language use." This statement is hardly surprising since anyone who knows children realizes that the topic being discussed influences their participation in the conversation. All people of all ages prefer to talk about things they are interested in, and children talk more about subjects with which they are personally involved. Moreover, the greater the degree of affect or personal involvement in the topic of conversation, the greater the likelihood of structural complexity.

Unfortunately, educational practices often fail to take into account what topics motivate students. Teaching methods designed without appreciation of this situational dimension often fall upon deaf student ears.

In selecting materials for speech therapy, the clinician must be aware of the effect of the topics presented by the materials on the responses of the children. Pictures depicting "Dick, Jane, and Sally" at work and at play may be quite suitable for the middle-class child, but they will be of little interest to the culturally different child. This is not to say that the therapist should feel limited in presenting materials which deal only with the immediate environment of the child. Cazden (1970) has found that novel, surprising, and incongrous items elicited much enthusiastic response from culturally different children. Therefore, it is incumbent upon the clinician to select materials and topics for conversation that are necessarily of interest to the children. And there may be no better way to find appropriate materials than to present assorted varieties of materials utilizing various methods of presentation and to observe the amount of interest each generates.

The rigid, conventional speech clinician will find it difficult to work with culturally different children, for imagination holds the key to capturing their interests. The therapist should often find it necessary to discard the well-worn picture stimuli in favor of objects and physical activities. Cameras, tape recorders, and slide projectors are examples of objects which may be foreign to many culturally different children but which, nevertheless, stimulate limitless fascination (and speech), especially when the children are allowed to operate the instruments themselves. Similarly, there is no limit to the number of objects and activities which the creative therapist can devise to capture the interest of the culturally different child, thereby opening a channel through which to elicit a variety of speech responses.

Task Context

When a person, child, or adult, speaks, he usually has a purpose or reason for speaking. Therefore, in looking at an utterance, it is useful to pose the question, What is the speaker trying to do?

Hopper and Naremore (1973) contend that the often found communication differences between different social classes may be primarily in the area of how language is used rather than in the sphere of linguistic development. For example, if the question "How are you today?" were asked, a middle-class speaker might respond, "Just fine, thanks," whereas a speaker from Appalachia might respond, "I be right fine." There can be no question that both speakers intended to convey the message that they are in good health, and both successfully did so. The response of the Appalachian would not be considered to be grammatically correct according to the rules of standard English. Yet an analysis of the response of the middle-class speaker reveals that, although it would be perfectly acceptable to all speakers of standard English, it is not syntactically correct—it is not a complete sentence!

Teachers and speech clinicians alike are guilty of placing what is perhaps too much emphasis on the way in which something is said rather than on *what* is actually being said. The basic reason we use language is to convey an idea. Therefore, it is well to remember that a speaker who loses the idea which he is trying to convey because of elaborate, though correct, lexicon and grammer is a *less* effective speaker than one who can convey his meaning regardless of linguistic form. As Hopper and Naremore (1973) state; "If we are careful to examine children's speech in terms of task context, we will often be less concerned with details of grammar and more concerned with sane and decent content."

Another aspect of task context deals with the goal which the teacher and/or clinician sets for the child, i.e., what they are asking him to do and the way in which they are asking him to do it. It is obvious that the particular task that the child is asked to perform will have an effect upon the manner in which he performs it. Some children will perform a task more easily than will other children, and, similarly, a child will perform some tasks more easily than he will other tasks. A child's familiarity with a task (how often he is exposed to similar tasks in his home environment) will determine how well and how easily he performs. Therefore, in evaluating a child's performance on a particular task it is important to consider the child's familiarity with that task.

Surrounding Physical Context

The physical context in which communication takes place is of great importance. Children are even more sensitive to physical context than are adults, and they use it more in their communication. They are, of course, apprehensive about new environments.

The social situation is comprised of a relationship between the place (locale) and time. Thus, if a particular child is in a familiar atmosphere, and if he happens to feel well (and feels like talking) at that particular time, then a speech sample obtained under these circumstances would contain more verbalizations with greater structural complexities than would a sample obtained from the same children under negative conditions of place and time.

Herman (1961) points out several interesting aspects of place and time (present and past as well as feelings at a particular time) that can be related to this context as well as several of the other contexts. The speaker himself is in an overlapping situation. He is located in the common part of two psychological situations that exist simultaneously for him. One situation may correspond to the person's own need or desire to speak a particular language; the other may correspond to the norms which may demand of him the use of another language. In the determination of which language he will use the forces operating may arise not only from the present situation, but also from the situation at large (background situation). This background situation is likely to be important when (1) the activity takes place in a public rather than a private setting, (2) the behavior in the situation may be interpreted as providing cues to group identifications (including social status) or conformity to group norms, or (3) the person involved in the activity wishes to identify (or to be identified) with a particular group or to be dissociated from it or desires (or feels obligated) to conform to the norms of a reference group. An individual's personal needs or desires are likely to be dominant under any of the following conditions: (1) where the setting is private rather than public, (2) where the situation provokes insecurity, high tensions, or frustration, or (3) where it touches the control rather than the peripheral layers of the personality. Finally, the immediate situation is likely to be dominant under the following conditions: (1) when the person is not concerned about group identifica- tions, (2) when the behavior is task-oriented, or (3) when well-established patterns of behavior characterize a relationship.

Thus, a child sitting in a therapy room will be influenced by his immediate surroundings in the room, by how he personally feels at that particular time, and by background (or past) experiences. At any one time one of these three situations is likely to be influencing him more than the others. The speech clinician must determine which of the variables is affecting the child and whether this effect is positive or negative. If the situational effects are felt to be negative, the therapist should carefully guard his observations made during that particular session, for they are not likely to be truly representative of that child.

THE REPORTING OF TEST DATA

The clinician should be aware that the test information presented in his or her report may effect the treatment or educational program devised for the child. If for some reason the clinician believes the test data are unreliable, it should be so stated and underscored in the report. Furthermore, in reporting data obtained from culturally-biased tests, i.e., tests not standardized on the population of which the child is a member (and most of the tests we use fall into this category), the data should be presented so that the reader may realize that (1) the test scores have been compared to middle-class norms and (2) to peer-group norms. Thus, in the first case, it would appear that a given child may be manifesting sub-standard skills relevant to middle-class children, and this information is important to the teacher or clinician who uses middle-class teaching strategies. In the second case, however, it would inform the teacher or clinician that in comparison to other children from the same socio-cultural environment, the child is manifesting acceptable skills.

For example, when testing a lower-class child with the Peabody Picture Vocabulary Test it is important that the tester realize that the test was normed with middle-class white children from Nashville, Tennessee. There is no reason to expect a normal lower-class child and perhaps a normal child from other distant geographic regions, to obtain normal scores on this test, i.e., scores ranging from 90 to 110. Instead, the tester will find generally an approximate 20 point difference in scores between the middle and lower class child; therefore a 75 ($\pm$ 5 points) score is frequently obtained by poor children on this (and other) tests. It is for this reason, in part, that the AAMD categorically states that the classification "mental retardation" necessitates a score of 69 or below; that the 70–90 range is not the retarded or slow range as has been conventionally defined. Furthermore, the AAMD criteria suggests that regardless of score (since so many of the scores are improperly obtained), if the child adapts to his socio-cultural environment as well as do his normal peers, he should also be considered normal

The cry heard from minority members a few years ago regarding the need for a moratorium on testing is valid. Too much harm has been done to poor children (and adults) because of improper testing methodologies, testing tools, and the reporting of such test data. It is time we recognized this harm and we alter our testing strategies.

ARTICULATORY DEVIANCES

Articulatory Testing and Its Effect upon the Poor Child

Throughout this text, we have suggested that there is a growing realization that part of the foundation upon which many of our data stand has relatively weak underpinnings. Our research data and subsequent clinical strategies designed to aid the poor and culturally different frequently are rooted in false or inappropriate assumptions. Conventional testing and treatment programs based upon these data need to be redefined. No where is this exemplified better than in the articulation testing and treatment programs of the speech clinician. We submit that a number of articulatory deviances of lower-class children are not in fact deficient productions but rather are normal for their social-class peers. A large proportion of the current treatment programs however, stress the concept of defect in the child, so they improperly attempt to remediate these culturally derived utterances. If a treatment program is to be truly effective, strategies must take into account more vigorously the social base upon which the child is reared.

Articulatory proficiency is evaluated commonly by standardized screening tests of articulation, such as the Templin-Darley test.* A reexamination of the standardization data of this test and others suggests that more rigorous definitions of social-class membership patterns may be

---

*Templin (1957) in her study used children from three different lower-class and three different middle-class groups, but the differences within the groups were "collapsed" and each group was treated as a whole entity. In other words the differences within the groups were considered as being nonsignificant.

necessary. Likewise, a more micromembership pattern and a comparison of ethnic differences might have produced different normative bases from which to make comparisons. The research data upon which many of these tests are dependent do not address themselves satisfactorily to these matters. Insofar as the Templin-Darley test is concerned, test norms were obtained solely from white subjects with only their father's occupation as the criterion to measure socioeconomic status (SES).

The overriding importance one attaches to test norms is exemplified perhaps in the manner in which articulatory deviances from the standard are treated. All sounds "malarticulated" on the particular test utilized are considered as manifestations of a defective pattern; little or no consideration is given to the possibility that the deviancy is a difference and not a deficit—that the test norm is not representative of the child's dialect community.

Treatment programs predicated on such culturally biased "normative" bases may be unsuccessful and even harmful. For instance, to say or imply to a child that the particular pattern of sound production he uses is improper and that it needs to be corrected, can be self-defeating if this same type or production is common to his peers. Furthermore, any articulatory changes that might occur would set him in phonological conflict with his peers and could be harmful to his interpersonal relationships. To explore this thesis in more detail, the author conducted a study of public school children in Knoxville, Tennessee.

The Knoxville Study*

An examination was carried out of the pattern (type and position) of articulatory deviations manifested by 197 randomly selected children diagnosed as speech defective attending the public schools in Knoxville, Tennessee. The social-class membership of each child was ascertained by a determination of his family's socioeconomic status (SES) and sociopsychological status. In addition, racial differences were noted for comparative purposes.

The questions asked. The answers to three questions were the objective of the study. (1) When measured by a conventional articulation test, does articulation proficiency seem to vary as a function of micro- or macro- SES categorizations? In our view this was the fundamental query.

*Part of this study is originally from Adler, S. Articulatory deviances and social class membership. *Journal of Learning Disabilities, 6,* 1973, pp 650–654. Reprinted by special permission of Professional Press, Inc.

In addition, (2) Does race appear to be associated with differences in number and type of articulatory deviances as obtained by a conventional articulation test? (3) Do race and SES interact in some fashion with respect to these articulatory deviances?

The data. The articulation test scores of a group of socially different children receiving speech therapy in the Knoxville public schools, all of whom were chosen at random, comprised our base data. The incorrect responses to items 19-43 on the Templin-Darley Articulation Test, previously administered by the public school speech clinicians, were compared according to the children's social-class membership. No attempt was made to choose selectively from among the many children receiving speech therapy for age, sex or etiology of deficit. The race and SES of the children are shown in Table 6–1.

Table 6–1

		SES		Race	
Macro		Micro		White	Black
Middle	104	Upper-middle	37	29	8
		Lower-middle	67	59	8
Lower	93	Upper-middle	73	64	9
		Lower-lower	20	16	4
	197		197	168	29

Results. In general, the research data relating articulatory performance to SES have shown only a higher number of articulatory errors as a function of lower SES (Winitz, 1969). Templin (1957) has reported that the common deficits in the spontaneous speech of these poor children were omissions and substitutions of consonants in all positions, with a prominent tendency to omit the final consonant.

Examination of item 7 in Table 6–2 tends to confirm these relationships. In this category race and micro-SES are collapsed so that all that is compared is the middle and lower classes. It can be seen that the lower-class children manifested a greater number of omissions and substitutions in all positions. There does not appear, however, to be a great distinction insofar as the omission of the final consonant is concerned. Furthermore, and of particular importance, the roles were reversed insofar as distortions were concerned. Here, it can be noted, the middle-class children manifested higher incidence figures in all three positions.

When attention is paid to the microstratifications of SES, as they interact with the white and black children (items 1-6 in Table 6-2), it can be seen that different kinds of articulatory pictures emerge. It is apparent that SES affects differently the error categories of both the white and black children according to the micro- or macro-categorization utilized. For example, the lower-lower-class white children manifested many more initial omissions and distortions than did white children from the upper-lower class; yet the distinction is lost in the macrostratification. Similarly, the distinction between the upper- and lower-middle-class with medial omissions and substitutions may be important, but they are lost in the conventional SES middle-class stratification. Other and similar distinctions can be found by comparing the data generated by the black children.

It is also apparent that there are differences in certain categories between the white and black children of similar SES; for example, the differences in medial and final omissions in item 5 where SES is collapsed and race only is compared. Contrarily, in item 6, where race is collapsed and micro-SES percentages are portrayed, it can be seen that upper-middle-class children are mainly responsible for the distortion pattern.

Table 6-3 shows the phonemes tested and the percentage of incorrect responses to these phonemes according to the race and SES of the child. The SES comparison within the white and the black sample of children shows that both groups of children, produced many voiced and unvoiced *th* deviances regardless of social-class differences, that r was incorrectly produced much more frequently by the white than the black children, that sibilants are more frequently differentially articulated by lower-lower-class white children as compared to upper-lower-class white children.

Why such differences were obtained is of fundamental importance. Can one presume that the r for example, is related to the dialectal pattern of the white children tested? According to Stewart (1967), white Appalachian children possess an intrusive r in their speech. One would expect, therefore, that this vestige of mountain speech would be found frequently in the speech of the white children who evolved out of and are a part of this culture. Since the test does not take this cultural standard into account, these children were penalized without regard for their linquistic heritage.

Discussion. It is interesting to note that Winitz's (1969) review of the research that pertained to SES and articulation performance does not differentiate SES on a microlevel nor did the researchers in his review

Table 6–2
Percent of Incorrect Responses According to Type and Position of the Articulatory Errors, the Race, and Ses of the Children (N = 197)

Race	Ses	Omission				Substitution				Distortions			
		Initial	Medial	Final	Total	Initial	Medial	Final	Total	Initial	Medial	Final	Total
(1)	UM	9.8	22.0	19.5	24.4	80.5	70.7	65.9	82.8	41.5	56.1	39.0	58.5
White	LM	9.2	30.6	19.4	31.6	78.6	83.5	63.3	91.8	40.6	51.0	29.6	61.2
	UL	11.7	43.6	37.2	57.4	87.4	90.5	76.8	94.7	32.2	48.9	24.4	54.3
	LL	19.0	38.1	38.1	47.6	81.0	81.0	66.7	90.5	50.0	38.0	23.8	57.1
(2)	UM	0.0	20.0	0.0	20.0	100.0	100.0	100.0	100.0	0.0	0.0	0.0	0.0
Black	LM	9.5	28.6	14.3	28.6	85.7	90.5	66.7	100.0	33.3	42.9	23.8	52.4
	UL	0.0	50.0	50.0	65.4	81.5	88.9	77.8	92.6	32.0	42.3	11.5	46.2
	LL	0.0	33.3	33.3	50.0	66.7	83.3	66.8	100.0	33.3	16.7	0.0	33.3
(3)	M	9.4	28.1	19.4	29.5	79.1	79.7	64.0	89.2	40.9	52.0	32.4	60.4
White	L	13.0	42.6	37.4	55.7	86.2	88.8	75.0	94.0	35.5	47.0	24.3	54.8
(4)	M	7.7	26.9	11.5	26.9	88.5	92.3	73.1	100.0	26.9	34.6	19.2	42.3
Black	L	0.0	46.9	46.9	62.5	78.8	87.9	75.8	93.9	32.3	37.5	9.4	43.7

Table 6–2 (continued)

Race	Ses	Omission				Substitution				Distortions			
		Initial	Medial	Final	Total	Initial	Medial	Final	Total	Initial	Medial	Final	Total
(5)													
White	M+L	10.9	33.1	26.5	40.4	80.8	82.2	66.7	90.2	39.6	50.9	29.1	58.9
+ Black	M+L	9.7	54.8	69.4	71.0	80.6	85.5	82.3	90.3	36.1	50.0	38.7	60.7
(6)													
White	UM	11.1	27.8	33.3	38.9	81.5	72.2	70.4	83.3	44.4	59.3	44.4	64.8
White	LM	9.6	36.5	30.4	40.9	79.1	85.1	65.2	93.0	41.1	51.3	33.0	62.6
+	UL	11.3	44.3	39.1	55.7	84.5	88.8	75.9	92.2	30.6	46.1	22.6	51.8
Black	LL	15.6	40.6	46.9	53.1	84.4	84.4	78.1	93.7	48.2	43.7	25.0	56.2
(7)													
White	M	10.1	33.7	31.4	40.2	79.9	81.0	66.9	89.9	42.2	53.8	36.7	63.3
+ Black	L	12.2	43.5	40.8	55.1	84.5	87.8	76.4	92.6	33.8	45.6	23.1	52.7

UM, upper-middle class   LL, lower-lower class
LM, lower-middle class   M, (the entire) middle class
UL, upper-lower class   L, (the entire) lower class

Table 6–3

Percent Incorrect Responses of the Phonemes Tested,
According to Race, and Ses of the Children (N = 197)

Phoneme	White				Black			
	LL	UL	LM	UM	LL	UL	LM	UM
m		.75	.33	.33		.98		
n		.45	.67	.67	1.18	.98	3.17	
ng		2.11	1.34					
p		.75	.50		1.18	1.96	1.59	1.72
b	.78	.60	.33		2.35	1.96	1.59	.57
t	2.33	2.41	1.34	1.34	7.06	2.94	6.35	4.60
d	1.55	3.47	1.00	1.34	1.18	1.96	1.59	1.72
k	.78	2.11	.84	.33	1.18	2.94		2.87
g		2.71	1.00		4.71	1.96	1.59	3.45
r	13.18	10.11	9.87	10.37	4.71	6.86	1.59	2.30
l	4.65	5.43	5.18	1.67		1.96	1.59	2.30
f	3.10	3.02	2.34	1.67	3.53	.98	1.59	1.72
v	3.87	7.24	5.67	1.00	8.24	1.96	7.94	6.90
th (thin)	10.08	15.38	12.54	9.36	10.59	14.71	14.29	10.92
th (then)	7.75	9.67	9.53	6.35	12.94	8.82	12.70	10.92
s	13.95	4.83	9.36	16.39	3.53	7.84	11.11	7.47
z	10.85	5.88	9.70	12.04	7.06	7.84	11.11	9.20
sh	11.63	6.79	6.69	13.04	10.59	10.78	4.67	6.32
h		.30	.33	1.34				
wh		1.21	1.51	.67	3.53	.98	7.94	5.17
w		1.51	.84	.33		1.96		2.30
j (yet)	2.33	3.32	2.84	1.67	1.18	1.96	3.17	2.30
ch (church)	4.65	4.68	7.36	10.03	4.71	10.78	3.17	7.47
dz (judge)	3.87	2.11	4.38	5.69	4.71	3.92	1.59	4.60
zh (azure)	4.65	3.17	4.52	4.35	5.88	2.94	1.59	5.17

always state the race of the children studied. It is not surprising that Winitz concluded that the relationship between SES and articulation defectiveness is a confusing one.

The data generated by this study augment this conclusion of Winitz. The varied percentage figures presented in Tables 6–2 and 6–3 may often be reflective of chance relationships, particularly with the black children, since such a small sample was used. Nevertheless, there is also good reason to suspect that many of these articulatory differences among or between the varied groups would be valid ones and that each region of our country containing different dialectal communities needs to supply their own normative bases for each of these communities. As Yoder (1970) has said, "there is the worrisome prospect that our testing procedures and instruments are sometimes revealing to us ethnic and social-class differences in language rather than distinctions in the speech capabilities or development of children" (p. 403).

It would seem that additional attention needs to be paid to this highly probable facet of testing programs. In particular, affirmative responses would seem to be relevant to the hypothesis we have posed in the text; i.e., microsocioeconomic status, race, and their interactions should be considered in evaluating articulatory deviances.

CONCLUSIONS

Although this chapter was not designed to be definitive in scope, it clearly indicates that more attention must be given to normative bases reflected in the social and racial membership patterns of different cultural communities. That children generate different articulatory patterns as a function of their unique linguistic environment should come as no surprise; it is also quite evident that different cultural environments create different dialect communities.

The continued utilization or inappropriate reporting of test data based upon cultural norms that are not representative of the children in question is untenable; this is implicit in the comparisons generated by the Knoxville study.

Two further matters of importance are apparent. (1) Definitive data need to be accumulated regarding the different normative bases noted above; these must be accumulated through the restandardization of conventional tests with different cultural groups, as the base sample. (2) The speech clinician and others should most cautiously interpret test data obtained from lower-class and culturally different children with respect to treatment programming.

REFERENCES

Adler, S. Data gathering: The reliability and validity of test data from culturally different children. *Journal of Learning Disabilities,* 1973, 6, 7, 429–434.

Allen, V. *Psychological factors in poverty.* Chicago: Markham, 1970.

Allen, V. Teaching standard English as a second dialect. In D. L. Shores (Ed.), Contemporary English: Change and variation. Philadelphia: J. B. Lippincott, 1972, pp. 237–256.

Bauman, R. An ethnogrpahic framework for the investigation of communicative behaviors. *ASHA,* 1971, *13,* 334–340.

Cazden, C. B. The neglected situation in child language research and education. In F. Williams (Ed.), *Language and poverty.* Chicago: Markham, 1970.

Fishman, J. A. *Language in sociocultural change.* Stanford, Calif.: Stanford University Press, 1972.

Herman, S. N. Explorations in the social psychology of language choice. *Human Relations,* 1961, *14,* 149–164.

Hertzler, J. O. *A sociology of language.* New York: Random House 1965.

Hopper, R., & Naremore, R. C. *Children's speech: A practical introduction to communication development.* New York: Harper & Row, 1973.

Hymes, D. Models of the interaction of language and social setting. *Journal of Social Issues,* 1967, *23,* 8–28.

Hymes, D. Introduction. In C. B. Cazden, V. P. John & D. Hymes (Eds.), *Functions of language in the classroom.* New York: Teachers College Press, 1972.

Mercer, J. R., & Brown, W. C. Racial differences in I.Q.: Fact or artifact. In Carl Senna (Ed.), *The Fallacy of I.Q.* New York: Third Press, 1973, pp. 56–113.

Roberts, E. An evaluation of standardized tests and tools for the measurement of language development. *Lang. Res. Found.,* 1971.

Stewart, W. A. *Language and communication programs in southern Appalachia.* Arlington, Va.: Center for Applied Linguistics, 1967.

Templin, M. C. *Certain language skills in children, their development and interrelationships.* Institute of Child Welfare, Monograph Series No. 26. Minneapolis: University of Minnesota Press, 1957.

Williams, E. *On the contribution of the linguist to institutional racism.* A paper presented at the Linguistic Society of America convention, San Francisco, Calif., 1969.

Williams, E., Whitehead, J.L., & Miller, M. Ethnic stereotyping and judgment of children's speech. *Speech Monographs,* 1971, *38,* 166–170.

Winitz, H. *Articulatory acquisition and behavior.* New York: Appleton-Century-Crofts, 1969.

Yoder, D. E. Some viewpoints of the speech, hearing and language clinician. In F. Williams (Ed.), *Language and poverty,* Chicago: Markham, 1970.

PART III

Bidialectal Education

7

Language Education

Language variation in American English is something that all speakers of our language notice in one way or another. People notice it and comment about it as they interact with individuals from different regions of the United States and different social and ethnic groups. Educators also confront it as they encounter the effect that dialect diversity may have on language skills relating to the education process. And professional linguists are concerned with it as they attempt to give a formal account of the rules of English.

—W. Wolfram and D. Christian,
Sociolinguistic Variables in Appalachian Dialects

THE CLINICIAN–TEACHER INTERFACE

A new breed of clinician and teacher is required who can effectively recognize and teach children equivalent linguistic utterances. The parochial concepts that consider the speech clinician as one who treats speech and language deficits only must be altered to include in the "job description" the teaching of speech and language skills particularly with "normal" children enrolled in intervention programs, such as in Head Start, or in early elementary school programs.

The speech clinician and teacher must work as a harmonious team; thus, clinicians may serve as consultants to the teacher or be teamed with the teacher to provide effective teaching–treating programs. Whatever the program, the training and self-concept of the clinician and of the teacher need to be altered to include these skills and particularly the attitude of cooperation.

It is necessary that the attitudinal problems and lack of rapport so common to teachers and diverse specialists be resolved. Too often these professional workers do not relate effectively to each other; too often are the diverse needs of the poor child—or any child—unmet or inappropriately catered to because of teacher–clinician biases. In our years of teaching both diverse habilitative specialists and teachers (preschool, early elementary, and secondary) we have witnessed this lack of cooperative effort, which inevitably affects the child's progress. To overcome this, we recommended the development of routine in-service programs where the problem can be addressed in an open manner. Unless the core problems are examined and obviated, the teaching–treating interface will not function to the optimal benefit of the children involved. It is incumbent upon administrators to recognize that one of the core problems relates to negative attitudes fostered by parochial sterotypes regarding each professional member's competence and abilities. Such negative perceptions will not allow for the development of effective bidialectal education programs.

GOAL OF A BIDIALECTAL LANGUAGE PROGRAM

Although recent research on phonology, grammar, and lexicon of culturally different language has begun to dispel many of the distorted assumptions about the language capabilities of minority-group children (i.e., that the language is error ridden and inadequate for logical thought), the majority of early education programs continue to direct their efforts toward changing the speech of these children so that it conforms to standard English while punishing the use of nonstandard forms. Not only have these efforts proved conspicuously ineffective, but the rejection of nonstandard forms is believed by many to have detrimental effects on the child's self-concept and to lead to the rejection of the school by children subjected to such an approach.*

Even though the majority of education programs continue to represent gross misconceptions about the linguistic capabilities of culturally different children, the more recent professional literature does reflect a growing acceptance of various social dialects as legitimate systems for communicating and learning, and attempts are being made to change the goals of some school language programs. Rather than trying to replace a child's dialect with standard English, efforts are being made to design teaching strategies that will facilitate the development of language skills in both the child's native dialect and standard English. The espoused goal of such programs is to increase language skills *in general*—to teach children to use standard English in appropriate contexts while respecting and maintaining the native dialect. This goal of bidialectalism is certainly preferable to that of eradicating different social dialects. Unfortunately, however, the goal is often too narrowly interpreted when translated to instructional objectives.

BIDIALECTAL PROGRAMMING

When teaching children with social dialects, educators have only a few choices available to them, but these choices entail drastically different teaching strategies— (1) the use of only standard English in the classroom and consequently the eradication of any dialectal differences; (2) instruction only in the dialect without any concentration on standard English; or (3) a bidialectal approach with instruction both in the dialect and in standard English (Wolfram & Fasold, 1974).

As we have contended throughout this volume, it is the theoretical framework of bidialectalism that provides the best alternative in devising teaching strategies for culturally different children. Compensatory education has utilized the first technique (teaching only through standard

---

*Some of the material in this section was presented by the author in an article, "Language Intervention and The Culturally Different Child," published in the *School Psychology Digest*, Nov.–Dec., 1978.

English) with apparently little success. Programs designed only around the second concept, instruction through dialect, handicap children by not exposing them to the prestigious "standard" or "establishment" dialect, which is the predominant medium of higher education, business, and government. The third approach—bidialectalism—advocates equating dialect and standard English at a functional level and not only teaching children to compare and contrast their own dialect and standard English, but also instructing clinicians and teachers in the crucial concept of "difference." The child's culture and language are respected in this approach, and his linguistic horizon is broadened to include another language variety. As Jaggar and Cullinan (1974) suggest, the "child's native dialect should be respected and maintained but . . . the goal of the language programs for the school is to help children who speak a nonstandard dialect to 'add' another dialect, i.e., standard English, to their repertoire."

There has been very little research that either supports or contradicts the bidialectal position, particularly for preschool-age children. Feigenbaum (1970) constructed a program for use in high schools, around the foreign language methodology of contrastive analysis. Labels are given to the different languages or dialects being taught (e.g., "formal" for standard English and "informal" for the nonstandard dialect), and students are taught, through exercises and pattern drills, to differentiate between the two. Leaverton (1969) and his associates in Chicago used the same methodology to design a first-grade reading program for black children that used dialect readers to explain the differences between "everyday" and "school" talk, Somerville (1975) noted that this program has had some success.

Research in teaching standard English as a second dialect before reading instruction begins is also sparse. Rystrom (1968, 1970) conducted two experiments with first-grade groups, one in California and the other in Georgia. Experimental groups of black children received dialect training 20 minutes a day for 8 weeks (1968) and for 6 months (1970). Pre- and post-testing with the Gates Word Reading Test and sections of the Stanford Achievement Test revealed no significant difference for the dialect-trained groups. Somerville (1975) properly points out that it was not until late into the school year that the studies were done and at the same time that reading instruction was being given. Rystrom (1970) reported that the simultaneous presentation of dialect training and reading instruction seemed to have been confusing to the children.

Contrastive Analysis*

Learning the sounds of a dialect, as well as its unique grammar and lexicon, should begin with ear training, that is, with hearing and comparing the standard and the nonstandard dialects.** Plummer (1970) has summarized some of the data perinent to contrastive auditory analysis (pattern-type drills, audiolingual approach), and his conclusions suggest that although such programs (e.g., Fries, 1954; Golden, 1964; Lin, 1965) are monotonous, they are useful—especially when the materials are made more relevant to the current idiom.

In a contrastive auditory program the contrast between the standard and nonstandard English form is presented, and the auditor is asked to repeat the standard form. Although many questions remain unresolved, both as to the efficacy of the concept and as to what age the exercises should be administered to a child, it does appear that such drills can be beneficial to many children of varying ethnic groups. In this way the phonological, syntactic, and lexical differences between the standard and nonstandard dialects can be distinguished. In order to prepare effective materials, one must find those language items in which standard English and nonstandard dialects differ, and these comparisons must be made with each of the dialects of the various subcultures. Fortunately, there has been some experimentation with syntactic constructions which points the way, for example, the work of Garvey and McFarlane (1968) with fifth-grade lower-class white and black children. Middle-class white controls can be utilized in such a program.

The Garvey and McFarland test format consisted of 50 sentences containing 14 different grammatical constructions, or 4 stimulus sentences per grammatical construction. The percentage of correct responses obtained, as a function of the repetition of these stimuli, were recorded and compared and are presented in the Table 7–1. The examples presented in this table are the present author's presentation of standard and nonstandard grammatical structures. It should be noted that the sentences are not

*A part of this section entitled "Language Intervention for Culturally Different Children" appeared in *Communicative Disorders: An Audio Journal for Continuing Education, 1,* p. 9, 1976.

**These concepts are discussed by Seville and Troike (1970), who also present a selected bibliography pertinent to the methods and materials which may be used in achieving such a goal. Labov (1969) and Houston (1969) discuss techniques one might utilize in such programs, particularly those involving phonological differences.

Table 7-1

Analysis of the Garvey and McFarlane Test Data; Percent Incorrect Responses on the Sentence Repetition Test

Grammatical Function	Lower-class white children	Lower-class black children	Middle-class white children	Examples (Transpositions in parenthesis)
Past Tense Verb	5.1	18.7	0.8	The boy passed the ball.
Plural Verb	28.7	54.1	1.6	The toys were (was) broken.
Possessive Noun	2.9	31.2	0.0	It was my sister's (sister) turn.
Copula	8.8	22.5	0.8	He is (omit is) working.
Reflexive Pronoun	54.7	53.3	11.6	The dog left by himself (hisself).
Demonstrative Pronoun	41.1	37.0	6.6	I've (I) seen that book already.
Singular Verb	19.1	56.1	0.8	When he falls (fall) he cries.
Embedded Question "If"	11.4	47.9	0.0	Let me see if (omit) I can find my dog.
Possessive Determiner	9.5	32.5	4.1	Whose (Who) doll is that?
Clause Introducer	26.8	35.0	8.3	She is the one who (omit who) got sick.

128

Table 7–1 continued

Grammatical Function	Lower-class white children	Lower-class black children	Middle-class white children	Examples (Transpositions in parenthesis)
Negated Auxiliary Verb	26.3	39.5	1.3	They aren't (ain't) here.
Embedded Question "Whether"	58.8	30.8	20.8	Ask Tom whether (if) he can go.*
Negative Concord	26.1	25.8	8.3	Sue doesn't have any (none)*
Plural Noun	5.1	22.9	2.5	Sally has on new shoes (shoe).
Relatives	31.9	19.5	15.8	She is the one who (that) fell down.

Source: Except for the last column, from C. Garvey and P. T. McFarlane, *A Preliminary Study of Standard English Speech Patterns in the Baltimore City Public Schools: Report No. 16* (Baltimore: Johns Hopkins University, 1968), p. 16. Copyright 1968 by Johns Hopkins University. Reprinted by permission. The last column with the examples of grammatical transpositions is done by the present author and is not intended to convey the dialectal pattern of a particular group.

*In black English, for example, the sentence might read as follows: "Sue don't have none", other sentences will require other transformations for different dialect speakers. Similarly, "he is working" (sentence no. 4) could be said by black lower-class speakers as "he working" or "he be working", the former statement refers to an employment being experienced now, as opposed to the consistency (chronic nature) of the latter statement. Interestingly, Applachian white children possess a similiar grammatical transposition in their use of "a" in place of "be", thus, "he a-working." In some instances children, white and black, have been heard to use both forms, e.g., "he be a-working" (Stewart, 1967).

intended to convey the dialectal pattern of any particular group, but only to indicate the nature of the discrete grammatical transposition. As can be seen in the table, more than half of the lower-class black children altered the singular and plural verb structures and the reflexive pronoun structure. Also, almost 48 percent of these children transformed the sentence whose grammatical function contained the embedded "if" question. Both the lower-class white and the lower-class black children transformed more than half of their reflexive pronouns. The poor white children transformed more than half of the sentences containing the embedded "whether" question, and approximately 41 percent of them transformed the demonstrative pronoun. Certainly these types of grammatical functions should receive careful scrutiny in testing or training black and white lower-class children (see also Rystrom, 1968).

There are many sound and word contrasts that are not auditorially perceived by culturally different children. It is also difficult to state whether this failure to perceive a given sound contrast is due to a phonological difference only in the dialectal pattern or whether it is also related to the grammatical differences in the dialects. If it is related to the grammatical constraints of the language, as in *50 cents,* where the plural of cents is omitted due to the inherent pluralization in the number 50, a test that would try to determine whether the child can make an auditory distinction between *cent* and *cents* may be invalid since there is no such word comparison in the lexicon of dialect speakers.

Similarly, one would have to take into account the fact that certain homophonous words are perceived as different by standard English speakers when different sounds are used in these words—for example, *pin* and *pen, cot* and *caught.* But lower-class black auditors with dialectal speech make no distinction between words containing these sounds. In view of these data, the use of conventional auditory discrimination testing materials and methodologies (same or different dichotomy) needs to be reconsidered when testing all dialectal speakers.

It is also apparent that before these children can be expected to use the sounds properly, a significant amount of attention will probably have to be given to discrimination training. Such training should emphasize the auditory distinctions inherent in the phonological and syntactical systems of *both* standard and dialectal English.

More explicitly, the training program might consist of the presentation of nonstandard dialectal forms and their equivalent standard English counterpart. The child should be informed regarding the distinction and be asked to indicate whether the word or phrase he hears is from his own language or from his school language. The differences in meaning between the contrasting words can be effectively tied in to this discrimination process where applicable, for example, *pin, pen*. Similarly, standard articulation, if indicated, could be taught at the same time.

Grammatical Differences

Although the overall structural difference between black dialect and standard English is obviously not as great as, for example, between English and Spanish, this does not make it easier for the black dialect speaker to learn standard English; contrariwise, the very fact that the differences are relatively discrete and subtle may make it quite difficult for the nonstandard dialectal speaker to tell which patterns are related to his dialect and which ones are not. According to Stewart (1969), this may help explain why many immigrant populations have been able to make a relatively rapid transition from their native language to standard English and why black dialect speakers are having difficulties in their acquisition of standard English.

One effect of the grammatical differences between the two dialects is exemplified in the low reading scores manifested by black children. That misinterpretations of the material read in standard English by black children do occur is quite evident when one considers the different meanings attached to the presence of the copula *be* as opposed to its absence. Certainly other factors than the differences in grammar may contribute to low reading scores, but it would be a mistake, in our opinion, to underplay the importance of this grammatical difference vis-à-vis reading scores in black culturally different children.

In essence, these grammatical differences should be utilized in an auditory contrastive analysis program as follows: (1) The child hears a standard grammatical function—e.g., Here are two pens. (2) He is then presented his nonstandard equivalent—Here are two pen. (3) He then is asked to repeat the standard equivalent. Numerous examples of this particular type of morphological alteration should be presented; at the same time, the child is taught that both grammatical forms are acceptable English—thus he is taught bidialectal English. For these kinds of programs to be maximally effective requires a total community effort on the part of teachers, parent, and school administrators as well as the children.

FUNCTIONAL BIDIALECTALISM

Functional bidialectalism as a goal for school programs has generally been defined as expanding children's language to include facility in a second dialect while maintaining the native dialect. For the speaker of black English, this means helping the child to develop competence in standard English while maintaining and facilitating competence in black English. It also means communicative competence, the ability to use appropriately either variety of the language, black English or standard English, according to the demands of the social situation. It means adjusting speech in terms of the setting, the topic, the participants, and the task at hand.

By comparing the standard English structure to be taught and the equivalent nonstandard structure, the student can learn how they differ. Feigenbaum's (1970) method for contrast and comparison between nonstandard English and standard English for teaching purposes caters effectively to this distinction. The instruction should include practice in sorting out standard from nonstandard. This practice can be provided when both standard and nonstandard are used in teaching. For many students, this sorting out is the beginning of a series of steps from passive recognition to active production.

Presentation.   One way in which the standard–nonstandard contrast can be employed is in presenting a lesson or an exercise. Two items, one standard and the other nonstandard, show the students the structure to be learned and practiced, and indicate where mistakes may occur. For example, the following two sentences may be written on the board or projected from a transparency:

He work hard.
He works hard.

The clinician would then ask how the two sentences differ and which one is standard and which is nonstandard. The clinician may wish to tell the class that the second sentence has an *s* on *works* and the first does not and that the first sentence is nonstandard and the second standard, but since the students are aware of the social uses of language, they should be able to provide the answers. Asking for their observation will make the activity more interesting.

Discrimination drills   A discrimination drill gives the students practice in discriminating between standard and nonstandard English on the basis of the feature being worked on. Pairs of sentences or words are presented to the students orally. The students indicate whether the two are the same or different.

Teacher Stimulus	*Student Response*
1. He work hard. He works hard.	1. different
2. He work hard. He work hard.	2. same
3. Paula likes leather coats. Paula likes leather coats.	3. same
4. She prefers movies. She prefer movies.	4. different
5. Robert play guard. Robert play guard.	5. same

In this drill the instructor must be certain that the students can hear the feature that distinguishes standard from nonstandard. If the students respond correctly to the five items in the drill, their attention has been directed to the feature and they hear it consistently.

Identification drills.   A general principle in second-language or dialect pedagogy is that production is easier for the students after they have learned to discriminate and identify what they will be called on to produce. The identification drill contributes to the preproduction work. It is more difficult than the discrimination drill in that the students are not presented with material to compare but are required to identify a single word or sentence without the assistance of a second item. The identification is standard or nonstandard.

Teacher Stimulus	*Student Response*
1. He work hard.	1. nonstandard
2. He works hard.	2. standard
3. Paula likes leather coats.	3. standard
4. Mr. Brown teaches geography.	4. standard
5. She ride on the bus.	5. nonstandard

The only indication of standard or nonstandard is the verb ending. If the students respond correctly, then they do hear the feature that distinguishes standard from nonstandard English and they can identify the two dialects on the basis of the feature.

Translation drills.   In a translation drill the students translate a word or sentence from nonstandard to standard or from standard to nonstandard. This may first be done by translating standard sentences to nonstandard sentences:

Teacher Stimulus	*Student Response*
1. He works hard.	1. He work hard.
2. Paula likes leather coats.	2. Paula like leather coats.
3. She prefers movies.	3. She prefer movies.
4. Robert plays guard.	4. Robert play guard.
5. He drives a motorcycle.	5. He drive a motorcycle.

Then nonstandard sentences are translated into standard sentences:

Teacher Stimulus	*Student Response*
1. He work hard.	1. He works hard.
2. Robert play guard.	2. Robert plays guard.
3. Mr. Brown teach English.	3. Mr. Brown teaches English.
4. She ride on the bus.	4. She rides on the bus.
5. He prefer movies.	5. He prefers movies.

The next drill is a combination of the two drills used above. In this drill the students make one overt response, but, in reality, they make two: the first is to identify the sentence as standard or nonstandard, and the second is to translate from one to the other.

Teacher Stimulus	*Student Response*
1. He works hard.	1. He work hard.
2. She prefer movies.	2. She prefers movies.
3. Robert plays guard.	3. Robert play guard.
4. Mr. Brown teaches English.	4. Mr. Brown teach English.
5. She ride on the bus.	5. She rides on the bus.

More complex translation drills can be constructed. The added complexity is the difference between the standard English verb forms with *he* and *they*. Since this difference does not exist in nonstandard English, translation in either direction will be challenging. The next drill is possible only if the students understand the status of a sentence, such as *They work hard,* and know how they are to respond to it in the drill.

Teacher Stimulus	*Student Response*
1. He works hard.	1. He work hard.
2. They like nylon jackets.	2. They like nylon jackets.
3. She prefers movies.	3. She prefer movies.
4. The player works hard.	4. The player work hard.
5. The men drive fast.	5. The men drive fast.

Response drills. The standard–nonstandard contrast and comparison can be carried into freer activities, in which the students have the opportunity of speaking more naturally. The drill types previously described provide very careful control of the linguistic material that the students employ: their responses are predetermined at the textbook–writing stage.

Other drill types and activities have less control and give the students the opportunity to speak in natural English. They still constrain the students' language but differently and less rigidly. For example, in the drill that follows the students are to contradict the statement with an appropriate response—standard statement and response or nonstandard statement and response.

Teacher Stimulus	*Student Response*
1. Your best friend work after school.	1. No, he don't.
2. He gets good grades.	2. No, he doesn't.
3. The teacher doesn't give too much work.	3. Yes, she does.
4. Her boyfriend don't drive too fast.	4. Yes, he do.
5. Your math teacher give good grades.	5. No, she don't.

In this drill the student's attention is focused on the grammatical feature that marks standard and nonstandard. In addition, the student has an opportunity to respond more naturally than in the previous drill types, which involve grammatical manipulation instead of conversation-like activity. We make certain that the students' responses will contain *do* or *does* because of the statement to which they reason. The additional change of negative to affirmative or affirmative to negative provides a further challenge.

Throughout the drills, as the controls are decreased, two objectives remain: distinguishing standard English from nonstandard and speaking accurate standard English when it is appropriate. These drills may also be used in teaching standard English pronunciation.

The drills are appropriate for young elementary-aged children; more basic drills for pre-school children are presented elsewhere. Teachers and clinicians may use this format in their teaching programs. It should be remembered that our primary goal is the development of adequate standard English speaking and writing skills in culturally-different children. We believe that through such exercises these goals can be obtained.

REFERENCES

Feigenbaum. I. The use of nonstandard English in teaching standard: Contrasts and comparison. In R. W. Fasold & R. W. Shuy (Eds.), *Teaching standard English in the inner city*. Arlington Va.: Center for Applied Linguistics, 1970.

Fries, C. C. Cumulative pattern practices. Ann Arbor: University of Michigan, 1945.

Garvey, C., & McFarlane, P. T. A preliminary study of standard *English speech patterns in the Baltimore city public schools: Report No. 16*. Baltimore: Johns Hopkins University, 1968.

Golden, R. I. *Changes in dialects: Instructional record for changing regional speech patterns*. New York: Folkway Record, 1964.

Houston, S. H. *Child black English in northern Florida: A socio-linguistic examination*. Atlanta: Southeastern Education Laboratory, 1969.

Jaggar, A. M., & Cullinan, B. E. Teaching standard English to achieve bidialectalism: Problems with current practices. *Florida FL Reporter*, 1974, 63-70.

Labov, W. Some sources of reading problems for Negro speakers of non-standard English. In J. C. Baratz & R. W. Shuy (Eds.), *Teaching black children to read*. Arlington, Va.: Center for Applied Linguistics, 1970.

Leaverton, L. The Psycholinguistic Reading Series: Board of Education - City of Chicago, Chicago, Ill., 1968.

Lin, S C. *Pattern practice in the teaching of standard English to students with a nonstandard dialect*. New York: Teachers College, Columbia University, 1965.

Plummer, D. A summary of environmentalistic views and some educational implications. In F. Williams (Ed.), *Language and Poverty*. Chicago: Markham, 1970, pp. 265–308.

Rystrom, R. C. *The effects of standard dialect training on Negro first graders being taught to read*. Final Report Project No. 81063. Washington, D.C.: U.S. Department of Health, Education, and Welfare, 1968.

Rystrom, R. C. Dialect training and reading: A further look. *Reading Research Quarterly*, 1970, *40*, 581–599.

Seville, M. P., & Troike, R. C. *A handbook of bilingual education*. Arlington, Va.: Center for Applied Linguistics, 1970.

Somerville, M. A. Dialect and reading: A review of alternative solutions. *Review of Educational Research* (Chicago Board of Education), 1975, *45*(2), 247–262.

Stewart, W. A. Continuity and change in American Negro dialects. *Florida FL Reporter*, 1968, *6*, 14–16, 18, 304.

Stewart, W. A. On the use of Negro dialect in the teaching of reading. In J. C. Baratz & R. W. Shuy (Eds.), *Teaching black children to read*. Arlington, Va.: Center for Applied Linguistics, 1970, pp. 156-219.

Wolfram, W. & Fasold, R. W. *The study of social dialects in American English*. Englewood Cliffs, N.J.: Prentice-Hall, 1974.

8
Preschool and K-3 Programming

By the age of six, when a child enters school, he has developed as much as two-thirds of the intelligence he will have at maturity.

—Maya Pines,
Revolution in Learning, Quoting
Benjamin S. Bloom of the
University of Chicago.

Realization of the changing needs of five year olds provides impetus in much rethinking of Kindergarten instructional programs.

—Elizabeth S. Meyers,
Helen H. Ball, and
Marjorie Crutchfield,
The Kindergarten Teacher's Handbook

PRESCHOOL CURRICULA

Education in early childhood from its beginning has been primarily concerned with enriching and supporting the optimum growth of children. Nursery schools, which were developed as an extension of home life to help enrich children's total development, stated psychological and physical nurture as objectives. With the advent of the "critical periods" hypothesis in the early 1960's, more and more attention was given to the field of early education as infant and toddler programs were born. For the optimum development of a child, it was assumed that physical and psychological environments must be enriched as early in life as possible because environmental effects are greatest in the early and more rapid periods of intellectual development. When the "critical periods" theory was beginning to take hold, history once again turned to a humanitarian impulse such as the one of the 1880's and 90's which spurred the birth of the kindergarten. It was in the early 1960's that similar social urgencies brought compensatory education on the scene.

With America's changing lifestyles, more concern is being given to compensatory early childhood education in general, and to children of low income families in particular. Statistics concerning the changing lifestyles report about 9,000,000 children are now being reared by single parents. The majority of these are poor and at least 10 percent are under 6 years of age. A majority of all American mothers with school age children are working outside the home, two-thirds of them in full-time jobs. It is quite evident that the curricula of preschool educational programs are of increasing importance to these mothers, and to others who make use of these programs.

COMPENSATORY CURRICULA

One of the most important questions to be asked of any educational intervention program or treatment strategy is whether or not the learner has sufficiently acquired the skills or educational content being transmitted to him. A justification of the continuance of any program is obviously in its success. Since the poor and culturally different child has apparently not demonstrated significant improvement in acquisition of skills or content—that is, the quality of his educational input still remains at a low level relative to his middle-class peer—it can only be assumed that program effectiveness has been minimal.

The various programs designed to enhance learning abilities and performance levels are based generally upon the malnutrition model, which holds to the point of view that the child must be "force-fed" those cognitive nutrients commensurate to those utilized by the "establishment." A variety of educational and clinical strategies have been employed relevant to this model, the thesis being that development of readiness or cognitive skills in poor children was distorted or impaired and that subsequent language learning and the acquisition of academic or content-type subjects were bound to be negatively affected.

Compensatory Programs—An Overview

Head-Start initiated compensatory programming for poor 5- to 6-year-old children in 1965. It was complemented by intervention programs that initiated training at younger age levels—3 or 4 years of age. At present infant education or stimulation programs have become the vogue. A variety of parent education programs have also been developed to supplement the various child and infant education programs.* Thus it was decided that "compensatory" programs be developed for disadvantaged children before they entered the compulsory school programs. The objective of such programs was to "enrich" these children so that their "readiness" level would more equate, or more nearly so, that of the "establishment" child, for whom our educational system is geared.

Hunt (1969), a protagonist of early environmental intervention, suggests that the various programs show fair levels of success—that they have not failed. But others do not support this premise; that the additional time given to the educational programming for the child allows for some demonstrable gains during preschool but does not carry over into elementary school.

Head Start programs were developed to provide an early education for the preschool child. It was hoped that with these opportunities, the educational problems of the poor child in elementary school would be, if not eliminated, at least significantly attenuated.

The results, however, do not appear to generally support this ideal. Although there are numerous exceptions, the fact remains that Head Start educated children seem to be experiencing the same rate of academic failure and disillusionment as do other poor children. The reason certainly does not lie with the skills or the enthusiasm of the Head Start staff but rather, as pointed out in the following pages, the failure of the compensatory philosophy they adhere to. It should also be noted that Head Start provides many other services to poor children and their families other than educational intervention. For example, the health and nutrition services and the parent education and counseling provided are of inestimable value to the participants in these programs.

Head Start initiated the first major effort to provide preschool programming for poor children. The program's expressed purpose was to

*These programs are discussed in more detail in Chapter 13.

provide education to children from low-income families in an effort to compensate for these children's inadequate experiental background and thus bring them up to the level of middle-class children by the time they entered school. A rather wide variety of philosophies and models characterized the different programs. Some were quite similar to the traditional nursery school, i.e., permissive and minimal structured learning situations; they provided a great deal of general enrichment such as field trips and verbal stimulation. Others provided highly structured learning environments by formally teaching cognitive and verbal skills.

There are a number of skills that almost all Head Start and the better Day Care Centers and nursery programs provide: the most important is the development of language skills. Since the preschool years are the most important for language development and allow for the rapid growth of oral language skills, it is obviously a developmental stage of much concern to preschool specialists. A number of different formalized learning as well as incidental learning techniques have been used to enhance the language skills of the children. For example, a process of heavy verbal bombardment with the teacher maintaining a steady stream of questions and comments has been used in some programs. Others have used games that encourage oral language usage, such as play-talking on the phone. Some programs systematically taught language skills to children using behavior modification techniques.

Another major goal of such programs is the teaching of percepts and concepts, particularly those categories or classes of things that are learned through visual processing activities. Examples are the teaching of color, size, and shape recognition, discrimination and sequencing. Less importance is attached to auditory processing; the skill we heavily emphasize in our Pediatric Language Laboratory program. If what is heard and understood—the auditory function of language—is basic to academic skill acquisition, then teaching programs must stress auditory as well as visual processing strategies.

Among other skills taught to children in preschool programs are gross and fine motor skills, social skills and self-help skills; as well as the attainment of a positive self-image, and an expectancy of success.

An analysis of the effectiveness of Head Start programming reveals that, in general children score higher on post-tests when completing Head Start than they scored on these same tests when starting the program. In comparison to middle-class children, they generally hold their own in the first and second grades, but they frequently fall behind their middle-class peers in the third, fourth, or fifth grades. (Jones, 1967).

Infant education programs came into being in response to the apparent failure of the other intervention-type programs. It was noted that one of the reasons for this lack of relative success was due to the child's established cognitive and linguistic behavior. It was suggested that, for intervention to be successful, it would have to be initiated before the child established these behavioral patterns—hence the need for infant education.

The Fallacy of the Compensatory Program

The essential fallacy of the compensatory program, according to Labov (1972), lies in the assumption that personal deficiencies account for the educational failures of the child. But when failure reaches such massive proportions, as it has in these programs, it is necessary to look at other possible causes, e.g., the social and cultural obstacles to learning and the inability of the school to adjust to the social situation. Operation Head Start is designed to repair the child rather than the school. To the extent that it is based upon this inverted logic, it is bound to fail.

A second area in which the compensatory approach is doing serious harm to our educational system concerns the consequences of failure and the reaction to it. The fault is found not in the data, the theory, or the methods used, but rather in the children who have failed to respond to opportunities offered them. When poor children fail to show the significant advance that the deprivation theory predicts, it is further proof—for those who support the contention—of the gulf which separates their mental processes from those of "the biologically superior middle class."

When intervention or enrichment programs such as Head Start failed in their stated purpose, programs were designed to initiate the training of these children very early in their lives through parent involvement in infant education programs. A few programs are currently underway, and if such programs fail, the only alternative in accounting for such failure is perhaps a genetic hypothesis—the hypothesis that posits a genetic gulf between the middle and lower classes, particularly the lower-class blacks. More specific and relevant reasons for these failures will be further discussed in the following sections.

Failure as Related to the
American School System

The American school system, whether public or private, is predominately a middle-class institution. It not only teaches middle-class values and ideals, but it operates in a middle-class fashion and uses middle-class methods in performing its role in American society. This is inevitable since the official ideology of the United States is a middle-class ideology, and the school system is an institutionalized arm of that middle-class society. The educators who staff the school system are themselves largely middle class or have adopted middle-class values—since they are products of the system, that is to be expected. Because they are based on middle-class values and ideals, the public school system and its methods have not made much headway in educating the economically disadvantaged. Though there has been scattered piecemeal success, the school system as a whole has failed in this effort.

Failure as Related to Compensatory Education for the Disadvantaged

Current educational programs for the economically disadvantaged are based on the assumption that the individual from a poor and/or different culture is actually culturally deprived. Therefore, attempts to alter the plight of the child have involved "enrichening" his environment or, as Williams (1969) put it, administering him a "dose of culture." The most widely endorsed strategy for helping disadvantaged children is one called "enrichment." In broad terms, enrichment attempts to compress into an educational program the maximum quantity of experience believed to contribute to the culturally privileged child's superiority in learning. Those educators who advocate this type of compensatory education (e.g., Bereiter & Engelmann, 1966; Bloom, 1965; Deutsch et al., 1967) claim that the poverty child lags behind his middle-class counterpart in preparation for school and that he is experientially, linguistically, and socially retarded: that is, he is culturally deficient or deprived. Thus, preschool intervention has been advocated by "deficit" theorists as a means for lessening the gap between the disadvantaged child's capabilities at school age and the requirements of a middle-class educational system. In order for the culturally deprived child to overcome his deficits (deficiencies), he must adopt the behavior, especially the language behavior, of mainstream society.

Williams (1969) states that teachers have certain evaluational reactions to their students' speech which are stereotyped versions of their attitudes toward the speaker. He speculates that a teacher bases much instructional behavior toward a child upon that stereotyped attitude. A child's speech may thus serve as an index and identification of his culture, and when the teacher encounters such a culturally different child, he or she perhaps subconsciously expects nonstandardness, reticence, and uncertainty from the child. Interestingly, the child may also have developed a particular stereotyped and negative attitude toward the teacher.

Teacher–pupil expectations affect teacher–pupil interactions. A child who is treated as though he were reticent, insecure, and a representative of that which is substandard will react as such. He will feel that, because of his inferior language behavior, he himself, and all that he represents, is inferior. Because he has to acquire his education in an unfamiliar and unnatural language, he will suffer frustration and educational alientation. His entire life style, which is also that of his parents and those with whom he associates, has been rejected by that institution which purportedly exists to supply him with the tools to succeed in American society.

Perhaps the most important factor in determining educational success is whether or not the child feels *he* has some control over his life. If the unique heritage from which he comes is destroyed by efforts to make him acceptable to an ideal social norm, the resultant human being can only feel powerless in a majority society.

Compensatory education, then, is an educational failure for most children, for it is destroying them psychologically and educationally by trying to prepare them for mainstream society. Concommitantly, it alienates them from the culture and language of their peer communities.*

A SAMPLE PRESCHOOL PROGRAM:
A TWO-PHASE APPROACH

In view of the apparent failure of compensatory programming to adequately prepare the child for a successful school career, and because aural-oral language is the touchstone on which successful academic

---

*Many states are now adopting compulsory competency testing and the attainment of specified scores for 8th grade as well as potential high school graduates. That is, before these children will be allowed to graduate they will have to demonstrate proficiency or, at least competency, in basic academic skills. We support such testing; we believe all high school graduates should be able to read and write with some basic skills. It is our conviction, however, that the larger majority of children who will fail the test and not be allowed to graduate until such time as the test is passed will be the lower-class or poor children. When such children fail these tests one, or possibly two or more times, dependent upon state laws, questions will inevitably be raised relevant to the genetic inferiority of these children and absolute statements made—"They are simply too dumb to learn." We submit, as suggested in the text, it is the professional worker and the teaching strategy employed that may be at fault—not the child.

achievement must rest, we initiated a noncompensatory program for preschool children in the early 1970s. Bidialectal programs were not new—an experimental program had been developed for black school-aged children in the Chicago public schools—and some programs had been developed for bilingual children (mainly Spanish-speaking children). Our program addressed the needs of preschool, mainly white, children attending three experimental and three control Head Start classrooms in Knox County, Tennessee.

The primary group used in this research on bidialectalism consisted predominantly of 4- and 5-year-old children. Most of the procedures presented in this section were developed and refined in an experimental pilot study performed in the Pediatric Language Laboratory (PLL), a preschool program sponsored by the Department of Audiology and Speech Pathology of the University of Tennessee. The program was conducted for approximately 7 months, from November through May.

The study team felt that before the actual teaching program began, it was essential to determine exactly what specific items of dialect are encountered in the black and white population in this Appalachian area. The work of other authors in cities in the North and in West Virginia (Labov, 1966, 1970; Wolfram, 1969, 1976) was used as a reference guide for the collection of the speech samples. These samples were collected for a period of approximately 2 months in both groups. Several methods were used: (1) spontaneous transcriptions recorded by teachers, clinicians, and the authors while the child was in the classroom, in therapy sessions, or in small play groups (this was the primary method used in the Head Start program), (2) analysis of certain tests such as the Peabody Picture Vocabulary Test to ascertain items differing from standard English; and (3) remote telemetry recordings that allowed taping of children in therapy or at play. The latter was used mainly with the PLL group. An effort was made to take samples from each child in both the school environment and the playground situation.

Once the samples were taken, they were analyzed by noting the similarities and differences of grammatical structures, lexical items, and phonological output among the different transcriptions of the children's speech as related to standard English. Standard English was operationally defined as the socially prestigious language patterns accepted and used by middle-class speakers (particularly, school teachers) in this area. Members of the child's cultural community were then questioned to ascertain if the dialectal features were still prominent in the area. A "dialectal difference" was defined as any phonological, syntactical, and lexical features manifested by the child which were in current use in the child's cultural community and which also differed from standard English. An effort was made to identify items that existed in the speech of both black and white children.

In general, the teaching strategy was designed around two broad ideas suggested by Labov (1973) and Wolfram (1970). Labov notes the advantages in first teaching the general items of the different dialects: "Some nonstandard forms are special cases that affect only one or two words of the language; but many are instances of general rules that operate in the nonstandard vernacular in a regular way and can affect the form of every sentence. It is plain that the more general rules should be introduced first in a teaching program." Wolfram makes the additional observation that it is important to teach the socially stigmatized variants first in any program. It is certainly easier to determine those features which are generally considered to be nonstandard and socially stigmatizing than to describe the complete nonstandard linguistic system.

The acceptance of mountain English and black English as distinct and valid linguistic systems by the teachers proved to be the most difficult aspect of this bidialectal program. To promote an understanding of these concepts, several in-service sessions were conducted which attempted to explain previous research and clarify issues involved in the programs. Three of the Head Start teachers were singled out for further training and instruction in the actual implementation of lesson plans. These teachers were visited at least once a week to eliminate problems, to check on the progress made by the children, and to supply the teachers with new lesson plans. Control and experimental teachers were paired as to their educational background and work experience.

The specific lesson plans for this program were centered around the contrastive analysis approach. Johnson (1971) describes the five steps inherent in the use of this approach: A child must (1) recognize that there is a difference between his language and the language he is learning, (2) hear the target language sound or grammatical pattern, (3) discriminate between his language and the target language at the conflict points, (4) reproduce the target language feature, and (5) practice the target language feature in oral drills. The labels of "school" talk and "everyday" talk* were used to

---

*A variety of terms have been used interchangeably with "everyday" talk; "other talk," "home talk," and "street talk," in particular, have been widely used as synonyms.

differentiate between standard English and the child's dialect. Figure 8–1 presents one of the lesson plans used in the Knox County program.

Special situations were created in order to facilitate the discrimination between "everyday" and "school" talk. Hand puppets were used in the early stages of the program, i.e., an "everyday" puppet and a "school" puppet. Later, pictures which represented a school or everyday environment were presented with the child identifying various speech patterns as appropriate to each. Finally, role playing was instituted, e.g., the child could assume the role of mother, father, teacher or businessman. Varied contexts made the material presented more entertaining for the children and sustained their attention for longer periods of time.

The program was divided into two interrelated phases: *Phase I*—a 15-minute formal language instruction period (Monday through Friday) in which the clinician-teacher compared and contrasted the features of the target language with standard English, using the lesson plans previously described; *Phase II*—Reinforcement of the differences between "school" and "everyday" talk by the teacher or her aide at various time throughout the day. (primarily in informal situations such as recess or lunch). Under Phase II the teacher verbally rewarded the child for the appropriate use of school or everyday talk and then asked the child to contrast what had been said with its opposite variety.

Evaluation of the Program

The Daily Language Facility Test was the evaluative measure for this program. Developed by John T. Daily, this test is designed "to provide a measure of language facility which is independent of vocabulary, information, pronunciation, and grammar." Besides measuring expressive use of language, the test can also be used to examine standard English usage by scoring sentences according to standard English criteria. It can usually be administered by a clinician in about 10 minutes. Children are shown three different pictures, one at a time, and asked to tell a story about what they see. There is no time limit. There is a warm-up, conversational period. If the child is not responding, the teacher is allowed to ask such questions as "What are they doing in this picture?" The teacher either records or transcribes what the child says. Each picture is assigned a score

Fig. 8–1.   A Lesson Plan Used in the Knoxville Head Start Program*

General Instructions:

Sometimes we talk different ways when we're in different places. At rest time we sometimes talk differently from the other times during the day. Today we're going to learn two kinds of talking: "everyday talk" (place tree on flannel board) and "school talk" (place school on flannel board). Is everybody ready to play?

Everyday Picture: This is our everyday picture. It's a picture we might use everyday. Here could be our swing and our house. We will put all of our "everyday talk" words on this side.

School Picture: This is our school picture. Sometimes we talk differently at school. We will put all of our "school talk" words over here.

An Example of a Lesson

Purpose: The purpose of this lesson plan is to contrast phonological, grammatical and lexical items of standard and nonstandard English.

I.   Materials: Level P Peabody Vocabulary Cards

(These cards allow you to present a picture representation of the words.)

A-13

H-2

T-5, or any of the pictures under 70Y Section

Vocabulary to be contrasted:

Everyday Talk	*School Talk*
hoss	horse (a-13)
his'n	his (H-2)
fetch	get (T-5)

Sentences to be contrasted:

1. I rode my *hoss*.	vs. I rode my *horse*.
2. This cot is *his'n*.	vs. This cot is *his*.
3. *Fetch* me the crayons (book, etc.)	vs. *Get* me the crayons, etc.

Variations:

1. *Traffic Signals*—Give the child two circles, one red, the other green. The red represents everyday talk; the green, school talk. Have the child operate them like traffic signals. The teacher will read an everyday (school) word or sentence while the child stands before the class flashing

*A different kind of lesson plan that may be used by Head Start teachers is presented in Appendix D.

Fig. 8-2   Linguistic Symbols Tested in The Clayton Study

	Receptive Language	Expressive Language	
Aural	Understanding what is heard PPVT	Talking DLFT	Oral
Visual	Understanding what is seen—reading DRT	Writing MPST	Graphic

Thus, the goal is to present to the children the idea that their *home* or *everyday* language and behaviors are acceptable and proper in that milieu and that another set of language patterns and behaviors should be used in school—i.e., school talk and school behavior.

At no time and in no way should their home talk or home behavior be labeled as incorrect, but only called what it is—*home talk*. After all, if a large group of people consistently use a certain linguistic utterance, then it is patently improper for us to call it—or think of it—as incorrect. Instead, it is necessary to look upon these constructions as being merely different.

The teacher must wholeheartedly understand this notion if the bicultural/bidialectal program is to be effective.

Overview.   There are three phases to the program: (1) contrastive analysis or aural–oral drill; (2) utilization of lesson plans employing home- and school-talk activities in the classroom; (3) informal promotion of the concept involved during the course of the school day's activities, i.e., labeling home talk as home talk when use by a child in response to a question and requesting his school-talk equivalent.

In essence, the program is designed to provide for an *equivalent* manner of talking and behaving, particularly the former. In traditional programs we label home talk *inferior* or *incorrect;* in the bidialectal program we label such utterances *different,* and we encourage the child to learn both modes of talking but to use them at appropriate times.*

Setting Forth the "why" of the program

It is our contention that the lexical differences inherent in mountain and standard English create many learning problems—particularly reading problems; and these problems are more prevalent than heretofore contemplated. By teaching the children these vocabulary equivalencies, we believe it will help them to appreciate better their reading lessons—and hence learn them more successfully.

The phonological and grammatical differences manifested by these children immediately label them as members of a certain culture. In and of itself, this labeling is of no harm; however, when the child becomes an adult and attempts to obtain a position where standard English is desired, the nonstandard speech pattern he uses may create an unfavorable image in the mind of the employer. Thus, we want to provide him with the skills to talk one way when he finds it necessary to communicate with members of the "establishment" but *encourage* him to keep and to use his native dialect when communicating with his peers. In other words, our objective is to make him an effective diglossic speaker, one who can *switch* dialects.

Presenting the "How"

Phase I.   Use of contrastive analysis is Phase I of the program. Three areas comprise the analysis: phonology, grammar, and lexicon. Appropriate examples are recorded on cards for the teacher to use.**

The cards for each area contain a contrasting method of saying certain words—all of which are used by most rural Appalachians. For example, on Card 1 you will hear, "Some people say 'across,'" followed by "but other people say 'crost'"; in turn, followed by, "if some people say 'across'." At this point, a child will be asked to press a button recording his response,

---

*Obviously there is much redundancy in the presentation of such information. We hope it will be of value to others preparing an in-service program. We gave the teachers a "hand-out" containing the above-noted information, and discussed these matters with them in much detail.

**An Electronic Futures, Inc. Flashcard Reader machine was used for presentation of these cards to the children. These contrasts and other lesson plans relevant to the above are presented in Chapter 3 and in Appendix E.

which should be, "it means the same as: crost." The other children in the class should then be asked if the child's utterance is the proper equivalent. Thus, if the child had happened to record "across," the other children, upon hearing his response, would have noted the fact that he should have used the everyday variant rather than duplicating the school utterance.

There is one set, or two cards, for each construction. Thus, as in the previous example, where we started out with the school language form and ended up with the child uttering, hopefully, the everyday language form on the complementary card (in this case, Card 2), we start out with the everyday language form and request the school language utterance from the child.

Children should be chosen randomly or by roll, according to teacher preference, and asked to respond to one set each (i.e., the two cards) of the phonological, grammatical, and lexical variants. The children may randomly choose from among the card sets in each of these three sections.

During the first week or two of exposure to this format (or perhaps for the kindergarten and first grades, three or four weeks or more) the child will undoubtedly require help in saying the proper "carrier phrase," i.e., "it means the same as," and the equivalent word, i.e., the everyday or school language variant.

The other children listening to this process should be encouraged to respond *following* the child's recording of the word variant; i.e., they should not clue the responding child regarding the proper variant to use but should acknowledge the propriety of the response after it eas been recorded.

If the child has correctly produced the proper phonological, grammatical, and lexical variants, he should be profusely and meaningfully rewarded. If only one or two of the three presentations produced by the child are correct, he should also be rewarded, but to a lesser degree. The goal is to reinforce the child's understanding of the two variants and their proper use. That is, either construction, everyday or school language, is appropriate and acceptable but only in certain circumstances.

The teacher should spend approximately 15 minutes per day on these drills.

Phase II*. In this phase the teacher follows lesson plans employing everday- and school-talk activities in the classroom.

---

*Note that in our Head Start research programs, we eliminated Phase I and initiated the program with Phase II.

The contrastive analysis program will be of little value unless it can be supplemented by classroom activities designed to encourage proper utilization of the terms. In Appendix (e) there are sample lesson plans, all of which employ the plural *s* concept in both everyday and school talk. The teacher may use these, alter them, and/or prepare others as he/she sees fit. Other lesson plans should be created utilizing the same format, or other formats, and involving other word constructions.

An approximate 15 minutes per day following the contrastive analysis lesson should be devoted to these exercises.

Phase III. The third phase involves informal promotion of the concept. During the course of the day's activities the teacher should be alert and responsive to the children's use of home language forms. When such an utterance is produced, the teacher may call on another child to note the proper school language variant. Liberal reinforcement should be used.

Evaluation of Program

Not only did the children in the program appear to verbalize more effectively but teacher evaluations indicated a plethora of desirable behavior changes in many of the children. Examination of the test data revealed that oral language proficiency increased significantly during the 3-month period; the other language forms were not statistically different between pre- and post-test data, but they did show some important trends. In particular, both reading and writing skills appeared to improve in most all the children enrolled in the experimental classes. Of most significance, perhaps, was the teacher appraisal of the program; they commented with much enthusiasm that many of their children demonstrated a lot more participatory behavior in the classroom, and that they were, frankly, surprised by the ability level exhibited by some of the children. It is fundamental, of course, that each participant in this program recognize the need for his or her absolute support for the philosophy being espoused. We recognize, as we are sure the reader does, that we have been nurtured by an educational concept propounding the desirability of standard English usage and the substandard nature of other forms. If the teacher maintains this conceptual thinking during interactions in the program, unavoidable harm will be done to the pluralistic concept we are attempting to utilize—which has a history of successful use in our country at different times and in different places.

CONCLUSION

To the author's knowledge the experimental Head Start and K-3 programs detailed in this chapter were among the first of their kind in use with lower-class and predominantly white preschool children. There are obvious problems with the bidialectal approach, but the initial gains reported in this research provide an incentive for overcoming any difficulties. The language and culture of the culturally different child needs to be respected in our educational system, and a bidialectal program provides an opportunity, as we have repeatedly emphasized, for teachers, clinicians, and children to learn of each other's language and culture.

The investigation of social dialects in American society has received a major impetus since the middle of the 1960s. The works of Labov (1968, 1973), Stewart (1967, 1968), Wolfram (1969, 1975), Baratz (1969), Dillard (1972), and others have detailed the linguistic regularities of not only "black English" but also the "mountain speech" of Appalachia. The major conception emerging form this research is that these varieties of English (black and mountain) are complete linguistic systems in their own right, with specific rules of grammar, phonology, and lexicon, and differ basically in the fact that they are stigmatized or less prestigious forms of standard English (Wolfram & Fasold, 1974). Our research has shown that bidialectal teaching programs can be successfully implemented when this concept is accepted.

REFERENCES

Baratz, J. C. Teaching reading in an urban Negro school system. In J. C. Baratz and R. W. Shuy (Eds.), *Teaching black children to read.* Arlington, Va.: Center for Applied Linguistics, 1969.

Bereiter, C., & Engelmann, S. *Teaching disadvantaged children in the preschool.* Englwood Cliffs, N.J.: Prentice-Hall, 1966.

Bloom, B. S., David, A., & Hess, R. *Compensatory education for cultural deprivation.* New York: Holt, Rinehart and Winston, 1965.

Deutsch, M., et al. *The Disadvantaged child: Selected papers of Martin Deutsch and associates.* New York: Basic Books, 1967.

Dillard, J. L. *Black English: Its history and usage in the United States*. New York: Random House, 1972.

Humt, J. M. *The challenge of incompetence and poverty*. Chicago: University of Illinois Press, 1969.

Hall, W. S. Black and white childrens' responses to black English vernacular to standard English sentences. In D. S. Harrison and T. Trabasso (Eds.), *Black English: a seminar*. Hillsdale, New Jersey: Laurence Erlbaum, 1976

Jaggar, A. M., & Cullinan, B. E. Teaching standard English to achieve bidialectalism: Problems with current practices. *Florida Foreign Language Reporter*, Spring/Fall, 1974, 63-70.

Johnson, K. R. Should black children learn standard English? *Viewpoints Bulletin of the School of Education*, Indiana University, 1971, *47*, 83-101.

Jones, J. P. *Child development*. Austin, Texas: Head Start Evaluation and Research Center, 1967.

Labov, W., P. Cohen, C. Robins, & Lewis, J. *A study of the non-standard English of Negro and Puerto Rican speakers in New York City*. USOE Final Report, Research Project No. 3288, Washington, D.C.: U.S. Government Printing Office, 1968.

Labov, W. The logic of nonstandard English. In J. E. Alatis (Ed.), *Georgetown monograph series on languages and linguistics*. No. 22. Arlington, Va.: Center for Applied Linguistics, 1970.

Labov, W. *Language in the inner city: Studies in the black English Vernacular*. Philadelphia: University of Pennsylvania Press, 1972.

Labov, W., & Cohen, P. Some suggestions for teaching standard English to speakers of nonstandard and urban dialects. In J. S. DeStefano (Ed.), *Language, society and education: A profile of black English*. Worthington, Ohio: Wadsworth, 1973.

Rosenthal, M. The magic boxes: Preschool children's attitudes toward black and standard English. The *Florida Froeign Language Reporter* Spring/Fall, 1974, 55-62, 92-93.

Stephens, M. I. Elicited imitation of selected features of two American English dialects in Head Start children. *Journal of Speech and Hearing Research*, 1976, *19*, 492-508.

Stewart, W. A. *Language and communication problems in southern Appalachia*. Arlington, Va.: Center for Applied Linguistics, 1967.

Stewart W. A. Continuity and change in American Negro dialects. *Florida Foreign Language Reporter, 1968, 6*, 14-16, 18, 304.

Williams, E. *On the contribution of the linguist to institutional racism*. A paper presented at the Linguistic Society of America convention, San Francisco, 1969.

Williams, F., J. L. Whitehead, & Miller, L. Relations between language attitudes and teacher expectancy. *American Educational Research Journal, 1972, 9*, 263-277.

Wolfram, W. *A sociolinguistic description of Detroit Negro speech.* Arlington, Va.: Center for Applied Linguistics, 1969 (a).

Wolfram, W. *Sociolinguistic premises and the nature of nonstandard dialects.* Arlington, Va.: Center for Applied Linguistics, 1969 (b).

Wolfram, W. Sociolinguistic implications for educational sequencing. In R. W. Fasold & R. W. Shuy (Eds.), *Teaching standard English in the inner city.* Arlington, Va.: Center for Applied Linguistics, 1970.

Wolfram, W. & Christian, D. *Sociolinguistic variables in Appalachian dialects,* Arlington, Va.: Center for Applied Linguistics, 1975.

Wolfram, W. & Fasold, R. W. *The study of social dialects in American English.* Englewood Cliffs, N.J.: Prentice-Hall, 1974.

9
Teaching Reading

Reading is only one important aspect of the total process of language development. Before a [normal hearing] student can read, he must have heard spoken language, acquired the ability to speak it, and understand the meanings it conveys.

—*The Alaskan Reader,*
The Northwest Regional Educational
Laboratory

The most important problem confronting educators, at the elementary level in particular, is the teaching of reading, which is but one facet of language teaching. The Coordinated Helps in Language Development (CHILD) Project, developed by the Portland (Oregon) Public Schools involves testing and programming for the following skills that cater to reading development:

1. Imitation of standard English
2. Identification and naming
3. Imitation of varying stress placed on words in a sentence
4. Expanding sentence length and complexity
5. Development of the concept of size, place, and location
6. Classification of objects in terms of concepts

The language differences of the culturally different student even extend beyond language proper: his patterns of nonverbal communications are not those of the middle-class speakers. As we have noted, eye contact, touch, posture, movement and paralanguage—signals not produced by the articulators or the vocal tract—are ways of expressing emotions and relating social processes.

When dealing with the culturally different, the teacher of English, particularly when teaching composition, is faced with differences in every aspect of language. Not all of these differences are of equal importance, however. Nonverbal communication is, of course, outside the realm of composition, and, phonology, no matter how obvious or stigmatizing, is relevant to composition only so far as it effects grammatical matters. Lexical differences would seem to be more serious: on first encounter, they do present barriers to communication, but these are barriers easily eliminated. To find out what a "pork chop" is, we merely have to ask. As far as the composition teacher is concerned, then, grammatical variations pose the most serious problems, for it is on grammatical problems that teachers fail students. If students are to write in "standard" English, they must master not a particular lexicon or a particular phonology, but particular sentence patterns and morphological systems.

When confronted with the language differences, the teacher of composition has been unable to deal with them—a more serious problem than the differences themselves. The chief reason for this failure is that instructors have failed to recognize that nonstandard varieties of English are just as valid and systematic as standard English: that is, instructors themselves lack the linguistic sophistication to deal with the problem. Lack of linguistic sophistication has led most teachers to a kind of malnutrition theory concerning these language differences: culturally different speakers lack proper grammatical training and, as a result, their language is some form of debased standard English.

The English teacher, then, faces two problems: the culturally different student has been nurtured in a different dialect, and the teacher does not sufficiently understand either the nature of language or the different dialect. The problems themselves suggest the nature of the solutions.

SOLUTIONS

First, it is imperative that teachers understand both the nature of language itself and the nature of dialect differences. Such understanding can best be achieved by requiring all future teachers to take at least two courses in linguistics, one of them perhaps in sociolinguistics. These courses would help shape and mold attitudes and would provide at least some familiarity with various dialects. Linguistics requirements will not solve our present problem, however: the teachers who are now teaching are certainly not going back to school. Apparently, the only ways to provide them with the relevant information is through extensive in-service programs and by flooding professional journals with relevant material.

Second, we must decide just how we are going to approach the problem. Three solutions have been proposed. The first of these maintains that "nonstandard" dialects, regardless of what research in linguistics shows, are inferior modes of communication and, as such, must be eradicated. This solution is based on invalid assumptions about language, and thus it can be dismissed. A second solution, recognizing the fact that no dialect is inherently better than any other, proposes that teachers merely leave the students' languages alone, appreciating the various dialects for what they are. Such a proposal suits the current political climate: pride in the black or mountain dialects is a part of black or Appalachian pride in general. Thus, those who tell us to leave these dialects alone accuse eradicationists and bidialectalists alike of racism: the attempts to change one's dialect—especially if one is black—is merely another way of trying to force the individual to become like middle-class whites, to lose his or her identity. This view overlooks three important considerations, however. First, "standard" English is the language of mainstream society; without a command of it one is isolated from that mainstream. Second, "standard" English is the language of instruction in the schools; it is the language in which all texts are written—without a knowledge of it, problems in reading and school are likely to occur. Most importantly, though, while there is no standard phonology, or even lexicon, there is a standard written grammar, a kind of "koine" which serves the whole of the English-speaking world; because of the standard written grammar, Americans can understand a book by Australians and vice versa. Therefore, there seems to be only one possible solution—bidialectalism. This solution assumes that students should learn to write "standard" English while maintaining the dialect of their nurture.

More linguistic sophistication and the establishment of an approach to the problem is not enough, however. English programs as they now stand must be reevaluated. The program must be based on the needs of the students: textbooks must be revamped to include materials for bidialectal teaching; teaching techniques and methods of evaluation likewise need to be revised.

A BIDIALECTAL PROGRAM FOR
ENGLISH COMPOSITION

The teacher of English composition is expected to teach students to construct a rhetorically sound essay—one that is unified, coherent, and stylistically appropriate—in any of the modes of discourse or patterns of exposition using "standard" written English (that "koine" previously discussed). These aims are certainly desirable: all students are expected to do written work such as homework, creative stories, research papers, essay examinations, etc. The training they receive in composition should prepare them for that work.

A way must be found to avoid dialect interference in composition. This can best be done by having students write in their own dialects for the first month or so of the school year. There are a number of advantages to this. First, it allows both student and teacher to concentrate on rhetorical principles and techniques of good composition. In this way, the student can develop good writing skills without the interference a "foreign" dialect causes; good writing skills can be mastered in any dialect. Second, if the student is allowed to write in the dialect of his nurture, chances are that he will draw his subjects from his own experience. As every teacher of composition knows, themes drawn from personal experience are likely to be more vigorous and interesting than those about subjects "foreign" to the student. The third advantage is psychological: students will probably make better grades and thus be encouraged to achieve in school. Furthermore, it is not unlikely that both teacher and student will come to a new appreciation of the so-called nonstandard dialect. The teacher will benefit in another way too. By the time he has received five or six papers, he will be able to analyze the grammatical, lexical, and morphological differences between the nonstandard dialect and the "koine" in which the students will eventually be expected to write.

The technique to be used in coming to grips with the various dialects is simply descriptive analysis. For example, if the teacher notes that all or most of his black students omit the plural sign s, the possessive sign s, and the third-person singular s, he should conclude that this is a difference in the grammatical systems of these students. At first glance, descriptive analyses would seem a monumental task, but it actually is not. There are only a handful of differences between the nonstandard dialects and the "koine". Furthermore, in the case of black English, there are a number of helpful hints which have already been compiled.

After 3 or 4 weeks the teacher might begin to introduce the "koine." The following suggestions might be helpful. Most important, do not call the "koine" standard English; it is certainly not that. If the instructor prefers a name less foreign, he might, for older students call it "editorial American English." Second, do not as of yet require students to write new themes in editorial American English; rather, have them "translate" old themes into it. In this way there should be no dialect interference; the learning of a new dialect should not affect the acquisition of composition skills. Third, emphasize, in classroom work, the differences between dialects and editorial American English. Using the material collected from student essays, the instructor should be able to illustrate and alert students to divergencies in the systems. The use of contrastive analysis and oral-aural drills on specific items—plurals, possessives, third-singular verbs, and negatives, for example—would prove particularly useful. The teacher might also begin a program of pattern analysis. Pattern sentences should be formulated that will illustrate grammatical and morphological problems such as those that follow:

The boys are tall.
The boy's dogs ran away.
He did not do anything.
The sprinter runs as fast as possible.

Students should be asked to find sentences which fit these patterns in their readings and to construct pattern sentences of their own. The next day students might be quizzed on them.

After about six weeks students should be required to write compositions in editorial American English. By this time, the students should have mastered most of the composition skills they need: that is, they should be able to write unified, coherent, logical, well-supported papers in any mode of discourse. Furthermore, they will have been systematically and progressively introduced to the new dialect; they will have "translated" about six of their papers into editorial American English and will have been alerted to almost all areas of difference.

We have approached our goals, then, by isolating them and proceeding toward them systematically. The student is taught skills in composition, then introduced to editorial American English, and then asked to write in it. No matter how good the approach, however, it will probably not succeed if the materials used in the course—i.e., the "reader"—are not geared to the culturally different student.

Almost every English class, at the secondary level in particular, makes use of a book of reading selections. These selections are supposed to serve two purposes; first, to provide illustrations of various modes of discourse and expository patterns; second, to provide models for the proper use of the language and rhetorical and stylistic techniques. Now if all papers are written in editorial American English and students are allowed to write in the dialect of their nurture, it is obvious that the reader cannot fulfill the latter of these functions. The problem, then, is to find a reader which, while furnishing illustrations of various modes of discourse and patterns of exposition, provides relevant models for students' language. That is, we need a reader that caters to the culturally different.

Many times readers are organized around particular themes. For example, one well-known reader at the upper secondary and college level is organized around work and leisure, another around cultural decay, and a third around the essay as an instrument of modern culture. The reader for our course might be organized around the theme of cultural diversity: that is, it should examine the various cultures that coexist in America. It might treat comparatively the various institutions which make up cultures. For instance, stories about the ghetto, hollow, barrio, and suburb might be included. There might also be essays on family life, literature, entertainment, and so forth. Most importantly, though, there would be selections on the various languages of these cultures. For high school students an essay like Kochman's "'Rapping' in the Black Ghetto"* might be particularly interesting. Furthermore, these essays should prove useful in approaching the study of language.

The readers, then, should reflect the variety of mores and values that permeate American society. Thus, in reading these selections, students should learn about something other than modes of discourse—though they should surely learn that too. The reader itself will establish a pluralistic base for our approach to composition.

Most importantly, though, a large number of selections must be written in dialects spoken by the culturally different. If this is the case, the students will have viable models to work with; if this is the case, the instructor can really illustrate the cultural diversity of our society.

Our readers, then, are organized around the theme of cultural

*In C. Laird and R. M. Gorrell (Eds.), *Reading About Language* (New York: Harcourt Brace Jovanovich, 1971).

diversity, reflect the various mores and values of different cultures, illustrate various modes of discourse, and are composed in a variety of dialects. The possibilities for discussion and the theme topics which arise from them should be infinite. For example, questions following the selections might be divided into three categories—questions on the mode of discourse, questions on the language, and questions on the institution and culture which the selections discuss. The teacher should always ask students how the languages of the readings differ from both their own—if indeed they do differ—and from editorial American English. In this way the students will be made aware of differences in systems. Furthermore, students can be asked to translate passages of the essays into other dialects. Questions on subject matter should provide topics for student essays. For example, the student may wish to compare and contrast an institution of his culture with one treated in the reader.

A reader geared to the problems, needs, and interests of the culturally different, will go a long way in solving the teacher's problems. When used with the approach and techhniques suggested, in our opinion, the results will be phenomenal. Moreover, our approach should eliminate many of the problems the composition teacher has in grading and evaluating the culturally different student. Dialect interference would be eliminated, grading norms would be altered so as to be based on the peer group, and we would not have to foster the myth of "correctness." Most importantly, though, the course is built upon the idea of progression. Goals are isolated and approached one at a time. When one has been met, students then began work toward the next. What we have, then, is a program that is pedagogically sound, psychologically beneficial, and structured to meet the needs of students.

Though teachers of English are presently faced with the most critical problem they have ever encountered, it is not a problem which cannot be solved. It is true that for the most part, they are teaching students whose values and languages differ from their own. However, if the teachers will take it upon themselves to obtain the necessary linguistic sophistication and sympathetic understanding, they will have provided themselves a solid foundation from which to work. If they will restructure their course—redefine aims, refine approach and technique, and revise materials—they can educate the culturally different, can teach them the composition skills necessary in future vocation or college work. The problems of the culturally different are not only theirs; they are ours. A reference list relevant to the needs of the teacher of English, is presented in Appendix F.

PART IV

The Emerging Roles of the Speech Clinician with the Culturally Different Child

11
Conventional Roles of the Speech Clinician

Even if we call the poverty child's language different, this still does not alleviate his problem within our society. Something still needs to be done about it.The reformulated question for us now is: How might the speech clinician work with the linguistically different child? We can speculate on a few answers to this.

—David E. Yoder
"Some Viewpoints of the Speech, Hearing, and Language Clinician" In Language and Poverty.

Identification of children with speech, language, and hearing disorders, evaluation of these children, and aiding children in the development of their speech and language skills has been the traditional and, in general, successful role of the speech clinician. The speech clinician, however, has also been a contributor to the psychological hang-ups many poor people have about their speech. For years it has been members of our profession who have helped label the dialectally different child as being "defective" in his speech. Rather than saying, "You possess the right to retain your dialect; its part of your culture and thus, part of your individuality", we have said implicitly or explicitly, covertly or overtly, "No, Johnny, you must talk as I do because my way is the right way." As we have argued in this book, it is the moral and ethical obligation of every speech clinician to understand these differences and learn more about them. Section A, Number 1 (a) of the American Speech and Hearing Association's Code of Ethics states:

The member must not provide services for which he has not been properly trained, i.e., not had the necessary course work and supervised practicum. Therefore, when a clinician offers professional services to any individual he should possess all relevant information concerning his client including knowledge relevant to this client's culture.

According to Bauman (1971), this obligation will help eliminate much of the cultural bias that exists in our clinical interactions. In particular, Bauman suggests the following be done: (1) The speech clinician should make him or herself familiar with the already extensive literature in the ethnography of communication. Before we can inform and appreciate others, we must have the information ourselves. (2) The clinician must evaluate his or her present goals and methods in therapy in terms of their congruence with the culture specific structuring of speech behavior by members of the speech community from which the clients come. (3) Ethnographic factors must be considered in formulating new goals and procedures for therapy. What may be the answer for the middle-class white is not always the best solution for the culturally different. (4) The clinician should evaluate critically the research in terms of its sensitivity to the ethnographic realities of the subjects involved; many of the data concerning the poor need to be carefully reevaluated regarding their reliability or validity. (5) Every effort to impart the ethnographic perspective to the students should be made so that they understand at least the notion that the organization of speech behavior is cross-culturally variable and that cultural difference does not mean cultural deficit.

TESTING

In assessing the language of culturally different children, the speech clinician must be cognizant of the limitations of the culturally biased tests currently in use. These tests, often standardized according to middle-class norms, present a distorted view of the language abilities of the culturally different. Before a test is utilized, two questions should be asked: (1) Precisely who comprised the standardization population? (2) What is the test attempting to describe or how valid is the test?

In Part II it was emphasized that it is patently unfair to compare a poor child's response pattern to the normative data generated by the middle-class subjects. Culture-fair evaluation tools are needed in order to make valid comparisons between a child's responses to those of his peers. Some progress in the development of such tools and tests has been made. Such procedures may enable the speech clinician to determine whether a child's speech performance does not agree with the norms of his peer community (thus, a genuine deficiency), or whether it agrees with the peer community norms but not with those of the standard, or middle-class, community (thus, a linguistic difference).

Valid Evaluation Tools

The speech clinician can obtain a valid evaluation of a child's communicative skills by using one or more of the following devices:

1. Spontaneous speech sampling
2. Structured speech sampling
3. Grammatical closure
4. Spontaneous written sampling
5. Sentence repetition task
6. Communicative function analysis

Spontaneous speech sampling. Use a tape recorder or manually record whatever the child says within a given amount of time. Analysis of this sample will give information regarding both quality and quantity of verbal output. Reliability is often questionable, however, and much care must be given to insure speech sample reliability.

Structured speech sampling. Use a picture(s) to elicit definite responses and grade the child on both the quality and quantity of the response. Daily has normed this task (the Daily Language Facility Test).

Grammatical closure. This procedure is also known as sentence completion task. The child is asked to fill in that portion of the sentence that is omitted (e.g., the Berko Test).

Spontaneous written sampling. In response to a picture a story is written. This is similar to structured speech sampling except that a graphic response is elicited. Obviously, this tool is useful when the child is old enough to respond appropriately (e.g., the Myklebust Picture Story Language Test).

Sentence repetition task. Repeating sentences is perhaps the most common method used to evaluate the language skills of children. It can distinguish among four types of children;

1. Those children who consistently use dialectal English and are delayed in language development.
2. Those children who consistently use dialectal English but possess normal language development.
3. Those children who consistently use standard English and are delayed in language development.
4. Those children who consistently use standard English but possess normal language development.

This technique allows the child to hear and repeat a sentence. It has been demonstrated that when asked to repeat simple sentences, children tend to omit portions of the sentence that are beyond their level of language development; thus, omissions can be used as an index of language development or of developmental delay. Therefore, when a child is asked to repeat a sentence containing a linguistic unit he is supposedly developmentally capable of producing, but, in fact, he omits it from his repetition, one can speculate that he is either developmentally retarded or linguistically different. If members of his peer group also tend to omit this unit, however, then it is obviously not part of his linguistic development. Also, if we know that dialectal-different speakers can repeat these sentences when they are spoken in dialect better than can establishment speakers, we can again assume these are valid linguistic utterances.

Anastasiow and Hanes (1976) have developed such a test; when words were omitted that were beyond the childrens level of development, the score obtained was called "function word omissions," but when the children changed portions of the sentence to conform to their dialect, they were called "reconstructions". The sentence repetition task we devised and used in our Head Start interactions is presented in Table 11–1. As can be seen, there were two kinds of sentences: standard English and nonstandard English. Pre-testing and post-testing on this test revealed that the experimental children were able to repeat more effectively the standard at the close of the program than could the controls; they incorporated more function words. Both groups did equally well on the nonstandard portion. Thus, we can conclude that our program was effective insofar as language development teaching strategies were concerned. This kind of test is very easy to administer and is reliable and valid.

Currently there are two common approaches for assessing a child's grammatical skills: through the analysis of spontaneous speech samples, or through the analysis of a sample of elicited imitations (sentence repetition tasks). Measurements of spontaneous speech can be made through a variety of tests:

Table 11—1

Sentence Repetition Test

Student Name _____Classroom _____

Age _____ Sex _____ Race _____

1. She's going to play.   11. I done it.

   _____   _____

2. She is eating.   12. They aren't supposed to eat this.

   _____   _____

3. What was you'ns adoin'?   13. He did it.

   _____   _____

4. He might be able to play.   14. I don't have any money.

   _____   _____

5. I might could go.   15. Where were you going?

   _____   _____

6. She isn't home.   16. I wonder was he walking?

   _____   _____

7. Why she be mean?   17. Her jumpin'.

   _____   _____

8. You not 'posed to do dat.   18. He ain't here.

   _____   _____

9. Why is he sad?   19. I don't have no butter.

   _____   _____

10. He gonna get hurt.   20. I wonder if she was running.

   _____   _____

1. *Mean Length of Response (MLR).* In this test from a sample of 50 sentences, the total number of words is determined and divided by 50. The relationship of a child's MLR to his language complexity seems to be taken for granted, but in fact are inferior indicators of the poor child's language complexity.
2. *Sentence Complexity Score (SCS).* In this test, one rank-orders the different types of sentences a child uses. The weight of the sentence type ranges from 0 (incomplete response) to 4 (complex response).
3. *Developmental Sentence Scoring (DSS).* In this test, eight grammatical features of a child's speech are scored: (a) indefinite pronouns, (b) personal pronouns, (c) main verbs, (d) secondary verbs, (e) negatives, (f) conjunctions, (g) interrogative reversals, (h) wh _____ questions. From the child's spontaneous speech, each of these features are scored from 0 (nonexistant) up to 8, depending on the number of complexities present in his speech. This is a complicated test and requires a good deal of practice before the examiner will become proficient in its use.

Measurements of elicited imitations (EI) attempt to evaluate a child's expressive grammar by having him repeat a series of sentences. Obviously, the child's short term memory (STM), as well as his dialectal patterns would influence the results of such tests.* Two well-known tests using this method are the (1) Carrow Elicited Language Inventory (CELI), and the Northwestern Syntax Screening Test (NSST). Neither test accounts for dialectal differences. The tests may score grammatical complexity as being absent, when in fact it may be present but its dialect is not that of the test instrument. There is no method of distinguishing between dialectal differences, and true language pathology.

Because nonstandard dialects tend to be simpler and more precise and eliminate the redundancies of standard dialect, poor children tend to use shorter sentences, more one-word responses, and tend to prefer simple sentences or incomplete sentences rather than compound or complex sentences. Nevertheless, such sentence structure is both complex and logical. However, the testing instruments mentioned do not show either the complexities or the logic of nonstandard English.

*See M. A. Simpson and H. L. McDade, "The use of delayed imitation to test grammatical performance," a paper presented to the American Speech and Hearing Association. San Francisco, California, 1978. Results from this study suggest that a three-second delay on the CELI provided the best predictor of DSS.

Communicative functions.   This type of analysis attempts to describe the way language is used in the communicative situation between the child and clinician (or teacher). A spontaneous communication sample is collected on videotape, and verbal and nonverbal responses are transcribed orthographically. The utterances are then categorized with respect to communicative intent, and the sequence of intents is plotted on a graph that is a modification of the one used for content and sequence analysis.

In a study by Tonkovich and Adler (1978) in the University of Tennessee Pediatric Language Laboratory, an analysis of communicative functions was applied to communication samples obtained from lower- and middle-class children. The following communicative functions were identified:

1.   Giving information in direct response to a question.
2.   Getting information.
3.   Getting the listener to do, believe, or feel something.
4.   Making a statement with the speaker as referent (e.g., I feel, I think, I'm going to).
5.   Making a statement with the listener as referent.
6.   Making a statement with a referent other than the speaker or listener.
7.   Using conversational devices (e.g., agreeing with speaker, interjecting).
8.   Entertaining (e.g., any riddle, nursery rhyme, joke, etc.).
9.   Function which is not discernable.
10. No response.

Using these categories, the authors classified utterances according to their communicative functions with 90 percent agreement using only the orthographic transcription of utterances, and with 95 percent agreement using orthographic transcription with the original videotape recording.

In analyzing the communicative functions of utterances in conversation, it is necessary to consider both the speaker and listener, as well as utterances which precede and immediately follow the utterance being analyzed. Nonverbal responses (e.g., shrugging shoulders, nodding head in approval) are transcribed, analyzed with respect to the function they served in communication, and plotted on the graph. The percentage of the speaker's nonverbal utterances is then calculated with respect to the child's number of total utterances.* Our study revealed significant differences as a function of the social class of the children.

The Use of Conventional Tests and the Appropriate Reporting of Data

Few of the more commonly used tests have been standardized on different ethnic and social-class children from different regions of the country. To do so is a very laborious task. We encourage the reader to make item analyses of the response patterns elicited from these various tests with the specific populations of children he or she interacts with; such information will allow the testor to compare a child's linguistic response to both standard and peer norms.

To use culture fair tests, however, which would not allow for a comparison with the middle-class norm would not be very helpful to the teacher or clinician attempting to teach middle-class responses. Similarly, a test report which does not compare the child's responses to his peer group—as is more commonly the case—would not validly reflect the child's skills.

Standardized tests should only be used by the speech clinician as an index of the child's progress in developing the additional language or dialect system of standard English. As Yoder (1973) points out, "Ironically, the more culturally biased such tests are, the more benefit they will be in this case, *so long as they are used as a basis for describing differences instead of deficits*" (italics added).

The speech clinician is faced with a challenging role as a diagnostician. To accomplish the unique demands of testing the culturally different child, the following should be done: (1) the clinician should educate himself regarding the customs, traditions, values, mores, and language patterns of the particular cultural group with which he is

*It was noted that the speech clinician involved in the study, used different language patterns when talking to the lower-class child as compared to the patterns used when talking to the middle-class control. It would seem obvious that clinicians must be very much aware of this potential alteration during communicative interactions; such differences could negatively affect therapeutic relationships with poor children. This study was presented by the first named author at the American Speech and Hearing Association Convention in San Francisco, 1978.

working;* (2) speech clinicians, especially in the schools, can combine forces and standardize the tests used with the children in their school district; (3) every speech clinician should compare the child's test score to both the standard- and peer-group norms, the latter norm to be obtained formally or, if necessary, be based upon an informal judgment.

REFERRALS

Jones (1972) feels that in serving the special needs of the culturally different child the speech clinician should be persistent in initiating referrals in cases where untreated medical, psychological, or other problems may have a direct bearing on observed speech, language, and hearing problems. It is the speech clinician's responsibility to become familiar with low-cost or free services which are available to children in inner-city or rural areas. The clinician must be willing to pursue these referrals in the face of occasionally indifferent, but more frequently, uninformed parents or agency personnel.

PUPIL PLACEMENT

In the past it was not uncommon for culturally different and poor children to be labeled "retarded" and be referred for placement in classrooms for the mentally retarded. In our roles as diagnosticians we must assume a more vigorous role in recommending proper educational placement for these children so that such inappropriate labeling and placement is no longer common. It is of interest to note that the American Association of Mental Deficiency now suggests that two criteria be used to ascertain retardation: (1) an IQ score of 69 or below as obtained on an inclusive test, such as the WISC or Stanford-Binet, administered by a licensed psychological testor and (2) an inability to relate properly to one's peer group, i.e., social adaptation is poor. When the speech clinician

*A child who possesses an articulation deficit according to his peer-group norms should perhaps be taught to say the sound (1) according to conventional or standard English norms and (2) according to his peer-group norms. For example, a black child who ways "Rup" instead of "Ruf" which is the equivalent of "Ruth" should be taught to say both the everyday and the school language equivalent of the word. As long as a child's cultural peers use nonstandard utterances, they should be taught to the client who omits them in his speech.

possesses information regarding these criteria, he or she should carefully appraise any label attached to the child to determine if it is justified.

TREATMENT

Traditionally, speech clinicians are known as professional workers who treat individuals possessing speech and language disorders; but if the conventional definition of "disorder" is questionable, then perhaps the propriety of our treatment programs is also questionable. Van Riper (1972) states "Speech is defective when it deviates so far from the speech of other people that it calls attention to itself, interferes with communication, or causes its possessor to be maladjusted." When using this definition to pass judgment upon a person's speech performance, the first part of the definition creates problems, it suggests that the speech of other [establishment] people is the norm, or at least has been so interpreted, when in reality it should be the speech of the peer group that is the norm. Thus, we have initiated therapy based upon an improper model. We conventionally compare one's speech performance to the middle-class standard and thereby label as "deficient" much that is in fact "different." To date, then, it would seem to be apparent that many clinicians have treated as pathological various speech and language utterances of poor children when many of the utterances are "different"—not deficient. Thus, an unjustifiable treatment program is arranged for such children. Such treatment programs must, we believe, frequently end in failure. Have our therapy programs for poor children been unsuccessful? Our experiences have demonstrated that therapy plans and programs for poor children have not been as successful as have those treatment programs devised for middle-class children.

Employing the Rosenthal and Hawthorne
Effects in the Therapy Program

As noted previously, the Rosenthal effect refers to the concept that therapeutic results are significantly influenced by the clinician's expectations; that is, the more one expects from a client, the more one will get from his client. The Hawthorne effect notes that the more attention you pay to a client, the better the response pattern. To utilize these concepts in the therapy program requires the clinician to expect the best from the patient while "showering" him with attention. Now such a behavioral interaction might seem to be fundamental to most therapy programs, but all too often we fear the clinician is "turned-off" by a poor child who manifests all kinds of behaviors considered to be rude, crude, or pathological. Such responses by the clinician, although covert rather than overt, nevertheless, dictate a therapeutic relationship that does not cater to the Rosenthal and Hawthorne effects. We suggest that these percepts be carefully considered when intereacting with any client—or, for that matter, in any interpersonal relationships.

THE DEVELOPMENT OF EFFECTIVE RURAL PUBLIC SCHOOL PROGRAMS

During the *ASHA* workshop on "Services to Neglected Populations in the Southeast," (1973), it was noted that a pressing need existed for speech clinicians to work with poor children and adults in these rural areas. It was reported that only 64.5 percent of the children identified as being handicapped were being served. We doubt that this statistic has changed much. There are still large numbers of communciatively impaired children whose needs are unmet.

Recent legislation, Public Law 94-142, has put all states under mandate to provide comprehensive and appropriate services to all handicapped children. To meet the needs of this legislation, new personnel will have to be hired and new programs provided in our rural areas. The question is "Who will work in these rural areas?" The geographic location, cultural isolation, low salary, and social isolation are all factors which affect the job market for hiring professionals. For example, a large rural population in the Southeast is located in the Appalachian mountain region. Traveling in this area of the country is difficult, especially when considering the weather conditions common to certain seasons of the year. The cultures of the people in these regions are unique and sometimes threatening to an outsider. The people have been isolated both geographically and socially, which often determines their acceptance or rejection of any new program. It can be seen that these factors might hinder the development of service programs in these areas. Yet effective programs can be implemented.*

*Professor Clare Maisel of the Department of Audiology and Speech Pathology of the University of Tennessee conducts a Public School practicum course in which students obtain diversified experience working in rural public schools. This program is entitled "The Satellite Public School Program" and is highly successful. In many ways it is a prototype of what a model rural Public School Speech program should be.

The implementation of a speech-language correction program begins with an identification phase in which all individuals both unserved and under-served must be located. To initiate this phase, the clinician should conduct a public information campaign to inform and educate the public as to the nature of the program being developed. One of the best media for this purpose is the newspaper (see Van Hattum, 1976, for more information). The best method would be to submit a pre-written article describing the nature or purpose of the program. Brief explanations of communicative disorders should be presented, and the relationship between speech and language to the educational process underscored. A well informed public is the key to success for a program of this nature.

During the identification phase, an attempt should be made to locate all individuals requiring services. The unserved can be located through referral services such as the Public Health Department or the Easter Seal Society, and through traditional speech-language-hearing screening within the school population. The screening procedures should serve to distinguish not only the linguistically deficient but also the linguistically different.

Once all individuals needing services have been identified, their need for services should be verified through more formal diagnostic testing procedures. Our previous discussion relevant to the reliability and validity of test instruments used should be considered. Considering the fact that the population within the rural areas primarily speak in a dialect native to their culture, most standardized tests would be a discriminatory means of verifying communication disorders within a cultural dialect group, if the results obtained were compared to standard norms, and would thus be invalid. Public Law 94-142 prohibits the use of discriminatory testing procedures for the purpose of identification and verification of communication disorders.

It is important that the tester know how to interpret the test for non-mainstream dialect speakers. The speech-language clinician should recognize the implications of these test biases and know how to account for and interpret the discrepancies in the test. As we have said, there is an imperative need that a test score obtained from such a discriminatory instrument be reported in terms of both the standardized norms and the individual's peer group performance to avoid all chance of penalizing a child because of cultural differences.

Using the diagnostic testing data as measures of the specific learning needs of the culturally different in the rural areas, the speech-language clinician could then determine the curricula best suited to the needs of the individuals involved. Public Law 94-142 requires an individualized education program (IEP) for each child evaluated. This IEP is required to be a written statement containing: (1) a statement of the levels of educational performance of the child at present; (2) a statement of annual goals, including short-term instructional objectives; (3) a statement of the specific educational services to be provided to the child and the extent to which the child will be able to participate in regular educational programs; (4) the projected date for initiation and anticipated duration of the services; and (5) appropriate objective criteria and evaluation procedures for determining, on at least an annual basis, whether instructional objectives are being achieved. Each child's IEP is developed during a meeting of the multidisciplinary team, (M-team) whose function it is to determine the appropriate treatment program for the child.

Several options exist for delivery of a treatment program; they include the traditional individual and group therapy procedures, and speech improvement and language development classes. In both programs, the bidialectal approach should be used; the relevance of this teaching-treating strategy should be explained to the M-team members so that they will support it.

The importance of the parental role in shaping communication and language development is well recognized. The speech-language clinician should be responsible for conducting home visits and establishing parent contact to insure understanding of the program and its goals, particularly, if the bidialectal approach is employed. For such a program to be effective, however, it must allow for intensive interaction, and that requires a job description that allows for such involvement.*

Throughout the time a program is in operation, it is the responsibility of the speech-language clinician to periodically assess the amount of change taking place as a result of the services provided by the program. Habilitative and educational procedures must be revised to meet the ever-changing needs of the children enrolled in the program. In addition, effective communication should be developed with the various agencies designed to help poor people, thereby enabling the clinician to cater to the changing needs of poor clients.

In summary, the effectiveness of a rural program depends on a number of factors, but the following two factors are of prime importance:

*If effective home involvement programs are to be implemented, it will require the clinician to visit these homes when, preferably, both parents are available. Thus, night or weekend visits. To accomplish this, the clinician must be allowed time-off during the regular work day, or the work day must be routinely altered to allow for such interactions to occur.

(1) knowledge of the cultural and cultural institutions, i.e., the learning styles of the children in these areas; (2) Knowledge of the power structure within the community. The power source may be the superintendent of the schools, or it may be a teacher, local professional, or even a non-professional, seemingly unimportant, individual. The power structure is useful in promoting the program and in securing funds for the program. In other words, the clinician must become politically involved to the extent that he can "sell" his ideas to the "powers-that-be." Unless such ideas can be implemented, they are of no value.

Working in rural areas provides the clinician with experiences unavailable to him in a regular clinical setting. It is a challenging experience. The need is there and it is the responsibility of the speech-language clinician to fulfill that need.

REFERENCES

ASHA Workshop on Services to Neglected Populations in the Southeast. Atlanta, Georgia, May 10, 1973.

Anastasiow, N. J. & Haynes, M. C. Language patterns of poverty children. Springfield, Ill.: Thomas, 1976.

Bauman, R. An ethnographic framework for the investigation of communicative behaviors. ASHA, 1971, 334-340.

Jones, S. A. The role of the public school clinician with the inner-city child. Journal of Speech, Hearing, and Language Services in the Schools, 1972, 3.

Tonkovich, J. D., & Adler, S. A study of pragmatics: A pilot study. Unpublished paper, University of Tennessee, Knoxville, 1978. Also presented as Content and sequence analysis of Communicative Interaction: A Research Tool, ASHA Convention. San Francisco, 1978.

Van Hattum, R. Clinical Speech in the Schools. Springfield, Ill.: Thomas, 1976.

Van Riper, C. Speech correction: principles and methods. (5th ed.). Englewood, Cliffs, N.J.: Prentice-Hall, 1972.

Yoder, D. E. "Some viewpoints of the speech, hearing and language clinician. In F. Williams (Ed.). Language and Poverty. Chicago: Markham, 1970.

12
Unconventional Roles of the Speech Clinician

It is necessary for the speech pathologist to understand the nature of the problem of teaching economically disadvantaged children in order to devise effective procedures for working with these children.

—J. C. Baratz,
"Language in the Economically Disadvantaged Child: A Perspective,"
ASHA, April 1968

IN THE SCHOOL SETTING

With the increase in the number of preschool children enrolled in day care facilities, a new emphasis is being placed on the development and needs of the preschool child in this setting. The Office of Education of the Department of Health, Education, and Welfare, estimates that 25 percent of the children in our educational systems are educationally handicapped; this number includes children who are defective in speech and hearing, as well as those children possessing learning disabilities of a cognitive-linguistic origin. It has been estimated that at least one-third of these children could be helped by appropriate preschool care. It then becomes the responsibility of day care personnel to provide the necessary educational and developmental services to meet the needs of the children, with developmental and remedial language programming as the core of such services. The Pediatric Language Institutes (PLI), a branch of the

Pediatric Language Programs at the University of Tennessee, is engaged in teaching such personnel in the East Tennessee area the developmental and remedial information required for them to develop such effective programs. The very positive response our clinicians receive from these professional and para-professional day care workers suggests we are catering to a basic need of these workers. A campus day-care center is directed by a member of our staff and allows for on-site visitations of these day care workers to our model program—our Pediatric Language Laboratory. In this program, twenty mild to moderate language retarded and language-different children receive help eight hours a day, five days a week. The multi-disciplinary staff is augmented by half-time and part-time student speech clinicians.

It is appropriate for the speech clinician to assume the role of clinical teacher in the classroom in order to meet the needs of the culturally different child more efficiently. This concept implies the need for a curriculum-oriented clinician who can teach as well as treat the children in his or her classroom. This new role for the speech clinician would be most advantageous in preschool programs located in Head Start, day care, nursery, and kindergarten centers.

If the communication needs of the preschool poor child are to be catered to successfully, it seems apparent that aural-oral linguistic symbols will have to be taught to the child in a more effective manner than heretofore has been the case. Speech-language clinicians possess the requisite expertise necessary for such developmental language teaching programs. In addition, the clinician can treat those children possessing deficiencies in their language skills, aural-oral as well as visuo-graphic (pre-reading and pre-writing) skills. Furthermore, the director of this program should possess expertise or at least interest in a variety of functions relevant to communication skills development.

In summary, rather than serve as an itinerant clinician serving the speech-language needs of children in a variety of settings or classes, it is envisioned that the speech-language clinician could teach and treat linguistic and possibly paralinguistic symbols to preschool aged normal and deficient children in self-contained classrooms such as Headstart or day care programs.*

---

*These matters are expounded upon in much detail in publications of the Pediatric Language Programs: Deborah King and Ann Lacy Hodges, "Pediatric Language Institutes—A Training Program: For Day Care and Other Pre-School Workers Emphasizing Communicative Skills," and Susan Dodson, Linda Logan, and Patricia Mallicote, "Pediatric Language Laboratory—A Day Care Center Program: for the High Risk Infant and Child. Second Edition.

Public Schools and the Learning
Disabilities Program

Poverty precipitates a higher incidence of language deficiencies and learning disabilities in children. It is our contention that there should be a significant involvement of speech-language clinicians to teach and treat poor children in self-contained classrooms or in resource room programs.

The field of speech pathology has undergone numerous changes since its birth approximately 54 years ago. The profession has become multi-faceted and has displayed a growing sophistication. In the 1930s, speech pathologists performed limited services. In the 1940s and 1950s, this profession expanded its areas of interest to include audiology. Concern with pediatric language problems has developed within recent years. Wepman (1975) reports that the professional interest in language was an outgrowth of society's need for an understanding of aphasia and aphasia therapy in the 1940s. The areas of interest expanded into psycholinguistics in the 1950s and 1960s. The increased interest in early childhood language and language disorders was reflected in the textbooks published in the late 1960s and 1970s.*

Recently speech pathologists have asserted a responsibility to provide services to learning and language disabled children (ASHA 1975, 1976). Public Law 94-142 (1978) has implications which have resulted in new roles for speech clinicians (Adler and Maisel, 1976; Butler, 1979). These specialists are now required to function as multidisciplinary team members and as consultants to other professionals. Furthermore, Adler and Maisel submit that speech-language clinicians must recognize the relationship of language to specific learning disabilities and participate in the remediation program of children with specific learning problems.

Speech clinicians, however, generally have not been considered qualified to provide educational services for the learning-disabled child. Possibly this misconception resulted because the speech clinician typically works with children outside the classroom. In addition, university training programs have not previously emphasized visuo-graphic language skills training. Wepman (1975) argues that the speech and language clinician should accept the challenge of today's society to provide services to the learning-disabled child in auditory discrimination, auditory memory, and auditory self-monitoring. By expanding this role to include remediation in

---

*Our textbook, *The Non Verbal Child: An Introduction to Pediatric Language Pathology*, Springfield, Ill.: C. C. Thomas, second edition, 1975, was first published in 1962 and was one of the first books in speech and hearing to be concerned with the child possessing significant language dysfunction.

the academic skill subjects involving the reading and writing needs of learning-disabled children, clinicians can increase their value to the educational system; this, however, necessitates additional training for the clinician in the visuo-graphic language skills.

Public Schools and the Speech Therapy Program

Speech clinicians can do much to influence their colleagues in the public schools and their attitudes toward the culturally different child.

From a simple setting as the teacher's lounge to a more structured in-service program, the speech clinician should respond to prejudicial attitudes with a firm counter argument based on a solid understanding and *feeling* for the pluralistic point of view. The clinician should be aware of current research in the area of the difference–deficit position and be able to use that knowledge in influencing colleagues' attitudes.

The speech clinician should be prepared to discuss standardization and norming techniques and their effect upon the culturally different child. He should be able to cite specifics about the testing situation and what procedures can be taken to make it a more culture-fair experience.

Pose to your colleagues some of the following questions: Are we, as members of the educational institution, attempting to narrow the range of acceptable learning behavior to a specific point which we have predetermined as "appropriate conformity"? Is not the most biased tenet of all the "median"? (usually based on reading scores). What about innate differences between individuals? Why are we able to accept some individual differences and not others? Why does society place hierarchical values upon these differences? Does higher IQ mean "better" or simply "different"?

The speech clinician can be an advocate for the culturally different child and can help colleagues interpret the culturally different child realistically in an attempt to help him "make it through" with the least possible stress. Why not focus on the strengths of the child rather than attempt to remake his weaknesses. Everyone concerned must begin to recognize individual differences, including language, and appreciate them for their uniqueness rather than attempt to change them.

One viable approach to the uniqueness of differences is to use bidialectal teaching strategies in oral language training. In contrast to other approaches, bidialectalism does not deny the legitimacy of the "other" language. It is not an attempt to eradication and replacement. Bidialectalism would offer all children educational experiences in both languages. If a classroom is integrated racially, ethnically, or socioeconomically, some classroom experiences can be heterocultural and organized around the languages the children speak. When teaching standard English, either oral or written, methods can emphasize parallel forms. And the clinician can be a consultant to the teacher initiating such a program. Figure 12–1 illustrates this and other roles relevant to the clinician.

A common question asked of the author by people interested in developing a bidialectal and bicultural program, is how they are to determine which language patterns are nonstandard and which are substandard for a

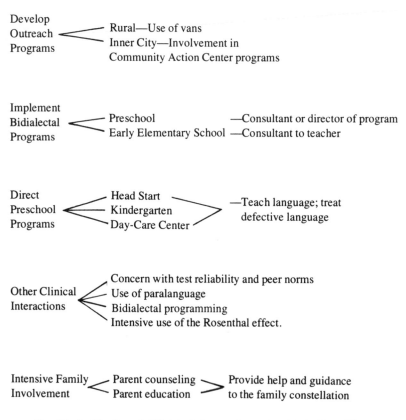

Develop
Outreach   Rural—Use of vans
Programs   Inner City—Involvement in
                  Community Action Center programs

Implement
Bidialectal   Preschool   —Consultant or director of program
Programs   Early Elementary School —Consultant to teacher

Direct   Head Start
Preschool   Kindergarten   —Teach language; treat
Programs   Day-Care Center   defective language

                  Concern with test reliability and peer norms
Other Clinical   Use of paralanguage
Interactions   Bidialectal programming
                  Intensive use of the Rosenthal effect.

Intensive Family Parent counseling   Provide help and guidance
Involvement   Parent education   to the family constellation

Fig. 12–1. The Speech Clinician's Innovative Role with the Poor Client

given dialect community. As our research has demonstrated the answer is to be found in the tabulation of those "different" patterns (phonological, grammatical, and lexical) that appear fairly consistently in the speech of most of the children from that particular dialect community. If a number of teachers in a given school, or a number of clinicians in a particular school system, were to compare such information over a period of time, they should be able to compile a valid listing of nonstandard and substandard utterances.

UTILIZING NONVERBAL BEHAVIOR IN THE THERAPY SETTING

It has been recognized that supervisors rate those workers who used more nonverbal movements as "better" clinicians. These "better" clinicians seem to use movements unconsciously. If all clinicians were aware of their nonverbal movements and purposely made more use of them, the impact should prove to be even greater.

It is important that, in the diagnostic setting, one gets the feel of the child's body rhythm to promote interactional synchrony. It has been suggested that the clinician play a game by pretending to be a mirror and to imitate the person's movements. Perhaps the clinician could tell the child that they are going to play Follow the Leader. It is the clinician's responsibility to get into the child's rhythm pattern. This involves an activity, performed for 3 to 5 minutes, to help the clinician adjust to the child's body rhythm. Quick adjustments to rhythm is a means of gaining rapport and promoting better communication. Also, imitation of the client's posture is recommended. If the child wishes to sit cross-legged on the floor, the clinician might do the same.

The clinician should make himself physically available to the child by bending, kneeling, or sitting. The child should be able to see that the clinician is giving of himself to make the child more comfortable. The clinician should be available so it is easy to touch the child to convey affection, approval, or motivation.

The clinician should learn to stroke the child rather than pat or "beat" him. Children seem to be irritated by constant patting. The clinician should not approach the child with hands behind the back, rather the hands should be in front of body. Hands, if possible, should not be used as a controlling device, such as using them to "herd" children from one place to another. It is better to invite a child to come sit in a chair rather than "herd" the child toward it with a light push on the back.

If the child's culture does not allow a close spatial relationship, hands can be used to extend out and bring the person in. This is a way to achieve close proximity without invading personal space. If the black child wishes to keep distant from the white clinician, closeness and warmth can still be transmitted by moving the materials closer to the child and keeping hands and arms extended. Yet actual body distance is not threatening to the child.

If even this spatial relationship makes the child uncomfortable, perhaps the distance can be reduced psychologically by increasing eye contact. In cases where both eye contact and close spatial relationships are undesirable, a mirror may be utilized. The clinician could have the child look into the mirror at the same time the clinician does, therefore gaining indirect eye contact.

Again, it is important to know what eye behaviors are characteristic of what cultures. Several investigators have suggested that there may be important differences between blacks and whites in eye behavior; that in poor black families, people look directly at one another less often than people do in middle-class white families. This would account for the fact that blacks meeting whites sometimes feel stared at, while whites feel that blacks are avoiding their eyes.

Yet another explanation could be due to the differences in body rhythms. Paul Byers, an anthropologist at Columbia University, analyzed a film made at a nursery school.

During a 10-minute sequence, one little black girl tried, by actual count, 35 times to catch the white teacher's eye and succeeded only four times, while a white child made contact eight times out of only fourteen tries. And it wasn't a case of favoritism. Analysis showed that the white child's timing was simply better: the little black girl kept looking at the teacher even when she was engrossed in helping another child, while the white girl saved her bids for attention, for the most part, for times when the teacher was free. Again and again in this film the teacher reached out to each of two little black girls, but each try at contact turned into a near miss, either because the woman herself hesitated, as if not sure her touch was welcome, or because the child, with a slight graceful ripple of the shoulders, shrugged off her hand. Byers believes the film demonstrates, not prejudice, but problem in interpreting body motion. (Davis, 1973, p. 118.)

Problems involving eye contact between two cultures could be due to misinterpretations of body motions or to lack of interactional synchrony. Perhaps the emphasis on body rhythms previously mentioned could help alleviate the problem

With children's special awareness of body language, it is imperative that we keep our emotions under control. One should be sure never to convey the information that we wish to be doing something else instead of giving attention to the child. While the child is talking to us, we should not be reaching for therapy material and preparing for what comes next. The child will often assume that we are simply not interested in him, although we know we can listen while doing something else. We should also be sure never to direct a frown at the child, even if we are frowning because of displeasure with ourselves and not the child. Children often remember angry looks much more than angry words. Again, the key is to remain aware of what the nonverbal cues are communicating.

Michael and Willis tested 80 children for their ability to send and interpret 12 common gestures and found middle-class children more skilled than those from lower socioeconomic classes (Knapp, Larson, & McCrosky, 1971). If this is true, a program to teach interpretation of gestures should be incorporated in all language therapy involving culturally different children. This could be done by playing a game similar to charades. The clinician could make a gesture and require the child to interpret the gesture.

As with the diagnostic methods, these therapy ideas cannot all be used in a single therapy hour. Many of the methods, such as those mentioned to communicate warmth, are only appropriate in a group setting. Similarly, methods such as imitation of posture apply only in the individual setting. Any clinician can use these methods. One must simply try which methods work best for particular clients. Some can be of value in any program involving either culturally different or culturally similar children.

A clinician may wish to make a videotape of the initial therapy session. If viewed objectively the clinician may be able to judge which methods may prove to be most useful as a means of obtaining the therapeutic goals. The justification for utilization of nonverbal cues in therapy is the results this procedure can achieve.

In view of the research, the evidence is overwhelming that the speech clinician should not ignore the importance of nonverbal cues in the therapy program.

OUTREACH SERVICES IN RURAL AND
INNER CITY COMMUNITIES

The increased use of mobile clinics to provide services to rural and inner-city residents is recommended. Because of great distance, poor roads, lack of transportation services, and other transportation problems, residents of many rural and inner-city areas are often unable to come to clinical centers for services; a mobile unit could take the services to them. The estimated initial cost of purchasing and equipping such a unit in 1979 was approximately $10,000 to $15,000 depending upon the quality of the unit. Yearly operating costs, exclusive of salaries, were estimated to be approximately $2,000 to $3,000.

One is able to develop effective programs by cultivating good relationships with Community Action Centers (CAC) generally located in nearby housing developments or rural areas. A significant problem confronting many of us is the lack of any significant experience on the part of the middle-class urban clinician with the inner-city or rural mores and value systems. Such ignorance frequently translates into prejudice, fear, hostility, apathy, and other pejorative attitudes. To negate this problem, contacts can be made with the local CAC to permit the development of service programs founded upon a relevant training program. A need exists for such training programs in all depressed areas. It would give speech clinicians direct experience with culturally different more and value systems. Furthermore, it would allow them to analyze dialectally different speech patterns. Labov (1959) states, "The situation we face is one of reciprocal ignorance, where teacher and student are ignorant of each other's systems, and therefore, the rules needed to translate from one system to another." This pluralistic concept is, of course, the theme undergirding this book.

Beyond providing for the speech disorders and speech differences in poverty-level children, the *elderly* poor make up a large population that requires hearing evaluations and many diversified speech services. To furnish such effective services will also require a training program for students which exposes them to these people and their problems. Carnell (1968) recommends an internship program in which the student lives in the target community (e.g., geriatric housing development) for a period of time. In this way the trainee will be able to become aware of and sensitive to every aspect and need of a community program. This is necessary for students who plan to seek jobs in depressed areas. A lack of sensitivity to the economic difficulties of others by people in the upper levels of society is created simply by isolation from the conditions at lower social levels; such insensitivity is potentially harmful to a therapy program because of the Rosenthal effect. Ayers (1970) contends that therapists do not understand the disadvantaged, their culture, life style, values, or attitudes and have virtually no accurate knowledge or experience in dealing with them. The lack of experience in particular, inevitably creates and perpetuates fear, anxiety, hostility, apathy, and indifferent attitudes. Our

Pediatric Language Clinic Program tries to solve these problems. This rural outreach program caters to the families of children with communication disorders. It attempts to relate effectively with the family by providing intensive education and counseling, as discussed below, and a sensitivity to the varied needs of these people.

FAMILY INVOLVEMENT

Parent Counseling

Most parents of exceptional children can profit significantly from intensive educational and counseling interactions. This is particularly the case with poor parents who frequently find it very difficult to relate effectively to middle-class workers. Yet these same parents may possess guilt feelings, negative feelings, fears, or anxieties that affect their self-concepts, and their relationships may trigger friction within the family with resultant unhealthy child-rearing and marital environments. The ability to cope with these feelings and problems is obviously of primary importance if a treatment program is to succeed in its goals.

The social worker is traditionally the person who is responsible for obviating the emotional problems relatively common to a family constellation in which a severely handicapped child is reared. If such a worker is unavailable, the clinician should be prepared to address these matters. Six areas of concern should be of major interest to this worker: child behavior, parent–child relationship, maternal self-concept, and financial, physical and emotional concommitants of the home environment.*

Of interest is the gradual emergence of guilt feelings and negative self-concepts by many parents. Given the opportunity to ventilate their

*We have employed a "crisis intervenor" in the University of Tennessee Pediatric Language Laboratory program. Her function is to cater almost exclusively to the socio–personal needs of the families whose children attend our program. Her time is taken up with crises involving (1) food stamps, (2) child-abuse problems, (3) marital problems, (4) taking the mother (and others) to various agencies, (5) interpretation of reports from these agencies, (6) arranging for needed food or clothing, and (7) many other similar needs. Our "crisis intervenor" collaborates frequently with representatives from other agencies when matters arise relevant to their disciplines. We have found that the financial, physical, and emotional needs of the poor mother are profound and require immediate and sustained attention.

feelings, they have evinced much cathartic behavior. These feelings must be handled carefully if the subsequent counseling interactions are to be healthy ones. To suggest, however, that the emergence of these or other emotions is potentially dangerous and such contacts should be avoided is generally unsatisfactory. Our work with the parents of the children needing therapy has clearly demonstrated the need for such counseling. In situations where the counseling is clearly beyond the competencies of the clinician, however, referrals should be made to other agencies specializing in such treatment.

Parent Education

It has long been our contention that the amount of time some habilitationists traditionally give to parental education is, at best, inadequate. To treat effectively a child's severe communication disorder, a significant amount of time must be alloted to the teaching of basic communication skills. Pragmatically, the only people capable of providing such amounts of time are the parents.

Therefore, one of the major goals of the language program should be to encourage *intensive parent involvement* in the treatment of each child. These attempts should be neither casual nor superficial; if at all possible, parents should be *required* to become active members of the habilitation team. Thus, a great deal of time and effort is necessarily devoted to parental education in our pediatric language programs, which cater almost exclusively to poor parents and their exceptional children. Parent education is provided in three basic forms: home visits, group and individual clinic meetings, and classroom participation.

The first aspect of our parent education is the home-visit program. Time must be alloted in the worker's treatment schedule to allow for such visits. Thus, rather than work a 5-day in-clinic schedule, the clinician might be allowed to work 3 or 4 days and use the other days for home visitation.* During these visits, the clinician is enabled to work with the parents in their natural environment. Lesson plans which are developed for each child and geared to the parents' level of sophistication are explained and demonstrated to the parents. Role playing is often utilized to ensure that minimum confusion and misapplications of therapy occur. If

---

*These visits should be made at a time when, hopefully, both parents are present, as well as any grandparents living in the home. This may necessitate night visits or visits on Saturdays; more frequently than not, our staff make their visits during the evening hours.

necessary, the home environment is physically altered; for example, part of a room may be rearranged to make it more conducive to the therapy interaction. More often, habilitation techniques are altered to fit the facilities found in each individual home.

The second aspect of a successful parent-education program involves individual and group conferences at the clinic. At these conferences group and individual lesson plans are presented and explained, and the parents are given the opportunity to ask questions regarding habilitation. Although conferences are held on a regular basis with every parent by each member of the habilitation team, parents are encouraged to interact with the staff whenever possible. It is incumbent upon the clinician to be sure he is, in fact, communicating with the parent; as a rule of thumb, we employ the dictum that it is never the parent's fault that communications were ineffective but rather our fault that we were unable to "get through" to the parents. All who have interacted intensively with culturally different and poor clients know full well the manifold difficulties that exist in developing such effective communications—but that should not deter from continuing to try to "bridge the gap."

The final aspect of parent education involves classroom participation. In this area parents act as "aides" in the classroom. Thus, they are enabled to become much more involved as a participant rather than as a spectator safely sheltered behind the one-way mirror. We employ the dictum that if students can be taught to be effective clinicians, so can parents be taught to be effective para–professional aides.

As can be expected, the majority of parents participating in a program will be the mothers. Yet, insofar as possible every attempt should be made to involve both parents as well as "kinfolk" living with the family in the habilitation process.

Infant Education   The very fact that a child is born into a poor family makes the child high-risk in terms of future development. Poverty breeds many deleterious health conditions, many of which can have a direct or indirect effect upon the infant's emerging communication or learning skills. Many of the infants we work with in our Pediatric Language Clinic program are referred to us by an Intensive Care Nursery (ICN) staff; by virtue of such ICN placement, they are immediately labeled as high-risk for future language-learning development.

Instead of waiting until such an infant matures and perhaps enters school with a variety of communicative and learning disabilities, an infant education (or stimulation) program can be devised for the parents of such infants. The program we use was devised by Dodson, Honeycutt, and Meeks (1978), and is used in our Pediatric Language Clinic Program.

The Infant Education Program:
An Education Program for Parents of
High-Risk Infants

I. *Population* High risk and handicapped infants (ages birth through 18 months) and their parents or primary caretaker.

II. *Rationale.* The early years are crucial in language development since it is during this time that a child acquires the motor, social and problem-solving skills which are prerequisite to learning oral language. Research has shown that parents of high-risk infants who are slightly below age level in the first months of life are often frustrated by their own lack of knowledge regarding their child's special needs, and their fears and anxieties build as they see their child developing at a very slow pace. The infant program is designed not only to give parents concrete suggestions for stimulating their infants in all areas of development but also to give them an opportunity to ask questions and ventilate their feelings. Group rather than individual sessions are held as a result of parents expressing a need to talk with other parents of handicapped children.

III. *Program Schedule* The parent-infant sessions are conducted once a week for six weeks. Two to six parents and their infants are enrolled.
   Each session consists of the following components:
   1. Informal discussion of the day's topic.
   2. Discussion of home activities carried out during the previous week.
   3. Demonstration of an activity based on the day's topic by the communication specialist.
   4. Demonstration of the same activity by the parent.
   5. Making a toy to take home.
   6. Discussion of home assignments for the next week.

   If the group consists of more than two infants and their parents, an aide keeps the infants during the initial discussion period.

IV. *Session Topics*
   1. "Understanding/Talking"—definitions of oral reception and expression and the differences between oral expression and articulation.
   2. "Exploring Baby's World"—how to give baby an opportunity to display his curiosity, encourage thinking skills and problem solving activities.
   3. "Baby Moves Around"—stimulating motor skills.
   4. "Toys You Can Make"—by exploring and playing with toys and

discovering their workings, children develop and perfect skills. Toys made from materials around the house will be demonstrated.

5. "Everyday Talking"—how to talk to baby and include him in activities while cooking, getting dressed, cleaning house, bathing, etc.

6. "Baby is a Person"—social and self-help skills.

V. *Goals*

1. To counsel parents regarding their child's over-all development, with an emphasis on oral language.

2. To teach parents to stimulate their children in the following areas of development: comprehension and expression of oral language, social, motor, problem solving skills.

VI. *Accountability:* Progress made by both the infant and parent will be measured in terms of behavioral objectives. A comparative study will be made on the average gains recorded for each performance objective.

1. *Infant Objectives*

(a) By the end of six month intervals, infants will show a gain of _____ months in the area of oral language comprehension as measured by the Birth to Three Scale.

(b) By the end of six month intervals, infants will show a gain of _____ months in the area of oral language expression as measured by the Birth to Three Scale.

(c) By the end of six month intervals, infants will show a gain of _____ months in the area of problem solving as measured by the Birth to Three Scale.

(d) By the end of six month intervals, infants will show a gain of _____ months in the area of social skills as measured by the Birth to Three Scale.

(e) By the end of six month intervals, infants will show a gain of _____ months in the area of motor skills as measured by the Birth to Three Scale.

2. *Parent Objectives*

(a) By the end of the six week session, parents of infants will show a proficiency of 80 percent in teaching activities as measured by a pre- and post-teacher made check list.

(b) By the end of the six week session, parents of infants will show a proficiency of 80% in understanding child development as measured by a pre- and post-teacher made test.

(c) By the end of six months, parents will increase in acceptance of their handicapped child by   percent as measured by a pre- and post-teacher made test.

VII. *Curriculum.* The following represents only a small sampling of activities carried out during each session as well as a sample lesson plan. Activities must be adapted to each individual infant and parent and their particular strengths and weaknesses.

Sample Session Plan. Group: three infants functioning at the 10-12 month level.

Goals	Activities	Materials
To give information to parents on developmental norms in the area of problem solving	Discussion with parents on the meaning of "problem solving". Give parents an "adult puzzle" to figure out. Discuss kinds of experiences they have had in order to figure out puzzle. As for concrete examples of their infants or other children's ability to "problem solve" or "figure out something."	Adult puzzle
To encourage infant's problem solving: object release into container	Demonstration of activities with infants. Put colored blocks into a shoe box which has had two squares cut out in the lid. Have the infant put the blocks in, open the lid and take them out.	Blocks and shoebox
Object permanence	Hide a favorite toy under a cloth. Encourage child to pull off cloth to find a toy.	Cloth, interesting toy
	Put objects in and take them out of clear plastic sack.	Blocks, key, comb, plastic sack from grocery store
To teach parents to stimulate their infants	Parents demonstrate the above activities	

Goals	Activities	Materials
To encourage parents to carry over activities into the home	Parents wrap contact paper around a "Pringle" can; cut square in the plastic top. Parents take can home for infants to put blocks in and take them out.	Contact paper no. of pringles cans, scissors
Home carry over	Assign home activities: Have child put objects into three different containers. Report back next week.	Written assignments on 3 x 5" cards

VIII. *Session Ideas*
   1.   Understanding and talking
        (Birth–six months)
        (a) While a child is in crib, shake rattle to one side for sound localization.
        (b) While changing diapers, hit powder and another can to each side of baby for sound localization.
        (c) Imitate baby's cooing right before baby goes to sleep in crib.
        (d) Tie jingling bells to crib.
        (Six–twelve months)
        (a) During bath time use short phrases such as "wash your face, hands, etc." Use short phrases while squeezing the washcloth and splashing the water.
        (b) Sit baby in a high chair while scrambling eggs for him to eat. Let him touch the eggs before they are cooked, then help him stir them with a spoon. Use short phrases such as "touch it", "it's sticky", "stir it", "it's hot", "open your mouth", "eat it".
        (c) Practice babbling or "talking" on a toy telephone.
        (Twelve–eighteen months)
        (a) Let the infant help make toast using language such as "get the bread", "it's soft", "spread the butter", "it's sticky", "let's toast it", "it's hot-don't touch", "get the knife", "cut the toast", "eat it".
        (b) Start a scrap book for the infant. Make it out of cotton cloth. Cut out of fuzzy fabric, animal figures or favorite objects. Go through the scrapbook and name the pictures.

2. Exploring baby's world
   (Birth–six months)
   (a) Give baby different objects to reach for and hold from around the house such as: tupperware top, plastic salt shaker with dice inside, tin pot pie pan, measuring cup with a long handle.
   (Six–twelve monhts)
   (See sample session plan.)
   (Twelve–eighteen months)
   (a) Provide containers of different sizes for nesting such as margarine tubs, cereal boxes, cans that fit into each other (without sharp edges), different sizes of hair rollers to nest.
   (b) Let the infant help stir cooking projects with a spoon.
3. Baby moves around
   (Birth–six months)
   (a) Encourage baby to turn from back to side by shaking a musical toy to one side just out of infant's grasp.
   (b) Pull into sitting position by holding baby's hands to strengthen neck control.
   (Six–twelve months)
   (a) Build strength by propping an ironing board against the sofa. Place a favorite toy half way up. Encourage baby to get the toy by crawling up (with supervision).
   (b) Encourage baby to pull himself over throw pillows or sofa pillows to get a favorite toy on the other side.
   (Twelve–eighteen months)
   (a) Pull socks half way off. Take infants hand and help him pull the sock completely off.
   (b) Play ball at home. Take infants arms through the motions of releasing the ball.
4. Toys you can make
   (Birth–six months)
   (a) "I see you" tube—cover empty toilet paper roll with contact paper.
   Six–twelve months
   (a) Make two or three balls from foil. Put balls in the recesses of an egg carton and move from one to another.
   (b) Make a poke box. Paste different texture pieces in the bottom of a shallow cardboard box. Cut circles out of the top of the box large enough for the child's finger to "poke" through.
   (Twelve–eighteen months)

(a) Make blocks out of large milk cartons.

(b) Cut a square or circle in the plastic top of a coffee can for the beginnings of form perception.

5. Everyday talking
    (Birth–six months)
    (a) Talk to baby during dressing, feeding, bathing and diapering.
    (Six–eighteen months)
    (a) In the bath—get a sponge to squeeze and drop in the water. Crochet a fish to go over soap—watch it float. Searching activities can be devised by visually following a bright toy, drop it in the water and see if the infant can find it. Pour water back and forth in cups and bowls.
    (b) In the kitchen—roll a rolling pin, feel and smell various orange and apple peeling, touch hot toast, provide a shelf with pans and utensils especially for baby to play with.
    (c) During housecleaning—put infant in a walker and let him help push vacuum cleaner and feel the hot air come out. Let the infant have his own cloth to polish "round and round" on the tables.

6. Baby is a person
    (Birth–six months)
    (a) Place a baby before a large mirror and encourage him to look and pat it.
    (b) Make a foot sock with eyes, nose and mouth sewn on to encourage foot play.
    (Six–twelve months)
    (a) Put cloth over baby's head. Remove and say "peepeye".
    (Twelve–eighteen months)
    (a) Give infant dust cloth or small comb and brush to encourage activity imitation.

In summary, our Pediatric Language Programs consist of three interacting units, all of which are funded currently through Title XX of the Tennessee Department of Human Services; this law requires that the participants in our programs be poor. We have had to develop new philosophies and strategies in order to be accountable, to perform our role successfully. Basic to these philosophies and strategies are the family-involvement concepts discussed above. There must be effective relationships with the families of our clients if we are to succeed in serving our stated function. To this end, the clinician must be willing to assume new roles, to discard the paracholistic notion that a clinician's function is merely to treat a client possessing a communicative dysfunction. The clinician must be willing to address unmet needs within the family constellation when there are no other team members able to cater to these varied needs. It is suggested that the clinician try to assume the role of these diverse specialists and at least attempt to help the family with its problems. Certainly this philosophy is espoused for all clients, but it is of particular significance and importance for the poor family who frequently does not know to whom to turn for help. We have learned in our Pediatric Language Programs (1) that tokenism for the poor client is wasted effort and (2) that accountability demands intensive involvement with the client's family.

CONCLUSION

A new breed of clinician is required: a pediatric language specialist. Appropriate coursework and practicum is required in early childhood language; its development, deficiencies, and differences. The clinician should be able to teach and treat in a self-contained classroom or resource room, normal as well as communicatively impaired preschool or early elementary aged children, and provide to the family and other paraprofessionals relevant education and counseling. In particular, the clinician should be able to do the following:

Children
1. To facilitate the acquisition of communication skills in normal preschool children.
2. To facilitate the acquisition of communicative skills in handicapped children.
3. To properly diagnose and treat the communicative disorders of bilingual and bidialectal speakers.
4. To properly diagnose and teach the "establishment" dialect to dialectally-different children.
5. To be aware of and utilize properly the paralinguistic components in the teaching-treating program.

Parents and Teachers
6. To implement programs with families and teachers to facilitate the communicative needs of normal preschool children.
7. To implement a parent-staff association program with families and teachers to facilitate the communicative needs of handicapped children.
8. To develop an educational counseling program and an affective counseling program with parents of exceptional children.

Programming
9. To develop, implement, and monitor programs for para-professionals working with communicatively handicapped children.
10. To work cooperatively with other professionals in the schools in designing   programs   and   instructional   strategies   for culturally-different children.
11. To develop interdisciplinary management skills; that is, to communicate effectively with different professional workers in the routine staffing of exceptional children.
12. To implement model programs for the speech-language clinicians participation in the classroom with communicatively handicapped children.
13. To be the primary service provider specialist in a self-contained classroom for the communicatively handicapped.

Other
14. To advocate the rights of all handicapped to an education and to facilitate positive community attitudes.
15. To be aware of and utilize properly the Rosenthal and Hawthorne effects.
16. To be aware of reliability and validity factors in test construction, test utilization, and data reporting.

REFERENCES

Adler, S. & Maisel, C. The 62% solution: The current status of language disorders and learning disabilities. *Tennessee Speech and Hearing Association Journal,* 1976, XX, 44-46.

ASHA Committee on Language 1973-74, Position Statement. *ASHA,* 1975, *17,* 273-278.

ASHA Task Force on Learning Disabilities, Position Statement. *ASHA,* 1976, *18,* 282-292.

Ayers, G. E. The disadvantaged: An analysis of factors affecting the counseling relationship. *Rehabilitation Literature,* 1970, 31, 194-199.

Butler, K. At the vortex: Myth and reality. *AHSA,* 1979, *21,* 3-6.

Carnell, C. M., Jr. Needs of the community clinic as related to training programs. *Rehabilitation Literature,* 1968, *29,* 198-203.

Davis, F. *Inside intuition—What we know about non-verbal communication.* New York: McGraw-Hill, 1973.

Dodson, S., Honeycutt, J., & Meeks, K. *Pediatric language clinic—An educational and counseling outreach program: For the family of the communicatively delayed infant and child.* S. Adler, (Ed.), University of Tennessee: Department of Audiology and Speech Pathology, 1978.

Knapp, M. L., Larson, C. E., & McCrosky, C. *An introduction to interpersonal communication.* Englewood Cliffs, N.J.: Prentice-Hall, 1971.

Labov, W. *Logic of nonstandard English.* In J. E. Alatis (Ed.), *Monograph series on language and linguistics.* Washington, D. C.: Georgetown University Press, 1969, 22.

Wepman, J. New and wider horizons for speech and hearing specialists. *ASHA,* 1975, 9-10.

13
Children and Poverty: Final Implications

Although the clinical mission of the speech specialist, by definition, is the diagnosis and correction of disorders in speech behavior, research in this profession is as concerned with the description and explanation of normal speech behavior as it is with the abnormal. In fact, one might venture the observation that the growth of research into normal behavior within the last decade or so has engendered a broadening of concern from the details of particular speech or hearing disorders to an overall concern with communication behavior itself.

—David E. Yoder,
"Some Viewpoints of the Speech, Hearing
and Language Clinician";
In, *Language and Poverty*

One of the myths fostered by our society and promoted by our institutions is that our society is composed of a homogenous people. We are, in fact, a pluralistic society of numerous subcultures of ethnic and class distinctions and of linguistic and behavioral differences. Until now, most reports on studies of subcultural linguistic differences have suggested that language intervention programs should be predicated upon the need to compensate for any deficiencies in language acquisition and usage, and thus upon the need for compensatory or enrichment educational programs. Relatively little attention has been paid by speech clinicians, educators, and others to the effects of cultural differences in language learning; in other words, compensatory programming is more popular than bidialectal teaching.

CULTURES AND SUBCULTURES*

A culture may be defined simply as a system of institutions. Furthermore, each institution has its own peculiar function as well as its interrelations with the other institutions. Some of the institutions which constitute a culture are religion, philosophy, the arts, politics, education, economics, and family life style, including language usage. A difference between peoples in only one institution (for example, politics) will have far-reaching effects in view of the institution's interrelationship with other institutions. Such differences affect the ethos of a cultural group and give vibrancy to its life style. Moreover, such differences are of immediate importance to speech clinicians. It is extremely vital that we recognize that a cultural *zeitgeist* (Ethos, or cultural life style) is manifested in its unique language style and to attempt to alter or change the language style is not only extremely difficult but also contrary to the prevailing mood of our times.

It is important to note that the acceptance of diverse behaviors, including bidialectalism, is a fundamental attribute of a pluralistic and democratic society. We should also remember that to understand well the nonstandard language of a subculture is to communicate with, and thereby have the option to interact effectively with, the spirit or ethos that pervades that culture. Yet, we would suppose that few people are capable of communicating and interacting effectively with any of the different cultural minorities that comprise our American society. We have stressed throughout this volume that subcultural differences account for these communication barriers.

It is only recently that interest has been expressed about the manner in which these differences have been analyzed (that is, in the analysis of the quality and quantity of verbal stimulation in the home), how these subcultural groups have been stratified (that is, socioeconomic class distinctions), and the results of comparisons between subcultural groups. How we (1) analyze the linguistic environment, (2) our use of stratification

---

*Much of this chapter is adapted from an article written by the author entitled "Pluralism, Relevance, and Language Intervention for Culturally Different Children," ASHA, 1971, 13, 719-725.

systems, and (3) the apparent irrelevance of our comparisons due to improper analysis and stratification have been discussed in this text and are summarized in this chapter. In addition, we shall consider (4) outreach and (5) intervention concepts.

ANALYSIS

Definitive, encompassing, and functional criteria would allow for an analysis and subsequent comparison of the nature and the type of the verbal stimulation inherent in the different levels of peoples within different subcultures. Most available information, however, is neither definitive, encompassing, nor functional because it has been based on retrospective questionnaires. Few of these have involved field observations of children, nor have such observations been undertaken to check on what mothers say their children did. The changing ethos of our American subcultures makes it mandatory that the psychosocial environment inherent in these subcultures be carefully and routinely reexamined through such observations. Although anthropologists (Mead, 1962), linguists (Sapir, 1921), and psychologists (Wyatt, 1969) have long been interested in field observations of child–adult verbal patterns, only rather recently have speech clinicians become concerned with such investigations. Wyatt is one of the few practicing speech clinicians who has concerned herself with field observations; neverhteless, her examples of mother–child verbal interaction are generally nonfunctional for cross-cultural comparative purposes (Wyatt, 1969, pp. 6–16).* Wolfram (1969) correctly commented, "Independent ethnographical description of behavioral patterns characterizing different social strata is required before any correlation of linguistic variables with these strata can be made."

More specifically, Jensen (1968) has said that the lower-class child, in comparison to his middle-class peer, has less verbal play and receives less verbal interaction and reinforcing behavior. Therefore, the lower-class child's speech and language development is retarded or deficient. Such assumptions are generally based on data obtained from retrospective questionnaires, not from field observations relevant to the nature of the

---

*Wyatt's major criterion involves the types and qualities of corrective feedback offered by the mother; we believe this is insufficient. A more molecular analysis of this concept is required as well as an appropriate rating system. Furthermore, the ratings need to be performed at different times and in different situations if reliable and valid comparisons are to be made with children and adults from different subcultures.

verbal interactions in specific homes. For example, as noted previously, Young's (1970) data, as obtained from her observations of black families in a small community in Georgia, tend to negate Jensen's assumptions. There is reason to believe that the lower-class child's verbal stimulation may be as effective or perhaps even superior to that of the middle-class child's. We simply do not know! Research data are needed involving systematic field study observations in culturally different home environments.

STRATIFICATION

The system of social-class stratification generally utilized in our research has been derived from conventional and socioeconomic systems that equate the visible symbols of prestige—wealth in its various forms—with status. Some inherently faulty assumptions appear in such stratifications. For example:

1. Indices of wealth (amount of money possessed, schooling completed, type of house owned or rent paid, type of occupation) are highly stable, that is, correlative, for members of different ethnic or racial groups.
2. Within definitive class cultures (for example, the lower class) one finds similar values, mores, and life styles.
3. Cultural distinctions based on economic inequities among social classes are democratic.

These matters have been discussed in some detail elsewhere, but it is important to emphasize that indices of wealth are not highly stable for members of different ethnic or racial groups. Furthermore, values, mores, and life styles are frequently different within definitive class cultures, and these differences are reflected also in the linguistic environments, that is, in the linguistic interactions between family and child. Therefore, the linguistic development of growing children may differ as a function of their social class. Cultural distinctions based on economic inequities among social classes naturally assume that those individuals who have more of something related to economic criteria are superior to others who have less; and thus, such distinctions cannot be considered democratic.

From these underpinnings emerges a concept of social malnutrition, a concept which relegates the lower class to an inferior status and which obviously institutionalizes class prejudice. This concept predisposes its user to think in value-laden terms—better, poorer; superior, inferior—or to think of deficits and deficiencies when dealing with children possessing so-called functional pathologies.

For example, Deutsch (1968) has written:

To categorize "conditions of life" within our own culture we can use the shorthand of socioeconomic status (SES) designations. In essence, relating SES to amount of stimuli available to the child means that we are hypothesizing that children who come from homes having a higher income and higher educational attainment on the part of the parents will, on the average, be exposed to a different and richer stimulus environment from those who come from less privileged homes (p. 78).

The implication that children emerging from middle-class homes are better than or superior to those children reared in lower-class homes is an example of institutionalized class prejudice. We do not question the fact that the stimulus environment is different; we question only the assumption that it is richer, better, or superior. Moreover, as Deutsch goes on to say, "There is very little work on the effects of environment defined in this way on any element of development or on any set of traits." What Deutsch is essentially saying is that we simply do not have sufficient information regarding subcultural "conditions of life" and their effects upon emergent behaviors to justify her statements. Although Deutsch is careful to suggest that this is an hypothesis, we believe few readers consider the statement hypothetical, but, in fact, assume that it is factual.

Middle versus Lower Class: Molar and Molecular Divisions

A reexamination of value systems and mores reveals significant differences in middle- and lower-class children. These differences are reflected in the varied ethnic and racial membership of the children as well as in the socioeconomic status of the family. Furthermore, these differences in value systems and mores create variations in life styles, variations which are reflected in language habits. The differences within classes may not, in most cases, be as gross as those between classes; nevertheless, the fact that there are differences has been well documented. Utilization of the conventional stratification systems smothers the intraclass differences. (In the past we have assumed these differences to be unimportant, but as we have discussed in Part III this assumption may be very incorrect.) Our research with articulatory deviances suggests the need to document these intraclass differences.

Flacks, (1969) has reported that there are now two dominant middle-class family styles in the United States. The overwhelmingly dominant type is one that continues to adhere to the values, aspirations, and interests of the capitalist culture. It places highest priority on material comfort and successful occupational attainment; it values respectability in overt behavior and self-discipline over impulse and emotion as necessities for achieving success, security, and status; it encourages educational achievement primarily because of its instrumental value; and it practices conventional religion and politics without enthusiastic engagement in either. Furthermore, it produces children who share these same beliefs and aspirations to a large extent and who do not appear to be skeptical about the American way of life they confidently plan to inherit.

The other dominant type of middle-class family is most apt to be found among highly educated professional people. This family, by its own report, encourages intrinsic intellectual, and aesthetic achievements more than it encourages concern for material comfort and status, something which it tends to regard as somehow vaguely distasteful or immoral. It rejects, at least verbally, conventional religious identifications and criteria for respectability. It values education for its own sake and tends to substitute the university for the church as the repository of highest values. Further, it is strongly liberal, supporting internationalism, civil rights, and government as an instrument of social change.

Of course, enormous variation occurs within these types, and no family completely fits either picture.

That important differences also occur within the lower class is demonstrated by Pavenstedt's (1965) study of poor white families in which she categorized families according to their stable or unstable family environment. Likewise, Young's (1970) study of black families suggests that differences in communication are a function of life style.

Do these differences in life styles and family environment within the middle and lower classes create differences in verbal stimulation, language development, and language usage? Our stratification systems have assumed that they do not, but that assumption rests, we believe, upon a foundation that does not stand after the closer scrutiny we have given it in this book.

Intraclass differences also have important implications regarding sampling and testing procedures with culturally different children. Zigler (1969), for example, has said; "You cannot safely attribute a difference in performance on a dependent variable to a known difference in subject characteristics (e.g., IQ), if the population also differs on other factors which could reasonably affect or have been demonstrated to affect performance on the dependent measure" (pp. 544–545). We believe that such differences do exist and that as a result much resultant bias is inextricably intertwined in some of the research data being reported in our professional journals. As we have suggested, of prime significance are the unfortunate but traditional methods of categorizing cultural and subcultural differences by analysis of the socioeconomic institutions which tend to denigrate behavioral differences and do not take into account linguistic differences.

For example, Haywood's (1970) discussion of sampling procedures points out vividly the importance of controlling behavioral variables related to personality characteristics and motivational relationships. That such variables are inherently and differentially related to the value system of different subcultural subjects is well known, but the variables are generally left uncontrolled. As a result, one might consider discontinuing the IQ or MA as a predicator variable and using instead each person in terms of his pattern of standardized behavioral performances. Scott (cited in Heal, 1970) counsels that "instead of seeking correlates of IQ or MA, the scientist should seek correlates of profiles of individual predictor variables." Such a desirable strategy requires an understanding of subcultural values, mores and linguistic systems, and the effect of these upon the subject's motivation and response behavior during cross-cultural testing situations. Differences among the speakers and auditors of different subcultures may cause communicative difficulties. That those differences may, therefore, account for significant amounts of variance in our research literature is of particular relevance to those studying communication development and its disorders.

In summary, the conventional stratification system utilized frequently by researchers, and based on socioeconomic differences, is both unreliable and undesirable. As is noted in more detail in Chapter 3, a system based on some other factor(s) would seem to be required. One might consider Banfield's (1970) concept of four classes of Americans, which extend from high to low on a psychological scale. People are separated by how much their orient themselves toward providing for a more or less distant future. Thus motivation, rather than the traditional socioeconomic variables such as education and income, might be the base for a definition of class membership, and a person who is poor, unschooled, and of low status might, thus, be upperclass.

COMPARISON

The traditional mode of comparison in the United States is to utilize the score of the middle-class child (and in particular, the middle-class white child) on a "standardized" test as the standard and to compare it to the score obtained by the culturally different child. Our argument, heretofore, against this procedure has been directed toward the impropriety of socioeconomic criteria as exclusive determinants of social-class levels. Another compelling reason to reject this mode of presenting comparative data is the inherent differences among various ethnic members of the same socioeconomic levels. In particular, note the research of Lesser, Fifer, and Clark (1965) with eight groups of middle- and lower-class Chinese, Jewish, black, and Puerto Rican children. Four tests were administered to each group of children. The findings indicated that, although social class and ethnic groups differ in their relative standing on different functions, only ethnicity fosters the development of a different pattern of abilities. Social-class differences within ethnic groups do not modify these basic patterns associated with ethnicity. These data strongly suggest that simply equating subjects on some socioeconomic level without controls for ethnic heritage may be invalid—that although all people are created equal, the equality is relevant only insofar as their opportunities for growth are concerned.

OUTREACH

During the past several years the role and function of the speech and language clinician in relation to the rest of society has come under serious scrutiny. A number of social critics have questioned whether the academic training of the clinician as well as the services performed are not symptomatic of institutionalized racism and classism. To negate this charge would apparently require a better understanding of the subcultural minorities of our country and an "outreaching"—that is, it would require the establishment of relevant service programs within the inner city, rural area, or wherever culturally different and poor children are found. In a previous publication (Adler, 1968) we suggested that the "facilities must be within transportation 'reach' of the population they are designed for, and thus should be conveniently located within the ghetto or rural area. Our present facilities too often, pose real transportation problems . . ." We also said:

The complexities of providing identification and care for [poor preschool-aged] children . . are many . . . . There are generally inadequate services for checking a child's hearing, vision, or other sense modalities. Similarly, neurological deficits in the various sensory, retentive, and discriminative functions often go unrecognized, as do motor problems that are minimal. . . .

There are many health centers, rehabilitation centers, treatment centers of various kinds [speech and hearing, remedial reading, etc.] whose operations are isolated by space and philosophy from each other, and from the people they are supposed to serve. . . .

If a coordinated program of inter-center cooperation could be effected . . . [it would allow for more relevant services to those who need them the most]. (Adler, 1968, pp. 53–54).

Suchman (1966) confirms vividly the need to reach out into the community and bring all kinds of needed services to the lower-income population. Such a philosophy is pertinent to members of all helping professions—certainly it includes the services of the speech pathologist and audiologist.

INTERVENTION PROGRAMS

Current intervention models generally follow the concept that the culturally different and economically poor child manifests a deficit in his speech and language usage; thus, intervention programs are generally compensatory in nature. The assumptions upon which such programs are created are surprisingly tenuous.

Another intervention model is currently being considered in the literature and elsewhere. This model presupposes that there are subcultural differences in languages and behaviors and that a bidialectal and a bibehavioral teaching strategy needs to be employed to minimize the differences. At the present time what is needed to make such programming effective is detailed mapping of the dialects and the behaviors of these children.

We see no reason to assume that culturally different and poor children could not benefit from both models; surely, both models deserve our consideration. Language intervention programs designed to both treat and teach language-impaired and language-different children are needed urgently, but such programs should cater to the sensibilities and needs of all children and their parents. Accomplishing these goals requires a redirection in the service programs and in the academic and clinical curricula of our university or college training programs.

The directions which language intervention programs will take depends on how we define the poor. To paraphrase Farber (1969), if we define the poor as a unique subculture (see Lewis, 1966), then questions arise as to whose way of life shall be preserved, whose values shall be implemented, and, even more crucially, who will decide. On the other hand, if the poor are conceptualized as only a *deviant* subculture, then poverty programs, exemplified by compensatory or enrichment programs, no longer ameliorate but rather destroy indigenous institutions that represent structures of lower-class environmental adaptation. Such programs no longer aid the poor but indeed come to constitute a literal war on the poor. Speech and language clinicians and others would do well to heed this dictum in their interactions with the poor.

REFERENCES

Adler, S. *The health and education of the economically deprived child.* St. Louis: Green, 1968.

Adler, S. Dialectal English: professional and clinical implications. *Journal of Speech and Hearing Disorders,* 1971, *36,* 90–100.

Banfield, E. *The unheavenly city.* Boston: Little, Brown, 1970.

Baratz, J. Should black children learn white dialect? *ASHA,* 1970, *9,* 415-417.

Deutsch, C. P. Environment and perception. In M. Deutsch, I. Katz, & A. R. Jensen (Eds.), *Social class, race and psychological development.* New York: Holt, Rinehart and Winston 1968.

Farber, B., Harvey, D., & Levine, M. *Community, kinship and competence: Research and development program on preschool disadvantaged children.* Final report, University of Illinois. ERIC Document ED036665, 1969.

Flacks, E. *The acquisition and development of values: Perspectives of research.* Bethesda, Md.: National Institute Child Health and Human Development, 1969.

Haywood, H. C. Mental retardation as an extension of the developmental laboratory. *American Journal of Mental Deficiency,* 1970, *75,* 1.

Heal, L. W. Research strategies and research goals in the scientific study of the mentally subnormal. *American Journal of Mental Deficiency,* 1970, *75,* 1.

Jensen, A. R. Social class and verbal development. In M. Deutsch, I. Katz, & A. R. Jensen (Eds.), *Social class, race and psychological development,* New York: Holt, Rinehart and Winston, 1969.

Lesser, G. S., Fifer, G., & Clark, D. H. Mental abilities of children from different social class and cultural groups. *Monographs of the Society for Research and Child Development,* 1965, *0,* 4.

Lewis, O. The culture of poverty. *Scientifica, American,* 1966, *215,* 19-25.

Mead, M. *Growing up in New Guinea.* New York: New American Library, 1953.

Pavenstedt, E. A comparison of the child-rearing environment of upper-lower and very low-lower-class families. *American Journal of Orthopsychiatry,* 1965, *35,* 89–98.

Sapir, E. *An introduction to the study of speech.* New York: Harcourt Brace Jovanovich, 1921.

Suchman, E. A. Medical deprivation. *American Journal of Orthopsychiatry,* 1966, *36,* 665–672.

Wolfram, W. A. *Social dialects from a linguistic perspective: Assumptions, current research and future directions.* Arlington, Va.: Center for Applied Linguistics, 1969.

Wyatt, F. L. *Language learning and communication disorders in children.* New York: Free Press, 1969.

Young, V. H. Family and childhood in a southern Negro community. *American Anthropologist,* 1970, *72,* 269–287.

Zigler, E. Developmental versus difference theories of mental retardation and the problem of motivation. *American Journal of Mental Deficiency,* 1969, *73,* 536-556.

Appendices

Appendix A:
Study Questions

Essay Questions

1. Oscar Lewis in the *Culture of Poverty* states that the culture of poverty is not just a matter of deprivation or disorganization, terms signifying the absence of something. It is a culture in the traditional anthropoligical sense in that it provides human beings with a design for living, with a ready-made set of solutions for human problems, and so serves a significant adaptive function.

   Discuss, as adaptive mechanisms, the language patterns, mother–child interactions, cognitive styles, and other aspects of the cultural life of the poor which you have encountered in your reading. Agree or disagree that the culture of poverty is not just a matter of deprivation.
2. Various educational strategies, designed for the poor, have been instituted in the past two decades, ranging from compensatory education to bidialectal. From the standpoint of language, discuss the major goals and assumptions of these different programs for "educating the culturally different." Evaluate the successes and failures of these programs, as you see them, with special attention to programs concerned with urban blacks and rural Appalachians.
3. Robbins Burling remarks that "black English is but one variety of English among others. More accurately, perhaps, it is one cluster of

varieties among many other varieties, for the speech of black Americans is no more unified than is the speech of whites."

Discuss the regional and social variation of American English with special consideration of the interaction between "nonstandard" versus "standard" varieties of language. Evaluate the research on the relationship of black speech to white speech.

4. Arthur Jensen in his article "How Much Can We Boost IQ and Scholastic Achievement?" argues, from the evidence of IQ tests, that blacks score consistently lower than whites due to genetically inherited traits.

Discuss the "nature–nurture" controversy. What are the implications of your arguments, when considering the use of intelligence tests and other clinical testing measures with the culturally different?

5. Assume you are professionally involved in an education and treatment program for culturally different children. Design a relevant program that caters to the childrens' needs both educationally and clinically. Justify your design. Cite references for your procedures and goals.

6. The author states that "the official ideology of America is a middle-class ideology, and the school system is an institutionalized arm of that middle-class society."

Do you agree? If not, what arguments can you use to refute the premise. (Keep in mind the programs already designed for the culturally different child.) What expectations do teachers have of their pupils? How does this affect teaching strategies?

Short-Answer Questions

1. According to the author's thesis, what are some of the problems that present learning difficulties for the "disadvantaged" child? Briefly evaluate this position from your own experience.
2. How would you define standard and nonstandard dialects?
3. Contrast the "malnutrition" model and the "cultural-disparity" model as applied to the lower-class culturally different child.
4. What are the major challenges, according to the author, that face the teacher–clinician in the immediate future? Do you agree with these predictions?
5. How would you define and describe a contrastive analysis program? How is it similar and different from previous models of early childhood education?

6. Describe various compensatory educational programs. What are some of the major fallacies of this approach, according to Labov? Do you agree?

7. Describe the philosophy behind the use of "everyday" and "school" talk.

8. What are the major goals of the pluralistic educator or clinician?

Appendix B:
Glossary

acrolect: the most prestigious form of any speech variety within the language (Nist, 1975, p. 75).

Appalachian English: the variety of English most typically associated with the working-class rural population found in Applachia, the region of the Appalachian Range, roughly from southwestern Pennsylvania south through the mountainous areas to and including Alabama (Wolfram, 1975, plate 51).

basilect: the generally recognized substandard form of any speech variety, regional, or geographical dialect (Nist, 1974, p. 75).

bidialectalism or **bidialectacism:** an approach in which standard English is taught, but with no effort to eradicate the student's nonstandard variety. This view rejects the notion that nonstandard English forms are inherently inferior (Wolfram, 1975, plate 225). Standard English is viewed as an "additive dialect to be used in certain social situations instead of a replacement dialect which eradicates the indigenous dialect" (Texas Education Agency, 1973, plate 29).

black dialect: a pattern of American Speech that is (1) Southern in origin and retains much of the regional flavoring of the south in addition to its own black characteristics and (2) contains many features common to all nonstandard speech. (3) The use of the double negative is especially prevalent. This dialect differs from standard English in phonemic structure, grammatical structure, and vocabulary.

children of the poor: Children can be said to be living in privation when (1) they have too little food to meet the requirements for growth, health, and energy; (2) they have too little clothing or shelter to give them material protection against cold, rain, and other natural phenomena; (3) they lack access to sufficient medical care to prevent illness or permit prompt recovery from both illness and its debilitating effect; (4) they lack schooling and training for the actual conditions awaiting them at the end of childhood; (5) the actual conditions of their existence are at great variance with those held to be typical and desirable by the dominant culture.

cognition: consists of perception, concept formation, language and all that is inherent in these functions and, in particular, judgments and value systems.

cognitive development: "the growth of those capacities which contribute to the process of knowing. Some important capacities here are perception, concept formation and problem solving." (Hirsch in Beck & Saxe, 1965, p. 66).

compensatory education: "a preventive and global intervention into the lives of people judged to have socioeconomic handicaps assumed to be predictive of unnecessarily limited school achievement and life chances" (Anderson in Stanley, 1963, p. 198–199). It "implies that something is lacking in the family, and so in the child, and that as a result the children are unable to benefit from schools" (Bernstein in Williams, 1970, p. 54). Compensatory education usually includes the primary objective of "improvement of the pupil's communication skills—listening, speaking, reading and writing" (Gorman in Beck & Saxe, 1965, p. 43).

correctness in American English: equals linguistic usage plus social acceptability (Nist, 1974, p. 73).

creolization: "a new language system restructured from a pidgin language" (Shuy in Williams, 1970, p. 345).

crystallized intelligence: "consists of knowledge and intellectual skills" and "increases with a person's experiences and with the education that provides new methods and perspectives for dealing with that experience" (Jensen, 1973, p. 175).

cultural deprivation: "refers to the situation in which the child's opportunity to utilize fully his intellectual potential or to achieve scholastically is impaired because of limited environmental experience, constricted language development and minimal valuation of intellectual or academic activities" (Friedman as quoted in Glaser, 1974).

cultural difference vs. cultural deprivation: The culturally deprived possess a substandard environmental background while the culturally different are defined as having a background which is ethnically different but not substandard (Hallman in Fagan, 1967). As a rule, *culturally different* will be used synonymously with *culturally deprived, underprivileged, socioeconomically deprived,* and *poor.*

cultural group: any group of people who share a common origin and exhibit a relatively constant set of genetically determined physical traits, or any group belonging to a population subdivision marked by common features of language.

cultural pluralism: as defined by the Conference on Education and Teacher Education for Cultural Pluralism, "a state of equal coexistence in a mutually supportive relationship within the boundaries or framework of one nation of people of diverse cultures with significantly different patterns of belief, behavior, color, and in many cases with different languages. To achieve cultural pluralism there must be unity with diversity. Each person must be aware of and secure in his own identity, and be willing to extend to others the same respect and rights that he expects to enjoy himself" (Stent et al., 1973, p. 14). "Cultural pluralism acknowledges the cultural and linguistic differences of children and the fact that a child's learning begins in his home and in his community. It accepts intrinsically the educational validity of this learning environment and builds upon it. Cultural racial, and linguistic differences are not viewed as negative components to be temporarily tolerated, but as integral, positive forces in American society" (Mazon, 1974, 1973). "A program for genuine cultural pluralism calls for an education which prepares people to make decisions in matters affecting their lives and to perceive the contraditions in their situation" (Platero in Stent, et al., 1973).

culture: a system of institutions (Adler, 1971); a system of symbols which orders experience and guides behavior (Diggs, 1974); "what a person has to know in order to live within a group on a minute-to-minute, hour-by-hour, day-by-day basis" and it is "based upon a systematic set of behaviors learned at the earliest ages and carried by every student into the classroom" (Abraham in Texas Education Agency, 1973, plate 15).

culture-free test: a test which attempts to purge all items believed to incorporate white Anglo-Saxon Protestant values (Jones in Texas Education Agency, 1973).

cumulative deficit: a phenomenon in which significant socioeconomic and race differences seen in measured variables become more marked as a child progresses through school (Deutsch et al., 1967).

cumulative learning view of mental development: the viewpoint that "emphasizes learning as the major causal factor in development . . . the sets of habits which we identify as intelligent behavior are seen as being built up through the acquisition of habits and chains of habits which interact to produce complex behavior. Thus mental development is viewed as the learning of an ordered set of capabilities in some hierarchial or progressive fashion, making for increased skills in stimulus discrimination, recall of previously learned responses, and generalization and transfer of learning" (Jensen, 1973, p. 117).

deficit position: an approach that contrasts poverty children with their middle-class counterparts in the area of language capacity (as well as other areas of function), moving from such contrasts to generalizations about the appearance of "developmental lags" thought to stem from a deprived environment. "This deprivation, or deficit, diagnosis of the poor suggests a kind of 'cultural injection' as an antidote for poverty, and that the earlier it is given, the better the results. Some have agreed that the language portion of the cultural antidote for poverty is by far the most critical" (Williams, 1970, p. 4).

Deutsch postulated the causes of such deficiency to be too much noise in the culturally disadvantaged home, too little directed and sustained action, lack of toys, books, etc., lack of adequate language models, and the use of language which was monotonous in structure and vocabulary (Bryen, 1974).

deprivation: a "lack of an adequate preparation, either cultural or social, which places a pupil at a disadvantage when compared with his peer group" (Rushton, 1975, p. 1) *Characteristics:* a "sense of low status, lack of power, cultural alienation, and limited economic opportunity" (Rushton, 1975, p. 2). See also *cultural deprivation.*

diagnostic teaching: a teaching approach in which disordered function is recognized, either through observation or testing, followed by remedial steps to habilitate deficiencies"

dialect: a set of speech habits which characterizes the speakers of a particular group or region. It is usually divided into three specific categories: phenemic structure, syntactic structure, and vocabulary. Dialects become different languages when they become mutually unintelligible; a language is divided into dialects when the speech of some of its speakers is perceived as different from that of others. See also *idolect; lect.*

dialectology: a branch of linguistics known as dialect geography, has long acknowledged variants in phonology (Cuber/Cuba), grammar (five pound/five pounds), and lexicon (bealed/running ear) as a function of regional geography. A linguistic atlas has been compiled to show these differences. Only recently, however, have dialectologists become concerned with sociocultural dialects. As a result, new ties are being fashioned between dialectologists and social scientists, educators, and habilitationists.

difference position: the viewpoint that dialectal variations are merely differences, not deficits. Standard English, under this outlook, would not be a replacement for a substandard form, but taught as a "second language" to be used when appropriate.

diglossia: the ability to switch from peer language to standard language, or the reverse. See also *switching.*
    Psychological bilingualism and societal diglossia: Diglossia refers to a societal pattern involving two or more languages, or dialects and should include the appropriate attitudes and values that accompany each of the languages or dialects. Both languages or dialects should be accepted as legitimate communicative forms. Thus a diglossic speaker may possess competency in his use of and cultural understanding of both languages or dialects.
    To be sure, diglossia is well accepted in multilingual societies in

which a number of different languages are commonplace; it is less well accepted in speech communities employing a different dialect of a language. In such cases a formal set of norms defining "correct" behaviors is "standardized"; all other dialects and behaviors then become "incorrect" and "substantard." Note, however, that all dialectal varieties of a language system are, in fact, nonstandard to the different cultural groups in the society, and a dialect is standard only to that segment of the society utilizing it. Thus, it is quite ethnocentric to suggest that one's own dialect and concommitant behavioral patterns are superior to other dialects or behavior patterns. Note also that the means by which a segmented speech community standardizes its norms is by institutionalizing them; that is, "establishment" control over the educational institutions, including the publication and utilization of commercial dictionaries and school grammars, allows for the perpetuation of its norms.

disadvantaged: used synonymously with the terms *culturally deprived, culturally alienated, culturally divergent, socioeconomically deprived, economically impoverished, poverty stricken, underprivileged, chronically poor, educationally disadvantaged, educationally disoriented,* and *experientially poor.* From an educational viewpoint, the term *disadvantaged* refers to children with a particular set of educationally associated problems arising from and residing extensively within the culture of the poor.

educability: the "ability for school learning. Educability is much more complexly determined than intelligence or learning ability. For one thing it depends . . . on a fund of prior knowledge, skills, and acquired cognitive habits. . . . But educability involves more than these intellectual abilities . . . A host of other factors must be taken into account. . . . These are usually described under labels, such as attitudes, motivation, work habits, regularity of school attendance, parental interest, and help in school work" (Jensen, 1973, p. 93).

educational aptitude: "the potential one may have for achieving success in the pursuit of education and/or schooling" (Jones in Texas Education Agency, 1973, plate 74).

educational options for minority groups: (1) define education as adaptation to the existing majority society and establish schools which embody the values of the dominant culture; (2) adopt the separatist pattern—encourage cultural isolation, leading inevitably to cultural and political fragmentation; (3) take cognizance of the presence of minority groups and introduce accommodations. This is often described as "meeting special needs" or "beginning where people are." The goal, however, is the same as in the first type—to prepare people to function within the dominant culture. Such an education perpetuates the "melting-pot mystique." (4) The final option sees education as "beginning where people are," but the goal is to provide what is best for their development. It does not prescribe what an individual or group can become (Davies & Cosby in Stent, 1973, pp. 137-138).

eradicationist vs. bidialectal approaches: The former philosophical position holds that only school talk or the standard English spoken by members of the "establishment" is desirable, and the social-regional dialectal "mix" of the less prestigious groups is considered substandard and needs to be eliminated or eradicated from the child's speech. Two major philosophical positions in opposition to this concept are the mandatory bidialectalism encouraged in this book, and the "free-choice" dialectalism of those opposed to the compulsory nature of bidialectalism. See also *bidialectalism*.

ethnic group: a group of people of the same race or nationality who share a common and distinctive culture.

ethnography: the process of constructing, through direct personal observations of social behavior, a theory of the workings of a particular culture. Because each culture is unique in its views and goals, there will be different response patterns manifested by culturally different individuals. This is particularly so with respect to language; people may value it differently, evaluate it differently, acquire it through different social mechanisms, and use it in different situations.

everyday or home talk: that dialect used by a cultural group, much of which is frequently considered substandard by the school teacher and an attempt is made to eradicate it by substituting school talk.

family environment: the physical, psychological, and linguistic environment in which a family exists; all of the conditions and influences which affect the lives of family members.

fluid intelligence: "a basic general brightness that can be marshalled for new learning and novel problem solving and adaptability; it is relatively independent of education and experience but it can be invested in the particular opportunities for learning afforded by the individual's life circumstances, motivations, and interests" (Jensen, 1973, p. 175).

formal grammar: the linguistic pattern utilized in formalized testing situations and in conversations with other than one's peers. See also *informal grammar.*

grammaticality: the "widest possible social acceptance and therefore credibility for the code in which a person casts his messages" (Nist, 1974, p. 97).

growth-readiness view of mental development: "certain organized patterns of growth of neural structures must occur before certain experiential factors can effectively contribute to development. The rate of intellectual development is seen as due primarily to internal physiological mechanisms and their orderly, sequential growth, rather than to inputs from the environment" (Jensen, 1973, p. 117).

handicapped English: "the result of the attempt of a native language to supplant the national language as the preferred resonant medium of communication" (Nist, 1975, p. 91). It is characterized by (1) an inadequate segmentation of reality and (2) an improper (or inappropriate) image of the self and various linguistic roles which this self must assume. It is distinguished by nonstandard and distractive phonology and/or grammar, and/or intonation, and/or speed of delivery (Nist, 1974).

Hawthorne effect: a phenomenon characterized by improved performance resulting from increased attention.

Head Start: "a national effort to expose disadvantaged youngsters to the stimulation of an educational experience under the guidance of trained adults who will help the youngsters to experience, practice, and enjoy the communication skills they tend to lack" (Withall in Fagan, 1967, p. 49).

home talk: see *everyday talk.*

human services: refers to and "includes all those activities involving direct person-to-person service including health, mental health, social service, education, recreation, child care, welfare, administration of justice and community organization. Much of this service is conducted by agencies of community, city, state, and federal government, as well as by private agencies, unions, and industry" (Miller, 1967, pp. 7–8).

idolect: a person's own individual dialect. Idolects group into dialects (Hart in Texas Education Agency, 1973, plate 27). See also *lect*.

informal grammar: the linguistic pattern that is used in spontaneous or peer-group conversation.

intelligence: not the innate ability of the individual but a label that binds together a series of behaviors and it is not different from any other label we use to describe and bind together behaviors of other varieties. Also, and of particular importance the behaviors that we bind together under this label of intelligence are going to be a function of the particular culture in which we find ourselves living.

intervention: "a conscious and purposeful set of actions intended to change or influence the anticipated course of development" (Sigel, Secrist, & Forman in Stanley, 1973, p. 26).

labeling: the process of associating distinctive names with discriminable attributes.

language: behaviorally, language includes all ways of behaving which allow for communication, and thus may involve (1) body movement (i.e., body language), including facial expressions and bodily stance; (2) suprasegmentals or prosody, including tonal and rhythmic differences; and (3) linguistic symbols. Developmentally, language symbols consist of discrete parts—sounds or letters, grammar, and lexical units—which develop within a social setting and are indigenous to that social environment, culture, or ecosystem.

language assimilation: refers to "studies of the nature and rate of change made in the language system of the outsider as he develops mastery of the new system" (Shuy in Williams, 1970, p. 345).

language codes: Bernstein (Williams, 1970) postulated the presence of two language codes:
(1) *restricted code:* "one which is used in day-to-day contact with friends, relatives,and people with whom we are closely associated. This does not require a complicated syntax or a

sophisticated vocabulary or grammar. It is the kind of language that is utilized in conversation with people who know the way we think and the ideas we have, but with whom we wish to communicate certain feelings. This can be done largely non-verbally through gesture and expression and does not require a complicated language code. All people have this restricted language capacity (Hirsch in Beck, 1965, p. 69).

(2) *elaborated language code:* "a more complicated syntax and a more accurate grammatical order, with logical modifiers and frequent use of impersonal pronouns and prepositions. This is the kind of language code which is increasingly important for learning as the child goes further in school" (Hirsch in Beck, 1965, p. 70). "The use [or abuse] of this distinction [between codes] has sometimes led to the erroneous conception that a restricted code can be directly equated with linguistic deprivation, linguistic deficiency or being non-verbal" (Bernstein in Williams, 1970, p. 26).

language enrichment: according to Deutsch "a language training program requiring the creation of a rich, individualized language environment where words are repeatedly placed in meaningful context, and where the child is allowed multiple opportunities for expressive language demonstrations as well as for receiving language stimuli under optimal conditions and being encouraged to make appropriate responses" (Cowles, 1967, p. 202). "The general philosophy of such programs has been to select those environmental features which seem most central for cognition and to offer these, in varying doses, to the disadvantaged child" (Williams, 1970, p. 65).

language functions: (1) a system of responses by which individuals communicate with each other (interindividual communication) and (2) a system of responses that facilitates thinking and action for the individual (intraindividual communication) (Hellmuth, 1968, p. 239).

learning set: "a set of habits which, when once thoroughly established, greatly facilitates the further learning of a variety of different tasks which subsume the particular habits comprising the learning set" (Jensen in Deutsch, Katz, & Jensen, 1968, p. 159).

lect: a term often used in preference to "dialect" since some speakers associate dialect only with regional or nonstandard varieties while "lect" may be used to designate any language variety.

markers of speech communities: Lower-class speech is characterized by restrictive patterns, while the middle-class pattern is said to possess a more elaborative code. More specifically, this is a more preditable pattern of linguistic utterances in the lower class due to the limited diversity of its verbal repertoire (Bernstein in Williams, 1970).

meaning: These are three kinds of semantic structure: "(1) implicative = relationship of linguistic signs to linguistic signs; (2) designative = relationship of linguistic signs to their nonlinguistic referents; and (3) expressive/pragmatic = relationship of linguistic signs and non-linguistic referents to the interpretive references in the behavioral responses of their users" (Nist, 1974, p. 25). Nist claims the disadvantaged are very deficient in their control of these semantic structures.

melting pot theory: implies homogeneity and denies cultural and ethnic diversity. It refers to a process in which the culturally diverse peoples which permeate this nation are somehow "melted down" into "something typically American" (Smith in Stent, 1973).

mesilect: the most pervasive version of any speech variety within the language (Nist, 1974).

nonstandard English: refers to English dialects which deviated from the standard in pronunciation, vocabulary, or grammar.

outreach: the promulgation of relevant service programs within the inner city or rural areas, or wherever the culturally different and poor children are to be found.

P.A.G.—progressive achievement gap: an observable phenomenon in which one group's performance measurement is increasingly depressed over time as compared to another group's performance measurement. This observable phenomenon is frequently explained by the hypothetical concept of "cumulative deficit" (Jensen, 1973, p. 296).

psyche needs: "the recognized needs of human beings for being with and interacting with compatible individuals (usually peers) whom they like and who like them" (Withall in Fagan, 1967, p. 49).

psycholinguistics vs. sociolinguistics: During the past decade and a half, psycho-linguistics has been profoundly affected by the impact of structural linguistics. Chomsky's contribution, among others, has generated much interest in the rules that guide verbal output and comprehension. These rules are created from the biogenetic inheritance of language patterns as well as from the uniqueness of the different speech communities in which the children are reared. Just as psycholinguistic performance models are being created, there is also a need to create sociolinguistic performance models. The juxtaposition of these models will undoubtedly allow for better understanding of language development as a function of one's cultural heritage. See also *sociology of language.*

Rosenthal (Pygmalion) effect: labels the tendency of the child to perform as he is expected to perform (Nist, 1974); often termed the "self-fulfilling prophesy."

rural poverty: conditions in sparsely populated country areas characterized by isolation, physical hardship, the lack of many of the benefits of even an old-fashioned industrialized society (such as plumbing, heat, adequate transportation), extremely poor schools and a general atmosphere of hopelessness. Rural poverty is tied to the long-term decline of the family farm, industrialization of the farm economy, the replacement of farm labor by mechanization and the exhaustion of the natural fertility of the land.

school talk: that dialect of English used by teachers in a given region of the country. It is commonly thought of as being "standard" or "prestige" English, but it has usually been altered by regional variants. Other frequently used synonyms describing school-talk dialect are *general American dialect,* and *broadcast English.*

segmentation of reality: in linguistics refers to "naming." The conditions for segmenting reality are (1) linguistic signs must be segmented, (2) linguistic signs must be repeatable, (3) linguistic signs must have built-in ambiguity, and (4) linguistic signs must be storable in human memory. (Nist, 1974, p. 129).

social class: those distinctions and differences that stratify people according to characteristics such as socioeconomic status, sociopsychological behavioral patterns, and sociolinguistic speech dialects.

social deprivation: "Environmental factors can be seen as socially depriving when at least two conditions are met: (1) when they are predominantly found within certain social groupings such as those defined by SES or race, and (2) when they are associated with impaired performance, e.g., lowered academic achievement. Social deprivation implies further that the association between social grouping and specific environmental factors is not strictly causal . . . but mediated by more basic environmental conditions such as unemployment, poverty, and inequality of opportunity in various areas. With the removal of such conditions, the association between social grouping and the socially depriving factor may vanish. Social deprivation also implies that the association between environmental conditions and performance decrement *is* causal, at least insofar as the deprivational factor hampers the learning of the performance in question" (Whiteman, Brown, & Deutsch in Deutsch et al., 1967, pp. 320-321).

socialization: "the process by which individuals, from birth onward, are given clues that permit them to define reality in a manner acceptable to their society. Socialization tells what *is*. It tells how to feel and act, and provides certain ranges of acceptable positive and negative behavior . . . In short, it defines situations and tells how to play roles" (Alman in Cowles, 1967, p. 8).

sociolinguistic testing *(Observation methods):* There are as many testing methods as there are people doing the testing. The basis of such testing, however, involves the determination of how people talk when they are being observed. But systematic observation frequently creates a bias. The goal should be to record people in their natural milieu without letting them know they are being evaluated. Such data gathering is available only to those workers recording speech patterns of babies through the utilization of tape recordings.

sociology of language (sociolinguistics): the study of the characteristics of language varieties, the characteristics of their functions, and the characteristics of their speakers, as these three constantly interact, change, and change on another, both within and between speech communities" (Fishman, 1971).

socio-needs: the needs to carry out or to participate in completing a task or in resolving a problem (Withall in Fagan, 1967, p. 49).

standard English: "the particular type of English which is used in the conduct of important affairs of our people. It is also the type of English used by the socially acceptable of most of our communities and, insofar as that is true, it has become a social or class dialect in the United States (Fries definition as quoted by Cazden in Hellmuth, 1968, p. 220).

swamping: "changes worked on the extant [language] systems by the newcomers" (Shuy in Williams, 1970, p. 345).

switching: synonomous with *diglossia*, the ability to "shift" from one dialect or language to another. Social mores allow the less prestigious dialect speaker to switch to a more prestigious (or standard) dialect, but the reverse is usually socially unacceptable. It is of interest to note that when switching takes the form of bi- or multilingualism (i.e., different languages), it is recognized as a desirable attribute, but dialect switching is generally considered an unimportant skill.

urban poor: people living in densely populated communities are "characterized by overcrowding, a lack of privacy, and unstable family and social relationships. Neighborhoods change, neighbors change, family members change. Life is spent in motion. Noise is ubiquitous. . . . Poverty in the city is lack of money coupled with high rent, high food costs, expensive clothing, and costly transportation. . . . City poverty means overcrowded and debilitated schools; streets proliferous with bars, drunks, sex perverts, prostitutes, addicts; crowds of people in motion without any apparent purpose" (Alman in Cowles, 1967, p. 7).

REFERENCES

Adler, S. *The health and education of the economically deprived child.* St. Louis: Green, 1968.
Adler, S. A sociolinguistic approach to functional mental retardation. *Exceptional Children,* 1971, *38,* 336–337.
Adler, S. Pluralism, relevance and language intervention for culturally different children. *ASHA,* 1971, *13,* 719–723.
Adler, S. The social class bases of language: A reexamination of socioeconomic, sociopsychological, and sociolinguistic factors. *AHSA,* 1973, *15,* 39.
Beck, J. M., & Saxe, R. W. *Teaching the culturally disadvantaged pupil.* Springfield, Ill.: Thomas, 1965.
Brooks, I. R. *A cross-cultural study of concept learning.* ERIC Document ED 115588, 1974.

Bryen, D. N. Special education and the linguistically different child. *Exceptional Children*, 1974, *40*, 589-599.

Cowles, M. (Ed.). *Perspectives in the education of disadvantaged children: A Multidisciplinary Approach*. New York: Harcourt Brace Jovanovich, 1967.

Deutsch, M., et al. *The disadvantaged child*. New York: Basic Books, 1967.

Deutsch, M., Katz, I., & Jensen, A. (Eds.). *Social class, race, and psychological development*. New York: Holt, Rinehart and Winston, 1968.

Diggs, R. W. Education across cultures. *Exceptional Children*, 1974, *40*, 578–583.

Fagan, E. R., (Ed.). *English and the disadvantaged*. Scranton, Penn.: International Textbook, 1967.

Fishman, J. A. *Advances in the Sociology of Language*. The Hague: Mouton & Co., 1971.

Glaser, K. *Learning difficulties*. Springfield, Ill.: Thomas, 1974.

Gordon, E. W., & Wilkerson, A. *Compensatory education for the disadvantaged*. New York: College Entrance Examination Board, 1966.

Gowan, J. C., & Demos, G. D. (Eds.). *The disadvantaged and potential dropout*. Springfield, Ill.: Thomas, 1966.

Hellmuth, J. (Ed.). *Disadvantaged child: Headstart and early intervention*. New York: Brunner/Mazel, 1968.

Jensen, A. R. *Educational differences*. London: Methuen, 1973.

Keach, E. T., Jr., Fulton, R., & Gardner, W. E. (Eds.). *Education and social class*. New York: Wiley, 1967.

Mazon, M. R. *Community, home, cultural awareness and language training: A design for teacher training in multicultural education*. ED 115588 1974.

Miller, H. L. (Ed.). *Education for the disadvantaged: Current issues and research*. New York: Free Press, 1967.

Nist, J. *Handicapped English: The language of the socially disadvantaged*. Springfield, Ill.: Thomas, 1974.

Rushton, J., & Turner, J. D. *Education and deprivation*. Manchester, Eng.: University Press, 1975.

Stanley, J. C. (Ed.). *Compensatory education for children two to eight*. Baltimore: Johns Hopkins University Press, 1973.

Stent, M. C., Hazard, W. R., & Rivlin, H. N. (Eds.). *Cultural pluralism in education: A mandate for change*. New York: Meredith, 1973.

Texas Education Agency. *The administrator's conference on language and cultural difference*. ERK Document ED 111169, 1973.

Williams, F. (Ed.). *Language and poverty*. Chicago: Markham 1970.

Wolfram, W. and D. Christian. *Sociolinguistic variables in Appalachian dialects*. ERIC Document Ed 112687, 1975.

Appendix C:
Some Examples of Culturally Biased Tests Favoring Poor Blacks and Rural Appalachians

SOCIOLOGY SURVEY ON *"THE BLACK DIALECT"**

1. If a "brother" is said to have a "do," he has:
   a. fast-moving cars
   b. a flunky
   c. a long jail record
   d. a process

2. An "uncle Tom" is:
   a. a militant black
   b. a black who always sides with a white
   c. a black who has a nephew
   d. anyone who is named Tom

3. A "clock" to a black means:
   a. a time device
   b. a dummy
   c. a rooster
   d. a place to stash dope

4. "Money don't get everything it's true:
   a. but what it don't get, I can't use.

*Compiled by Alex Rowan as part of a class requirement at the University of Tennessee, Knoxville. Correct answers are supplied on page 263.

      b. but I don't have none so why worry about it."

      c. so make it with what you got."

      d. but neither does peace."

5.   Which word "don't" belong?
   a. Splib
   b. Blood
   c. Jive
   d. Spook

6.   What does it mean when it's said to "pimp"?
   a. to sweet talk a woman
   b. to walk cool
   c. to break out in the face
   d. to work

7.   Today, if a black thinks something is truly hipped, he would call it:
   a. neat-o
   b. terrific
   c. cool as a roach on a poach
   d. super bad

8.   The phrase "I ain't studin' you" means:
   a. I don't care what you think
   b. I am not studying about you
   c. I am not looking for nothing to go right
   d. I've never had sex with her.

9.   Your "Ace-Boon Coon" is:
   a. a card playin' friend
   b. your best huntin' dog
   c. your cute buddy
   d. an outfit of clothing

10. If Bobbie Jo's head's bad,
   a. she needs her hair fixed
   b. she has a headache
   c. she has been drinking
   d. she's in love

11. When a black says, "to be or not to be," he:
   a. means that in order to be somebody, you've got to be white
   b. is speaking from Shakespeare

c. means that you are either black or you're not.
d. is in love

12. "Henry broke Gary's face." What happened?
a. Henry hit Gary in his face
b. Henry out-talked Gary
c. Gary hit Henry in the face
d. They hit each other

13. When Mama doesn't want me to talk back at her,
a. She would say, "Don't give me no lip!"
b. She would say, "Button your lip!"
c. She would say, "Don't talk to me!"
d. She would say, "Give me a lip-lock."

14. "What's hapnin!" means:
a. Hello
b. What do you want
c. What is occurring here
d. I can't see for looking

15. If Larry's arms are "talking" he needs:
a. To stop taking dope
b. Someone who understands sign language.
c. To stop using his hands to talk
d. Right Guard (deodorant)

16. "A pain in the butt" might be called a:
a. Splib
b. Hassle
c. ass ache
d. problem

17. "To make a hussle" means:
a. to play hard
b. to work
c. to win praise
d. to make a lady

18. A "gig" is:
a. something to ride in
b. a job

    c. an ugly girl
    d. your pad or house

19.   Billie Holiday's dude was named:
    a. Charles Geter
    b. Willie Mays
    c. Wilber Hawkins
    d. Lewis McKay

20.   If a black is agitating a fight between two other blacks, he is
    a. mean
    b. bambooseling
    c. copin' a plea
    d. signifying

21.   When two blacks want to get married, the guy usually asks the girl:
    a. Let's mate
    b. is heaven our bond
    c. you and me, baby
    d. let's get married

22.   A "Deuce-and-a-quarter" is a brother's
    a. pay check
    b. good hand in a card game
    c. half-brother
    d. ride

23.   To "lean" means:
    a. to come to me with your problems
    b. to lean over while one drives
    c. to lean over while one walks
    d. to walk humped back

24.   If a child asked you, "How stands the sky"? You should answer:
    a. the sky is big
    b. that's not what you meant to say
    c. no one knows how high the sky is
    d. the sky is blue

25.   To "cop-a-plea" means:
    a. that one is pleading for something
    b. to find something

    c. to make an excuse
    d. to tell on someone

26. A "mack":
    a. is a pimp
    b. fights a lot
    c. is anyone that you don't know
    d. is a common person

27. A "blue-eyed soul brother or sister" is:
    a. a child who has one parent who is black and another parent who is white
    b. a child with blue eyes that has two black parents.
    c. a white person with "soul"
    d. a black person who thinks that he is white

28. "Superfly" refers to:
    a. dope
    b. a strong fly
    c. blackness
    d. "Shaft"

29. Something that "holds papers" is a:
    a. sissy bag
    b. Whitey's judgment case
    c. brief relief
    d. folder

30. When a brother says "the Douzens," he means:
    a. someone is talking about someone else's parents
    b. his family
    c. that his gang has twelve members
    d. that having children is cheaper by the dozen

THE DOVE COUNTERBALANCE GENERAL INTELLIGENCE TEST

(A measure of cultural involvement in "poor folks" and "soul" cultures; answers are on page 263)

1. "T-Bone Walker" got famous for playing what?
    a. trombone

   b. piano
   c. "T-flute"
   d. guitar
   e. hambone

2. Who did "Stagger Lee" kill (in the famous blues legend)?
   a. his mother
   b. Frankie
   c. Johnny
   d. his girlfriend
   e. Billy

3. A "Gas-Head" is a person who has a_____.
   a. fast moving car
   b. stole of "lace"
   c. "process"
   d. habit of stealing cars
   e. long jail record for arson

4. If a man is called a "Blood," then he is a_____.
   a. fighter
   b. Mexican-American
   c. Negro
   d. hungry hemophile
   e. redman or Indian

5. If you throw the dice and "7" is showing on the top, what is facing down?
   a. "seven"
   b. "snake eyes"
   c. "boxcars"
   d. "little joes"
   e. "eleven"

6. Jazz pianist Ahmad Jamal took an Arabic name after becoming really famous. Previously, he had some fame with what he called his "slave name." What *was* his previous name?
   a. Willie Lee Jackson
   b. LeRoi Jones
   c. Wilbur McDougal
   d. Fritz Jones
   e. Andy Johnson

7. In "C.C. Rider," what does "C.C." stand for?
   a. civil service
   b. church council
   c. country circuit, preacher an old time rambler
   d. country club
   e. "cheatin' Charlie"

8. Cheap chitlings (not the kind you purchase at a frozen-food counter) will taste rubbery unless they are cooked long enough. How soon can you quit, cooking them to eat and enjoy them?
   a. 45 minutes
   b. 2 hours
   c. 24 hours
   d. 1 week (on a low flame)
   e. 1 hour

9. "Down home" (the South) today, for the average "Soul Brother" who is picking cotton (in season) from sunup until sundown, what is the average take home earning for one full day?
   a. $ .75
   b. $ 1.65
   c. $ 3.50
   d. $ 5.00
   e. $12.00

10. If a judge finds you guilty of "holding weed" (in California), what's the most he can give you?
   a. indeterminate (life)
   b. a nickel
   c. a dime—10 years
   d. a year in County
   e. $500.00

11. "Bird" or "yardbird" was the "jacket" that jazz lovers from coast to coast hung on:
   a. Lester Young
   b. Peggy Lee
   c. Benny Goodman
   d. Charlie Parker
   e. "Birdman of Alcatraz"

12. A "hype" is a person who:

    a. always says they feel sickly
    b. has water on the brain
    c. uses heroin
    d. is always sick
    e. is always ripping and running

13. "Hully Gully" came from
    a. "east Oakland"
    b. Fillmore
    c. Watts
    d. Harlem
    e. Motor City

14. What is Willie Mae's last name?
    a. Schwartz
    b. Matsuda
    c. Gomez
    d. Turner
    e. O'Flaherty

15. The opposite of "square" is:
    a. round
    b. up
    c. down
    d. hip
    e. lame

16. Do the Beatles have soul?
    a. yes
    b. no
    c. gee whiz or maybe

17. A "handkerchief head" is
    a. a cool cat
    b. a porter
    c. an Uncle Tom
    d. a hoddi
    e. a Preacher

18. What are the dixiehummingbirds?
    a. a part of the KKK
    b. a swamp disease
    c. a Modern Gospel Group

d. a Mississippi black, paramilitary strike force

e. deacons

19. "Jet" is:

a. an "East Oakland" motorcycle club

b. one of the gangs in West Side Story

c. a news and gossip magazine

d. a way of life for the very rich

20. Hattie May Johnson is on the County. She has four kids and her husband is now in jail for nonsupport as he was unemployed and was not able to give her money. Her welfare check is now $286 per month. Last night she went out with the biggest player in town. If she got pregnant, then nine months from now, how much more will her welfare check be?

a. $80

b. $2

c. $35

d. $150

e. $100

Fill in in the Missing Word or Words That Sound Best

21. "Tell it like it

a. thinks I am"

b. baby"

c. try"

d. is"

e. y'all"

22. "You've got to get up early in the morning if you want to:

a. catch the worms"

b. be healthy, wealthy, and wise"

c. try to fool me"

d. fare well"

e. be the first one on the street"

23. And Jesus said, "Walk together children:

a. Don't you get weary. There's a great camp meeting."

b. for we shall overcome."

c. for the family that walks together talks together."

     d. by your patience you will win your souls" (Luke 21:29)

     e. mind the things that are above, not the things that are on Earth."
       (Col 3:3)

24. "Money don't get everything it's true:
    a. but I don't have none and I'm so blue"
    b. but what it don't get I can't use"
    c. so make do with what you've got"
    d. but I don't *know* that neither"

25. "Bo-Diddley" is a:
    a. a game for children
    b. down-home cheap wine
    c. down-home singer
    d. new dance
    e. Moejoe call

26. Which word is most out of place here?
    a. Splib
    b. Blood
    c. Grey
    d. Spook
    e. Black

27. How much does a "short-dog" cost?
    a. $ .15
    b. $2.00
    c. $ .35
    d. $ .05
    e. $ .86 − tax

28. A "pimp" is also a young man who lays around all day.
    a. yes
    b. no

29. If a pimp is up tight with a woman who gets State aid, what does he
mean when he talks about "Mother's Day"?
    a. second Sunday in May
    b. third Sunday in June
    c. first of every month
    d. none of these
    e. first and fifteenth of every month

30. Many people say that "Juneteenth" (June 19) should be made a legal holiday because this was the day when:
    a. the slaves were freed in the US.A.
    b. the slaves were freed in Texas
    c. the slaves were freed in Jamaica
    d. the slaves were freed in California
    e. Martin Luther King was born
    f. Booker T. Washington died

A CULTURALLY BIASED TEST FAVORING
THE RURAL APPALACHIAN: I*

1. Ginseng or "sang" is:
   a. a leaf of a tree
   b. a square dance
   c. an herb used by the Chinese
   d. a drink made from the ginger leaf

2. After it has been topped, tobacoo is ready to cut when it:
   a. turns yellow
   b. is green
   c. dries
   d. turns brown

3. Women weren't allowed in a coal mine because:
   a. it was against the law
   b. it was bad luck
   c. they distracted the miners

4. When you see mice running toward the exit of a coal mine, it means:
   a. danger of a cave-in or leaking gas
   b. they're hunting someone's lunch
   c. it's going to rain

5. Red-eye gravy is:
   a. gravy with red food coloring in it
   b. gravy made with ham grease (or water and coffee)

*Devised by K. Rogers and D. Stulberg as part of Operation Mainstream, in Oak Ridge, Tennessee, 1970.

       c. unaged moonshine

       d. fish sauce

6.   Cracklin's are:

       a. made from beef

       b. pork rind and fat

       c. fireworks

       d. chicken feed

7.   A twig from a small willow or sassafras limb chewed up at the end is for:

       a. chewing gum

       b. a toothpick

       c. a switch

       d. a toothbrush

8.   Bee gum is:

       a. made from honey comb

       b. tree sap used for chewing

       c. an early American bee hive

       d. a sweetgum tree that attracts bees to its fruit.

9.   Dogwood is generally used for:

       a. a building material:

       b. shuttles for looms

       c. firewood

       d. furniture

10.   A barrel rim or goop, and a piece of wire, "A click and a wheel" is:

       a. a child's toy

       b. a singing frame

       c. used part of a bike wheel

11.   Sour mash is:

       a. a fertilizer

       b. an ingredient for moonshine

       c. a woven fence

       d. a home remedy for rheumatism

12.   "Annie Over" is a:

       a. neighbor

       b. game played with a rubber ball

       c. folk tale

       d. song

13. Carbide is:
    a. added to water to make acetylene gas
    b. used to make baking powder
    c. used to make extra copies of a newspaper

14. Flax seed is used to:
    a. get something out of your eye
    b. feed chickens
    c. feed hogs

15. A pounding is:
    a. driving a nail
    b. gifts to a new neighbor
    c. a one-pound chicken

16. A peach tree fork is used for:
    a. finding oil
    b. a stirring fork in cooking
    c. finding water
    d. pruning peach trees

17. Leather britches are:
    a. threaded dried green beans
    b. britches worn by mountaineers
    c. part of a harness

18. Hogs head, ears, and sage make:
    a. sausage
    b. steamed pudding
    c. souse meat
    d. frankfurters

19. The best time for killing hogs when the meat is to be cured is:
    a. around Thanksgiving when temperature is below 32 degrees
    b. after Ground Hog Day
    c. anytime
    d. before killing frost

20. Hog jowl and black-eyed peas are:
    a. New Year's dinner eaten for good luck
    b. a remedy for the croup
    c. Thanksgiving dinner eaten for good luck

21. Sorghum is made from:

     a. sugar cane
     b. sugar beets
     c. sorghum cane

22. Lye, grease, water, and bacon rind are used for making:
     a. cracklins
     b. soap
     c. black strap molasses

23. Flying ginny is:
     a. a name of an early airplane
     b. a children's game
     c. a title of a children's story
     d. a slow mule

24. A tow sack is:
     a. a foot covering
     b. a burlap bag
     c. a foot bandage

25. Kiverlid is:
     a. a bed cover
     b. a hat
     c. a kitchen utensil

26. Flower Garden, Chicken Track, Wedding Ring, Dutch Girls are:
     a. names of songs
     b. quilt patterns
     c. square dances
     d. children's games

27. Light bread is:
     a. hot bread
     b. store bread
     c. corn bread
     d. cream puffs

28. Mole beans are:
     a. a variety of shellout beans
     b. for poisoning moles
     c. molded beans

29. An Appalachian asking for a "plug" would most likely mean:
     a. a broken down mule

    b. chewing tobacco
    c. a stopper for a sink drain

30. Johnny Johnson got his racing training:
    a. delivering groceries
    b. working as a mechanic in an auto shop
    c. delivering moonshine
    d. as a pit man at the tracks

31. "Sang," dock root, whiskey, poke root are ingredients for:
    a. anything that ails you
    b. making moonshine
    c. country soap

32. "Long John" is the name for:
    a. underwear
    b. a famous freight line
    c. a short gun
    d. a famous literary character

33. Trees generally used for pulpwood are:
    a. dogwoods
    b. pines
    c. oaks
    d. sugar maple

34. Poke salad generally refers to
    a. berries of poke plant used for dye
    b. tender greens of poke
    c. greens bought at the store

A CULTURALLY BIASED TEST FAVORING
THE RURAL APPALACHIAN: II*

1. A greasy poke best serves a person who:
    a. has a cold
    b. has sore muscles
    c. is hungry

*"Mountain Quiz" in "The Mountain Call," Christmas 1974, *II*, 1, page 6.

    d. is pregnant
    e. is tired

2. A dotey person is:
    a. crippled
    b. fat
    c. in love
    d. lazy
    e. senile

3. Burley is usually cured:
    a. by the processor
    b. in flue forms
    c. in open air barns
    d. on the stalk
    e. a year after it is cut

4. The word blinky refers to:
    a. a child's toy
    b. an early frost
    c. an eccentric woman
    d. soured milk
    e. spoiled canned goods

5. A bealed head refers to:
    a. a bloated cow
    b. a festering pimple
    c. a hairless condition
    d. a rotten cabbage
    e. a swollen face

6. A man who has granny trouble can look forward to:
    a. obstaining from sex
    b. the birth of his child
    c. having only daughters
    d. his mother in law moving in
    e. a stomach condition

7. Jumping jig refers to:
    a. dance
    b. escaped convict
    c. groom
    d. racial slur
    e. toy

8. To back an envelope is to:
   a. address it
   b. apply a return address
   c. mail it
   d. put postage on it
   e. seal it

9. A back set is a (an):
   a. brace
   b. farm tool
   c. ignorant person
   d. low chair
   e. relapse

10. Which of the following belongs least with the others?
    a. dodger
    b. grits
    c. hush puppy
    d. pone
    e. scrapple

11. Southern mountain people usually express the political feelings by:
    a. voting independently
    b. seldom voting
    c. rejecting traditional candidates
    d. voting strongly democratic
    e. voting strongly Republican

12. An anxious bench might be found in:
    a. church
    b. county jail
    c. grocery store
    d. hospital
    e. one room school

Answers

Survey on Black Dialect: 1d, 2b, 3a, 4a, 5c, 6b, 7d, 8a, 9c, 10c, 11b, 12b, 13a, 14a, 15d, 16b, 17b, 18b, 19d, 20d, 21d, 22b, 23d, 24c, 25a, 26c, 27a, 28d, 29a, 30a. *The Dove Test:* 1e, 2e, 3c, 4c, 5a, 6d, 7c, 8c, 9d, 10c, 11d, 12c, 13c, 14c, 15d, 16b, 17c, 18c, 19d, 20c, 21d, 22c, 23a, 24b, 25c, 26c, 27e, 28a, 29c, 30b. *Appalachian I:* 1c, 2a, 3b, 4a, 5b, 6b, 7d, 8c, 9b, 10a, 11b, 12b, 13a, 14a, 15b, 16c, 17a, 18c, 19a, 20a, 21c, 22b, 23a, 24b, 25a, 26b, 27b, 28b, 29b, 30b, 31a, 32a, 33b, 34b. *Appalachian II:* 1c, 2e, 3c, 4d, 5e, 6b, 7e, 8a, 9e, 10e, 11e, 12a.

Appendix D:
A Supplemental Language Intervention Lesson Plan for Head Start and Other Preschool Teachers*

The following lessons are designed for classroom use in teaching oral, standard sentence structure to children with nonstandard language. No specific effort is made to teach listening skills, vocabulary, or concept development—although these may coincidentally improve. Time required in teaching a lesson is 15 to 30 minutes depending upon the number of children, the teacher's facility with the lessons, and the children's response rate.

Initiating the Program

The format of each presentation is adaptable to the presence or absence of nonstandard language. If it has been determined that a nonstandard construct exists, fill in the blanks provided with the appropriate nonstandard usage *before beginning the programs*. If it has been determined that no nonstandard construct is generally used by the class, the parenthesized statement can be ignored. Furthermore, if it has

*Obtained, with permission, from a term paper by Gladys Hof, a former student of the University of Tennessee.

been determined that nonstandard language is used, a brief discussion of "school talk" and "everyday talk" should precede the structured program itself.

The teacher then presents a picture and an associated verbal stimulus (the nonstandard equivalent may then be presented). The child responds with an appropriate standard sentence; the teacher reinforces that response. Each language lesson follows essentially the same format. Pictures needed, examples given, teacher stimulus/child response are clearly provided for each step in each lesson. Lengthy explanations regarding grammar are not necessary. The teacher might use hand signals to indicate the appropriate times for listening and the appropriate times for the child's response.

It is suggested that a regular period be established as "language time" and one lesson taught at that time. It is suggested that each step be repeated twice, if there is enough time. One lesson every two days is ideal as this allows the teacher time to reinforce and follow up on the model sentences in other classroom activities.

Reinforcement

If the response is correct, the teacher should drop a lima bean in a small paper cup that the child is holding. Verbal reinforcement must also occur—"good" or "thank you" or "that's good (school) talk," etc. If the child does not respond as desired, a bean is not given. The teacher should say nothing and go to the next child.

After the lesson is completed, the children having full cups of beans should be allowed to select a "prize" from several in a box kept for that purpose—marbles, toy rings, a page of stickers, or anything else of small monetary value that would be meaningful to them. If a child's cup is not full, he can redeem it at a later date when it is. Special privileges may also be given as a reward for a "full cup."

For the first three to five lessons each child should be reinforced (verbally and with a bean) simply for participation—such as listening attentively, approximating the response desired, or saying anything (in the case of the withdrawn or low-verbal child). The teacher's assistant can score the responses. The Language Lesson: Response Record for each lesson taught should be used. This record should be kept and used as a reference to determine overall class performance as well as each child's individual performance.

LANGUAGE PROGRAM—"IS" VERB

Step A. Instructions

1. If nonstandard language is used by the children, begin with a simple discussion explaining "school talk," "other talk."
2. Select and arrange in the following order these Peabody (Level 1) pictures: B-1, B-3, B-8. B-21, B-26, B-29, B-31, B-32, B-42, B-44, A-4, A-13, A-15, A-17, A-24, A-29, A-36, A-40, A-46, A-50.
3. Place the stacked pictures on the chalk rail, B-1 (bird) facing outward.
4. Say: "I'll say a sentence: The bird is yellow." (Option: Next use the nonstandard equivalency if one exists.)
5. Move B-1 to the back bringing forward B-3 (dog).
6. Say: "I'll say another sentence: The dog is brown." (Option: Next use the nonstandard equivalency if one exists.)
7. Rearrange the pictures in the original order, B-1, B-3, B-8, etc.
8. Say: "I'll say the sentence and you say it after me: The bird is yellow." (Option: Repeat the nonstandard equivalency. Then say: "You say it in 'school talk'."
9. The first child then says: "The bird is yellow."
10. Go through all 20 sentences this way, one picture for each child. Repeat the order if more than 20 children. Reinforce and record each response. At completion of Step A, go to Step B.

Stimulus—Response Sequence for Step A

Picture No.	Teacher	(Teacher: using non-standard construct. Then: "You say it in 'school talk.'"	Child
B-1	The bird is yellow.	_____	The bird is yellow.
B-3	The dog is brown	_____	The dog is brown.
B-8	The chick is yellow.	_____	The chick is yellow.
B-21	The sheep is white	_____	The sheep is white.
B-26	The bird is red.	_____	The bird is red.

Stimulus—Response Sequence for Step A (continued)

Picture No.	Teacher	(Teacher: using non-standard construct. Then: "You say it in 'school talk.'")	Child
B-29	The crow is black.	_____	The crow is black.
B-31	The fish is green.	_____	The fish is green.
B-32	The fox is brown.	_____	The fox is brown.
B-42	The turtle is green.	_____	The turtle is green.
B-44	The bear is white.	_____	The bear is white.
A-4	The boy is eating.	_____	The boy is eating.
A-13	The girl is sweeping.	_____	The girl is sweeping.
A-15	The lady is talking.	_____	The lady is talking.
A-17	The teacher is writing.	_____	The teacher is writing.
A-24	The man is painting.	_____	The man is painting.
A-29	The man is sawing.	_____	The man is sawing.
A-36	The boy is jumping.	_____	The boy is jumping.
A-40	The girl is sitting.	_____	The girl is sitting.
A-46	The boy is throwing.	_____	The boy is throwing.
A-50	The girl is waving.	_____	The girl is waving.

Step B Instructions

1. Use the same pictures in the same order as in Step A.
2. Place the stacked pictures on the chalk rail, B-1 (bird) facing outward.
3. Say: "Now I'll say one word, is, and you say the whole sentence, 'The

bird is yellow'." If including nonstandard construct, say only its verb
equivalency.
4. Give another example using the second picture, B-3 (dog).
5. Rearrange the pictures in the original order.
6. Say "is" and let the first child respond with "The bird is yellow."
7. Go through all 20 sentences this way, one picture for each child. Repeat
   the order if more than 20 children. Reinforce and record each response.
   Language Program "IS" is completed at the end of Step B.
8. Accept *any* correct predicate adjective. (Fourth word in child's
   response.)

Stimulus—Response Squence for Step B

Picture No.	Teacher	(Teacher: using non-standard equivalent. Then: "You say it in 'school talk'."	Child
B-1	is	_____	The bird is yellow.
B-3	is	_____	The dog is brown.
B-8	is	_____	The chick is yellow.
B-21	is	_____	The sheep is white.
B-26	is	_____	The bird is red.
B-29	is	_____	The crow is black.
B-31	is	_____	The fish is green.
B-32	is	_____	The fox is brown.
B-42	is	_____	The turtle is green.
B-44	is	_____	The bear is white.
A-4	is	_____	The boy is eating.

Stimulus—Response Sequence for Step B (continued)

Picture No.	Teacher	(Teacher: using non-standard equivalent. Then: "You say it in 'school talk'."	Child
A-13	is	_____	The girl is sweeping.
A-15	is	_____	The lady is talking.
A-17	is	_____	The teacher is writing.
A-24	is	_____	The man is painting.
A-29	is	_____	The man is sawing.
A-36	is	_____	The boy is jumping.
A-40	is	_____	The girl is sitting.
A-46	is	_____	The boy is throwing.
A-50	is	_____	The girl is waving.

Comments: _____

_____

_____

_____

_____

_____

_____

LANGUAGE PROGRAM—"ARE" VERB

Step A Instructions

1. If nonstandard language is used by the children, review "school talk," "other talk."
2. Select and arrange in the following order these Peabody (Level 1) pictures: C-21, C-22, E-15, C-2, E-6, C-25, E-19, C-51, F-7, C-57.
3. Place the stacked pictures on the chalk rail, C-21 (shoes) facing outward.
4. Say: "I'll say a sentence: 'The shoes are brown.'"
   (Option: Next use the nonstandard equivalency if one exists.)
5. Move C-21 to the back bringing forward C-22 (pants).
6. Say: "I'll say another sentence: 'The pants are green.'"
   (Option: Next use the nonstandard equivalency if one exists.)
7. Rearrange the pictures in the original order.
8. Say: "I'll say the sentence and you say it after me: 'The shoes are brown.'"
   (Option: Repeat the nonstandard equivalency. Then say: "You say it in 'school talk.'")
9. The first child then says: "The shoes are brown."
10. Go through all 10 pictures this way, one picture for each child. Repeat the order if more than 10 children. Reinforce and record each response. At completion of Step A, go to Step B.

Stimulus—Response Sequence for Step A

Picture No.	Teacher	(Teacher: using non-standard construct. Then: "You say it in 'school talk.'"	Child
C-21	The shoes are brown.	_____	The shoes are brown.
C-22	The pants are green.	_____	The pants are green.
E-15	The beans are white.	_____	The beans are white.
C-2	The gloves are brown.	_____	The gloves are brown.
E-6	The lemons are yellow.	_____	The lemons are yellow.

Stimulus—Response Sequence for Step A (continued)

Picture No.	Teacher	(Teacher: using non-standard construct. Then: "You say it in 'school talk.'")	Child
C-25	The boots are black.	_____	The boots are black.
E-19	The carrots are orange.	_____	The carrots are orange.
C-51	The mittens are blue.	_____	The mittens are blue.
F-7	The beans are green.	_____	The beans are green.
C-57	The glasses are brown.	_____	The glasses are brown.

Step B Instructions

1. Use the same pictures in the same order as in Step A.
2. Place the stacked pictures on the chalk rail, C-21 (shoes) facing outward.
3. Say: "Now I'll say one word, *are,* and you say the whole sentence: The shoes are brown.'" If including nonstandard construct, say only its verb equivalency.
4. Give another example using the second picture, C-22 (pants).
5. Rearrange the pictures in the original order.
6. Say "are" and let the first child respond with "The shoes are brown."
7. Go through all 10 sentences this way, one picture for each child. Repeat the order if more than 10 children. Reinforce and record each response. Language Program "are" is completed at the end of Step B.
8. Accept any adequate predicate adjective (4th word in child's response).

Stimulus—Response Sequence for Step B

Picture No.	Teacher	(Teacher: using non-standard construct. Then: "You say it in 'school talk.'")	Child
C-21	are	_____	The shoes are brown.

Stimulus—Response Sequence for Step B (continued)

Picture No.	Teacher	(Teacher: using non-standard construct. Then: "You say it in 'school talk.'"	Child
C-22	are	_____	The pants are green.
B-15	are	_____	The beans are white.
C-2	are	_____	The gloves are brown.
E-6	are	_____	The lemons are yellow.
C-25	are	_____	The overshoes are black.
E-19	are	_____	The carrots are orange.
C-51	are	_____	The mittens are blue.
F-7	are	_____	The beans are green.
C-57	are	_____	The glasses are brown.

Comments: _____

_____

_____

_____

_____

_____

_____

LANGUAGE PROGRAM—"IS/ARE" VERBS

Step A Instructions

1. If nonstandard language is used by the children, review "school," "other talk."
2. Select and arrange in the following order these Peabody (Level 1) pictures: B-1, C-21, B-21, C-22, B-26, E-6, B-31, E-19, B-32, C-51.
3. Place the stacked pictures on the chalk rail, B-1 (bird) facing outward.
4. Say: "I'll say a sentence: The bird is yellow.'"
   (Option: Next use the nonstandard equivalency if one exists.)
5. Move B-1 to the back bringing forward C-21.
6. Say: "I'll say another sentence. 'The shoes are brown.'"
   (Option: Repeat the nonstandard equivalency. Then say: "You say it in 'school talk.'")
7. Rearrange the pictures in original order.
8. Say: "I'll say the sentence and you say it after me. 'The bird is yellow.'"
   (Option: Repeat the nonstandard equivalency. Then say: "You say it in 'school talk.'")
9. The first child then says: "The bird is yellow."
10. Go through all 10 sentences this way, a new picture and new sentence for each child. Repeat the order if more than 10 children. Reinforce and record each response. At completion of Step A go to Step B.

Stimulus—Response Sequence for Step A

Picture No.	Teacher	(Teacher: using non-standard construct. Then: "You say it in 'school talk.'")	Child
B-1	The bird is yellow.	_____	The bird is yellow.
C-21	The shoes are brown.	_____	The shoes are brown.
B-21	The sheep is white.	_____	The sheep is white.
C-22	The pants are green.	_____	the pants are green.
B-26	The bird is red.	_____	The bird is red.

Stimulus—Response Sequence for Step A (continued)

Picture No.	Teacher	(Teacher: using non-standard constrct. Then: "You say it in 'school talk.'")	Child
E-6	The lemons are yellow.	_____	The lemons are yellow.
B-31	The fish is green.	_____	The fish is green.
E-19	The carrots are orange.	_____	The carrots are orange.
B-32	The fox is brown.	_____	The fox is brown.
C-5	The mittens are blue.	_____	The mittens are blue.

Step B Instructions

1. Use the same pictures in the same order as in Step A.
2. Place the stacked pictures on the chalk rail, B-1 (bird) facing outward.
3. Say: "Now I'll say another word, *is,* and you'll say the whole sentence: 'The bird is yellow.'" If including nonstandard construct, say only its verb equivalency.
4. Move B-1 to the back bringing forward C-21.
5. Say: "I'll say another word, *are,* and you'll say the whole sentence: 'The shoes are brown.'" If including nonstandard construct, say only its verb equivalency.
6. Rearrange the pictures in the original order.
7. Say "is" and let the first child respond with "The bird is yellow."
8. Go through all 10 sentences this way. Give one stimulus word ("is" or "are" plus the optional nonstandard equivalency) and one picture to each child. Repeat the order if more than 10 children. Reinforce and record each response. Language Program "Is-Are" Verbs is completed at the end of Step B.
9. Accept any adequate predicate adjective (4th word) in child's response.

Stimulus—Response Sequence for Step B

Picture No.	Teacher	(Teacher: using non-standard construct. Then: "You say it in 'school talk.'")	Child
B-1	is	_____	The bird is yellow.
C-21	are	_____	The shoes are brown.
B-21	is	_____	The sheep is white.
C-22	are	_____	The pants are green.
B-26	is	_____	The bird is red.
E-6	are	_____	The lemons are yellow.
B-31	is	_____	The fish is green.
E-19	are	_____	The carrots are orange.
B-32	is	_____	The fox is brown.
C-51	are	_____	The mittens are blue.

Comments: _____

_____

_____

_____

_____

_____

_____

_____

ACTIVITIES TO SUPPLEMENT
THE LANGUAGE PROGRAM

The criterion for teaching a skill is its usage. Therefore, language skills taught should be observable in the child's self-generation of them in peer-group speaking situations. The gap between the structured language program in the classroom and everyday, spontaneous speech can be bridged by effective use of supplemental language activites.

Initially, the teacher should deliberately structure the environment so that the desired response is elicited. Positive reinforcement should be used at all times. For example, "Can you tell me something about that book? . . . it *is* red . . . it *is* big . . ."; "Who are your friends? . . . My cousin *is* my friend . . . John and Mary *are* my friends . . ."

Gradually the teacher should be observing, reinforcing, and discussing language usage in totally unstructured language situations, for instance when:

1. having "show and tell."
2. describing situational pictures and, consequently, using strings of sentences.
3. painting or drawing, then telling a story about it.
4. playing during free time.
5. singing, i.e., "This *is* the way we wash our hands . . ."
6. playing the game "Give us a hint," where one given descriptive hints about an object until the others guess.

CONTINUING LANGUAGE PROGRAMS

Main verbs, in their progressive order of development, can easily be integrated into a suggested form of language programming.

1. *-s* and *-ed:* play*s*, play*ed*
2. Copula and auxiliary: *am, was, were*
3. *Can, will, may* + verb: *may go*
   Obligatory *do* + verb: *don't go*
   Emphatic *do* + verb: *I do see*
4. *Could, would, should, might* + verb: *might come, could be*
5. Obligatory and emphatic *does, did* + verb
6. Passive with *get* and/or *be*, any tense

7. *Must, shall* + verb: *must come*
   Have + verb + en: *I've eaten*
   Have got: I've got it.
8. *Have been* + verb + *ing*
   Had been + verb + *ing*

SUPPLEMENTAL READINGS AND RESOURCES
FOR THE HEAD START TEACHER

Griffin, L. (compiler). *Multi-ethnic books for young children* (1970). National Association for the Education of Young Children, 1834 Connecticut Avenue, NW, Washington, D.C. 20009.

Peabody Language development kits. American Guidance Service, Publishers' Building, Circle Pines, Minnesota 55014.

Project Head Start, speech language, and hearing program: A guide for Head Start personnel. U.S. Government Printing Office, Washington, D.C., 20402.

White, D (compiler). *Multi-ethnic books for Head Start children* (1969). Part I, Black and integrated literature. National Laboratory on Early Childhood Education, Urbana, Illinois 61801.

Appendix E:
Sample Lesson Plans Used in the
University of Tennessee
Experimental Elementary School
Program (K-3)

LESSON 1

A. Structure: Plural noun—*s*.
B. Instructional Objective: The students shall be able to use the plural noun upon demand in "school talk."
C. Behavioral Objective: The students shall be able to distinguish between a set containing one object and other sets containing more than one object.
D. Procedures and/or Activities:
   1. Place on the floor five large, brightly colored construction paper circles.
   2. Request students to remove shoes.
   3. Secure schoolhouse and apartment upon chalk board.*
   4. Elicit from students the number of circles (sets) on the floor.
   5. The response of "five circle [set]" will be placed under the apartment. The response of "five circles [sets]" will be placed under the schoolhouse.

*The teacher can use the term "apartment" for city children, and "house" for rural children.

6. Small, colorful *s* will be placed at the end of the plural noun under the schoolhouse.
7. Request one volunteer from class to step into one circle.
8. Ask class how many boys or girls are in the circle.
9. The response of "one boy" or "one girl" will be placed under the schoolhouse *and* apartment.
10. Request two volunteers to step into another circle.
11. Ask the class how many boys or girls are in this circle.
12. The response of "two boys" or "two girls" is placed under the schoolhouse. The response of "two boy" and "two girl" is placed under the apartment.
13. Small, colorful *s'* s are placed at the end of all plural nouns under the schoolhouse.

F. Materials:
1. Poster-board schoolhouse and apartment.
2. One large construction paper *s*.
3. Fifteen small construction paper *s'* s.
4. Blindfold.
5. Ditto.

LESSON 2

A. Structure: Plural noun—*s*.
B. Instructional Objective: The students shall be able to use the plural noun upon demand in "school talk."
C. Behavioral Objective: The students shall be able to:
1. Distinguish between single and multiple sounds.
2. Count and list objects found on the treasure hunt demonstrating use of the plural noun.
D. Procedures and/ Activities:
1. The schoolhouse and apartment will be attached to the chalk board.
2. A group of pictures (spread out) will be placed at one end of the chalk board. These pictures correspond to sounds on a tape recorder.
3. As the tape recorder and single or multiple sounds are played, each child will be designated a turn.
4. After the child hears his sound or sounds (i.e., one bell or several cows mooing), the child will respond by saying "cow*s*" or "cow."
5. If the child gives the correct "school-talk" response, he finds his

picture and places it under the schoolhouse. If the child gives the "everyday-talk" response, the child will find his picture and place it under the apartment.

6. No penalty is given for everyday talk.
7. The class will prepare to go outside on a treasure hunt discussed earlier in class related to a science project, unit study, etc. Objects to be collected could be the following: 2 acorns, 1 feather, 3 nuts, 4 stones, 5 flowers, etc.
8. When class returns, they will write in their science or unit notebooks the "treasures" and number of each found. The list of words will be written on the board.
9. The teacher will check each child's notebook as the class writes, giving individual attention and reinforcement.

E.   Evaluation: The listing of objects in notebooks using the plural noun where needed will be the evaluation.
F.   Materials:
1. Poster-board schoolhouse and apartment.
2. Tape recorder and tape of sounds.
3. Pictures on cards to match sounds on tape.
4. Paper bags for treasures.
5. Notebooks.

LESSON 3

A.   Structure: Plural noun—*s*.
B.   Instructional Objective: The students shall be able to use the plural noun upon demand in "school talk."
C.   Behavioral Objective: The students shall be able to produce the plural noun in context form.
D.   Procedure and/ Activities:
1. Attach schoolhouse and apartment to the chalk board.
2. Distribute various numbers of objects to class, i.e., paper clips, scissors, rubber bands, pencils, blocks, pieces of paper, crayons, etc.
3. Tell the students that you will ask them the question, "What do you have?" They are to respond. "I have [number of objects]."
4. Give several trials to make sure everyone knows the pattern in which he is to respond.
5. If the response is in the correct pattern using the plural noun, the child will go stand under the schoolhouse. If the response is not in

the requested pattern or the plural noun was not used, the child goes to stand under the apartment.

6. At the end of the game, note who is at "school" and who is at "home."

7. If time allows and/or interest is high, additional sentence patterns may be used, i.e.,

Teacher: "*Do you have 6 crayons?*"

Student: "No, I have 3 crayons."

or

"Yes, I have 6 crayons?"

This may be used to reinforce a unit of money (pennies, dimes, nickels, quarters, etc.) or measurement (inches, feet, yards).

E. Evaluation: The results of the game will be the evaluation.

F. Materials:

1. Poster-board schoolhouse and apartment.

2. Various objects found in classroom to be distributed to students.

LESSON 4 (NONSENSE STORY)

Nonsense stories could be written in the mountain English (or other nonstandard) language patterns used by the children. These language patterns could be obtained from language experience lessons, class discussions, interviews with the children, or responses from stimulus pictures.

These stories could be used in a sequence developing the concept of "school talk" and "everyday talk." Only the grammatical rules and structure discussed earlier will be presented, e.g., omission of final *s*.

The pictures in the nonsense stories could be used as stimulus pictures which allow each student to write his own story in either school talk or everyday talk. This would depend on the developmental phase and skill level of each child.

LESSON 5

A. Structure: Noun pluralization (tapes 5–8).

B. Instructional Objective: The students shall be able to respond with the standard English pluralizations of nouns upon demand in school talk.

C. Procedure and/or Activities:
    1. Place house and schoolhouse on the board.
    2. Student draws a picture from a box.
    3. Student describes picture saying, "This is two *postes/posts*."
    4. Student goes and stands beneath appropriate heading and repeats his response.
    5. The next student must give the corresponding pluralization. For example, if student 1 said *postes,* student 2 must respond with *posts.*
D. 1. Student draws a house or a schoolhouse from a box. Then he draws a picture from the other box.
    2. The student must respond according to the first card drawn. For example, if a student draws the schoolhouse, he must respond with *posts* and vice versa.
    3. As long as the student responds correctly, he may continue drawing from both boxes.
    4. When the response does not match the card drawn from the first box, the student must go stand under the heading corresponding to his response. When his turn arrives again, he may start drawing again if he can use the appropriate response.
E. Remember—no response is incorrect or wrong. Instead of correcting the child, remind him that you had asked for school talk rather than everyday talk (or vice versa) and ask him to try again. If he cannot respond correctly, ask another student to help him with the response. Then have the first child repeat the desired response before returning to his seat.
F. Materials:
    1. Poster-board schoolhouse and house.
    2. Two small boxes.
    3. Pictures (small) of house and schoolhouse.
    4. Pictures cut from magazines or line drawings representing pluarlized nouns.

LESSON 6

A. Structure: Pronouns, emphatic demonstrative.
B. Instructional Objective: The student shall be able to respond with standard English demonstrative pronouns upon demand in "school talk."

C.   Procedures and Activities:

    I-1.   Place the schoolhouse and the house on the board.

    I-2.   Two students come to the front of the class and are given two objects (books, pencils, erasers, etc.) that are alike.

    I-3.   The teacher will say, "Billy and Bob have pencils. Which one do you have Billy?"

    I-4.   If the student's response is, "that'n/this here," he stands beneath the house.

    I-5.   If the response is, *"This one,"* the student stands beneath the schoolhouse.

    I-6.   The teacher may also ask, "Which one does Bob have, Billy?"

    I-7.   A response of *that' n/that there* will place the student beneath the house, etc.

    II-1. Utilize the same physical set-up as in I–1 of this lesson.

    II-2. Have the student choose between using everyday or school talk.

    II-3. Upon receiving the question, "Which one do you have?" or "Which one does he have?" the student must respond in the type of talk he chose.

    II-4. The other student at the front of the class must respond in the talk not chosen by the other.

    II-5. The second student is then given a chance to choose response modes.

    II-6. As each student responds, he must stand beneath the appropriate heading.

D.   Remember—do not label a response incorrect or wrong. Also, have other students volunteer the desired response and then have them aid the first student in utilizing the desired response. Use the children as their own teachers.

E.   Materials:

    1. Poster-board schoolhouse and house.

    2. Sets of similar objects, such as books, chalk, erasers, etc.

LESSON 7

A.   Structure: Pronouns, disjunctive possessive.

B.   Instructional Objective: Student shall be able to use standard English possessive pronouns upon demand in "school talk."

C.   Procedures and Activities:

    I-1.   One student stands at the board between the schoolhouse and house.

I-2. Objects, or pictures of objects, belonging to the student are placed on a table in front of the teacher.

I-3. Each child comes to the table and picks up an object.

I-4. The teacher asks, "Whose [object name] is this?"

I-5. A student responding "The ball is his'n" goes and stands beneath the house. There the response is repeated.

I-6. A student responding "The ball is his" stands beneath the schoolhouse and repeats his response.

II-1. The class is divided into two parts—one-half are schoolhouse, one half are house.

II-2. Students take objects and hand them to the subject at the board.

II-3. Those who say "The ball is you'n" stand under the house.

II-4. Those who say "The ball is yours" stand under the schoolhouse.

III-1. The class is divided into two parts—one-half are schoolhouse, one-half are house.

III-2. Again a student is placed at the board.

III-3. Each child takes an object belonging to the subject.

III-4. Those in the schoolhouse half of the class must produce the object and say "This is his" or "This is yours."

III-5. Those in the house half of the class must produce the object and say "This is his'n" or "This is you'n."

III-6. Everytime this plan is used be sure to alternate those students in the schoolhouse and house groups.

D. Be sure every child has a chance to respond. Those who used everyday talk during one session (particularly in part II) should be asked to use school talk the next time. If a child does not respond with the desired form, remind him to use school talk, do not correct him or label his response *wrong*.

E. Materials:

1. Poster-board schoolhouse and house.

2. Objects belonging to student, such as books, pencils, notebooks, etc.

LESSON 8

A. Structure: *hit/it*.

B. Instructional Objective: The students shall be able to use the standard English pronoun "it" upon demand in "school talk."

I-1. Place schoolhouse and house on the board.

I-2. Show the class pictures of objects and ask, "What is this?"

I-3. Call on those who volunteer. If a child says, "Hit's a ball," let him stand beneath the house and repeat the question and the response.

I-4. If the answer is, "It's a ball," let him stand beneath the school and repeat both the question and the response.

II-1. Place schoolhouse and house on the board.

II-2. Use a game spinner with a picture of a house and a school placed over the numbers.

II-3. Have a child come forward and spin the pointer. If it lands on house, he must respond in everyday talk. If it points to school, he must use school talk.

II-4. Show the child a picture and ask, "What is this?" Place him under the house or school upon response and have him repeat it.

C. After your students have become proficient in utilizing "it" as the subject of a sentence, alter the position of "it" within the sentence (for example, move "it" from subject to object). Try to allow every student in your class to respond.

D. Materials:

1. Poster-board house and schoolhouse.

2. Spinner from game with pictures of house and school pasted over pictures of various single objects.

LESSON 9

A. Sturcture: *them/those*.

B. Instructional Objective: The students shall be able to use the standard English usages of "them" and "those" upon demand in "school talk."

I-1. Place schoolhouse and house on the board.

I-2. Divide the class into four groups.

I-3. Hold up an object that belongs to group one and ask a student in group 2, "Whom does this belong to?"

I-4. If the student says, "It belongs to *them boys*," place him beneath the house, and repeat the question and response.

I-5. Go to group 3 and say, "Who is in group 2?" If the student says, "Those boys are in group 2," place him under the school, and repeat both the question and the response.

II-1. Place house and school on the board.

II-2. Show the class two pictures of objects that are identical except for an obvious difference (e.g., balls with stripes and balls with polka dots).

II-3. Have a student draw a house or a schoolhouse from a box.

II-4. Ask the student, "Which balls have stripes on them?" as you show him the pictures.

II-5. The student must respond according to the house or schoolhouse which he drew and then he should stand under the appropriate heading.

C.   The pictures used in Part I-1–I-5 may be used with Part II-1–II-5 of this lesson. Work with Part I until you believe your students can discriminate between the two language patterns presented before requiring them to respond in a specific manner.

D.   Materials:

1. Poster-board house and schoolhouse.

2. Pictures of groups of objects identical except for some obvious difference.

3. A small box.

4. Small pictures of house and schoolhouse.

LESSON 10

A.   Structure: Verbs, strong preterites.

B.   Instructional Objective: The student shall be able to use the standard English past tense of verbs upon demand in "school talk."

I-1.   Place the schoohouse and house on the board.

I-2.   Preset pictures of present verb action.

I-3.   The teacher, upon presenting the picture, will say, "John is *climbing* the hill."

I-4.   Present picture of past verb action.

I-5.   The teacher, upon presenting the picture, will say, "John made it. Now what did John do?"

I-6.   Teacher will call on a student who should respond, "He *climbed/clum* the hill."

I-7.   Those who respond with school talk will stand underneath the schoolhouse and will repeat both the present and past tenses of the verbs that coincide with the pictures.

I-8. Those who respond with everyday talk will stand beneath the house. They will repeat their responses.

II-1. Place small pictures of house and schoolhouse in a box.

II-2. Each student must come forward and draw when it is his turn.

II-3. Upon drawing, the student will stand under the schoolhouse or the house, whichever corresponds with the card he picked.

II-4. The teacher presents the present and past action cards, and the student responds.

II-5. Those who drew the house must respond in everyday talk. Those who drew the school must respond in school talk.

D. Materials:

1. Poster-board schoolhouse and house.
2. Line drawings, on poster board, of present and past verb action (e.g., is driving, drove; is climbing, climbed; is breaking, broke)
3. Small box.
4. Small drawings of house and school to be drawn from the box.

LESSON 11

A. Structure: Verbs, weak preterites.

B. Instructional Objectives: The student shall be able to use the standard English past tense of verbs upon demand in "school talk."

C. Procedures:

I-1. Place the schoolhouse and house on the board.

I-2. The teacher performs a task saying, "I am drawing the picture."

I-3. The teacher calls on a student and asks, "What did I do?"

I-4. The student responds, "You *drew/drawed* a picture."

I-5. The student stands beneath the heading that corresponds with his response.

I-6. The student then repeats his response.

II-1. Each student draws a house or a schoolhouse from a box.

II-2. The teacher performs a task saying, "I am catching a ball."

II-3. The teacher calls upon the student saying, "What did I do?"

II-4. If the student has drawn a schoolhouse (school language is required), he must answer, "You caught the ball."

II-5. If he or she has drawn the house, the response should be, "You ketched the ball."

II-6. After the child's response the remainder of the class is required to answer the corresponding form not used by the student.

D. Remember to add to your list of verb forms that your children use those which are not presented on the cards. In the more advanced class you may want to have your students conjugate verbs in both everyday and school talk.

E. Materials:
1. Poster-board schoolhouse and house.
2. Objects needed to perform tasks (chalk and slate for drawing, a ball for catching, etc.)
3. A small box.
4. Small drawings of schoolhouse and house to be drawn from the box.

LESSON 12

A. Structure: Double comparative and superlative.

B. Instructional Objective: The students shall be able to use standard English comparatives and superlatives upon demand in "school talk."

I-1. Place the schoolhouse and house on the board.

I-2. Present the first of a three-picture series. (For example, have Goldilocks trying the bears' bowls of porridge with obviously increasing distaste.)

I-3. The teacher shows the first pictures and says, "This porridge tastes bad."

I-4. A student chosen by the teacher repeats the response and is shown the second.

I-5. If the student says, "This porridge tastes *worser*," he stands beneath the house and repeats both responses when the appropriate pictures are displayed.

I-6. This exercise may be performed with all students before the superlative is introduced.

I-7. Introduce the superlative in the same manner as the comparative.

II-1. Place the house and schoolhouse on the board.

II-2. Have the children act out parts of a play (Goldilocks, for example) in both school and everyday talk.

II-3. Have an everyday talk Goldilocks under the house and a school-talk Goldilocks under the schoolhouse.

II-4. Both students will "taste" the first bowl of porridge and make a face. The class will ask, "How does it taste [school talk/everyday talk] Goldilocks?"

II-5. Appropriate Goldilocks will say "It tastes bad." The class will question other students similarly.

II-6. Both Goldilocks taste the second bowl and are asked how it tastes. They should respond appropriately.

II-7. Other fairy tales may be used as themes.

D. You may help your children make a book of fairy tales in which one page is in school talk and the facing page (utilizing the same illustration) is in everyday talk. You might also put on short skits, identical ones except that one utilizes school talk while the other uses everyday talk.

E. Materials:

1. Poster-board house and schoolhouse.

2. Three-picture action series, such as Goldilocks tasting porridge, etc.

3. Play materials needed for acting out fairy tales.

LESSON 13

A. Structure: Prepositions; *a-* is used.

B. Instructional Objective: The students shall be able to use standard English prepositions upon demand in "school talk."

C. Procedures and Activities:

I-1. The house and schoolhouse are placed on the board.

I-2. Pictures are presented to the class (e.g., a man going to do something or going somewhere, people giving each other things, etc.).

I-3. Students volunteer as the teacher asks, "What's happening in this picture?" If the desired responses (those containing forms of "going" or "giving," for example) cannot be obtained, the teacher may ask, "Where are they going?" etc.

I-4. Upon a student's response, the teacher places it under the appropriate heading ("a-going" or "a-giving" under house and "going" or "giving" under school) and asks the student to repeat it.

II-1. The teacher presents the pictures and asks, "Who can describe the picture using everyday/school talk?

II-2. If there are no volunteers the teacher may call on a child to give the appropriate response.

II-3. Never say a response is wrong. The teacher should say, "Sue, we wanted you to use school talk instead of everyday talk [or vice versa]. Give us the school talk that means the same as He's a-going to town."

D. Be sure and collect lists of other similar forms your students might use such as "a-riding," "a-walking," etc. You can do this by presenting pictures of such action and asking for descriptions of the action. If several students use a form, list it.

E. Materials:

1. Poster-board house and schoolhouse.
2. Pictures of people in action, such as going to town, or giving each other objects.

LESSON 14

A. Structure: Agreement of subject and verb.

B. Instructional Objective: The students shall be able to produce standard English agreement between nouns and verbs upon demand in "school talk."

C. Procedures and Activities:

I-1. Place schoolhouse and house on the board.

I-2. Present action pictures found in textbooks, coloring books, or other sources found in the classroom.

I-3. A student comes forward, and the teacher asks, "What is he doing?"

I-4. If a child responds "He go/going to town," he stands beneath the house.

I-5. If a student responds, "He is going to town," he stands under the schoolhouse.

I-6. As each student stands beneath the appropriate heading (house or school), he repeats his response.

I-7. Upon repetition of the response the teacher asks for another student to give the equivalency of that response in the corresponding dialect.

II-1. Divide the class into two halves.

II-2. Tell both groups that they are to respond with school talk.

II-3. Each time a student in a group responds to an action picture with school talk, he moves to the back of his group, and lets the next child in line try.

II-4. When a child responds with everyday talk, he goes and stands under the picture of the house and his team loses its turn.

II-5. When the "turn" has returned to his team, the next child must use school talk properly to get the child out of the house and into the school.

II-6. The child who used everyday talk must repeat the school-talk response before he can return to his group.

II-7. Use this activity and require only everday-talk responses. In this exercise a school-talk response would result in a team losing its turn and a child standing under the school.

D. Do not worry if some children who did not use everyday talk begin to use some everyday talk constructions. This is merely reciprocal learning, and we expect the standard English speaker to learn the Appalachian dialect just as we expect the Appalchian speaker to learn standard English. Just remind your students to use "school talk" at school.

E. Materials:

1. Poster-board house and schoolhouse.

2. Action pictures from books or materials that the teacher already possesses.

Appendix F:
A Reference List for
Teachers of English

RELEVANT REFERENCES FOR THE TEACHER OF ENGLISH

Toward a Theory of Language

*Baker, R. J. The linguistic theory of usage. *Journal of the Canadian* Linguistic Association, 1961, *6*, 209–212.

*Bloomfield, L. Secondary and tertiary responses to language. *Language*, 1944, *20*, 45–55.

Brooks, C. Telling it like it is in the tower of babel. *SR*, 1971, *79*, 136–155.

Bush, D. Polluting our language. *AMSCH*, 1972, *41*, 238–247.

*Dykema, K. W. Where our grammar came from. *CE*, 1961, *22*, 455–465.

Eskey, D. E. The case for standard language. *CE*, 1974, *35*, 769–774.

Evans, B. Grammar for today. *Atlantic Monthly*, 1960, *205*, 79–82.

Follett, W. Grammar is obsolete. *Atlantic Monthly*, 1960, *205*, 73–76.

Funkhaser, J. L. A various standard. *CE*, 1973, *34*, 806–827.

Goodman, K. Language differences and the ethno-centric researcher. *ERIC* Document, Ed 030107.

*Hill, A. A. Prescriptivism and linguistics in English teaching. *CE*, 1954, *15*, 395–399.

---

*Reprinted in H. B. Allen, *Readings in applied English linguistics* (2nd ed.). New York: Appleton-Century-Crofts, 1964.

Hill, T. Institutional linguistics. *Orbis*, 1958, *7*, 448–449.

Hill, A. W. Introduction to linguistic structure. New York: Harcourt Brace Jovanovich, 1958.

Hoffman, M. J. Bidialectalism is not the linguistics of white supremacy. *The English Record*, 1971, *21*, 99.

Joos, M. *The five clocks*. New York: Harcourt Brace Jovanovich, 1967.

*Kenyon, J. S. Cultrual levels and functional varieties of English. *CE*, 1948, *9*, 31–36.

Krutch, J. W. Who says its English? *Saturday Review of Literature*, 1967, *50*, 19–21.

*Malmstrom, J. Linguistic atlas findings versus textbook pronouncements on current American usage. *EJ*, 1959, *48*, 191–198.

McDavid, R. I. Historical, regional and social variation. In A. L. Davis (Ed.), Culture, class and language variety. Champaign, Ill.: National Council of Teachers of English, 1969.

*McMillan, J. B. A philosophy of language. *College English*, 1948, *9*, 385–390.

Pixton, W. H. Response to CCCC executive committee's resolution 'the students' right to his own language.' *College Composition and Communication*, 1972, *23*, 298–300.

Sledd, J. H. On not teaching English usage. *English Journal*, 1965, *54*, 698–703.

Sledd, J. H. After bidialectism, what? *English Journal*, 1973, *62*, 774–778.

Sledd, J. H. Bi-dialectalism: The linguistics of white supremacy. *English Journal*, 1969, *58*, 1307–1315.

Sledd, J. H. Doublespeak: Dialectology in the service of big brother. *College English*, 1972, *33*, 439–456.

Smitherman, G. English teacher, why you be doing the things you don't do?. *English Journal*, 1972(A), *61*, 59–65.

Smitherman, G. "God don't never change," black English from a black perspective. *College English*, 1972(b), *33*, 828–833.

Smitherman, G. Grammar and goodness. *English Journal*, 1973, *62*, 774–778.

Students' right to their own language. College Composition and Communication Special Issue. 1974, *25*.

Taylor, M. U. The folklore of usage. *College English*, 1974, *35*, 756–768.

Williams, C. *On the Contribution of the Linguist to Institutional Racism. ERIC* Document, ED 039511, 1969.

*Womack, T. Teachers' attitudes toward current usage. *English Journal*, 1959, *48*, 186–190.

Reference Works

Francis, W. N. *The structure of American English*. New York: Ronald, 1958.

Fries, C. C. *American English grammar*. New York: Appleton-Century-Crofts, 1940.

Jespersen, O. *Essentials of English grammar*. University, Ala.: University of Alabama Press, 1969
Kurath, H. & McDavid, R. I. *The pronunciation of English in the Atlantic states*. Ann Arobor: Univ. of Michigan Press, 1961.
Leonard, S. A. *Current English usage*. Champaign, Ill.: N.C.T.E., 1932.
Marckwardt, A. A. & Walcott, F. G. *Facts about current English usage*. Champaign, Ill.: National Council Teachers of English, 1938.
Oxford English Dictionary. Oxford, Eng.: Clarendon, 1933.

Historical Studies

Algeo, J. *Problems in the origins and development of the English language* (2nd ed.). New York: Harcourt Brace Jovanovich, 1972.
Greenough, J. B. & Kittridge, G. L. *Words and their ways in English speech*. New York: Macmillan, 1924.
Krapp, G. P. *The English language in America* (Vols. 1, 2). New York: Century, 1925.
Laird, C. *Language in America*. New York: Harcourt Brace Jovanovich, 1970.
Mencken, H. L. *The American Language* (4th ed.). New York: Knoff, 1941.
Pyles, T. *Words and ways of American speech*. New York: Random House, 1952.

Black English

Burling, R. *English in black and white*. New York: Holt, Rinehart and Winston, 1973.
Kochman, T. "Rapping" in the black ghetto. In C. Laird & R.M. Gorrell (Eds.), *Reading about language*. New York: Harcourt Brace Jovanovich, 1971.
Labov, W. *The social stratification of English in New York City*. Arlington, Va.: Center for Applied Linguistics, 1966.
Labov, W. *Language in the inner city: Studies in the black English vernacular*. Philadelphia: University of Pennsylvania Press, 1972.
Labov, W. Some features of the English of black Americans. In R. W. Bailey & J. L. Robinson (Eds.), *Varieties of present-day English*. New York: Macmillan, 1973.
Taylor, O. L. *An introduction to the historical development of black English: Some implications for American education*. ERIC Document ED 35863, 1969.
Wolfram, W. Some illustrative features of black English. *ERIC* Document ED 045957, 1970.

Sociolinguistics

Card, W. & McDavid, V. G. Problem areas in grammar. In A. L. Davis (ed.), *Culture, class and language variety*. Champaign, Ill.: National Council Teachers of English, 1969.

Davis, A. L. Culture, class and the disadvantaged. In A. L. Davis (Ed.), *Culture, class and language variety*. Champaign, Ill.: National Council Teachers of English, 1969.

Fasold, R. W. & Shuy, R. W. *Teaching standard English in the inner city*. Arlington, Va.: Center for Applied Linguistics, 1970.

*Fischer, J. L. Social influences on the choice of a linguistics variant. *Word*, 1958, *14*, 47–56.

McDavid, R. I. A checklist of significant features for discriminating social dialects. In A. L. Davis (Ed.), *Culture, class and language variety*. Champaign, Ill.: National Council Teachers of English, 1969.

McDavid, R. I. Go slow in ethnic attributions: Geographic mobility and dialect prejudices. In R. W. Bailey and J. L. Robinson (Eds.), *Varieties and present-day English*. New York: Macmillan, 1973.

*McDavid, R. I. Some social differences in pronunciation. *Language Learning*, 1957, *4*, 102–116.

Shuy, R. W. *Social dialects and language learning*. National Council Teachers of English, 1964.

Shuy, R. W. Language and Success. In R. W. Bailey & J. L. Robinson (Eds.), *Varieties of present-day English*. New York: Macmillan, 1973.

Tucker, G. R. & Lambert, W. E. White and Negro listener's reactions to various American-English dialects. *Social Forces*, 1969, *47*, 463–468.

Williams, F. (Ed.). *Language and poverty: Perspectives on a theme*. Chicago: Rand McNally, 1970.

Wolfram, W. *Sociolinguistic premises and the nature of nonstandard dialects*. *ERIC* Document ED 033370, 1969.

Wolfram, W. & Fasold, R. W. *The study of social dialects in American English*. Englewood Cliffs, N.J.: Prentice-Hall, 1974.

Nonverbal Communication

Austin, W. M. Nonverbal communicationl In A. L. Davis (Ed.), *Culture, Class and Language variety*. Champaign, Ill.: National Council Teachers of English, 1969(a).

Austin, W. M. The suprasegmental phonemes of English. In A. L. Davis (Ed.), *Culture, class and language variety*. Champaign, Ill.: National Council Teachers of English, 1969 (b).

Duke, C. R. *Nonverbal behavior and the communication process*. *ERIC* Document ED 088090, 1972.

Tarone, E. *Aspects of intonation in black English*. *ERIC* Document ED076983, 1972.

Dialect Differences and the Teacher of Composition

Bailey, R. W. Write off vs. write on, dialects and the teacher of composition. In R. W. Bailey & J. L. Robinson (Eds.), *Varieties of present-day English*. New York: Macmillan, 1973.

Bentley, R. H. On Black dialects, white linguistics and the teaching of English. In C. Laird & R. M. Gorrell (Eds.), *Reading about language*. New York: Harcourt Brace and Jovanovich, 1971.

Crystal, D. Dialect mixture and sorting out the concept of freshman English remediations. *Florida Foriegn Language Reporter*, 1972, *10*, 1–2, 43–46.

Feigenbaun, I. The use of nonstandard English in teaching standard contrast and comparison. In R. W. Fasold and R. W. Shuy (Eds.), *Teaching standard English in the inner city*. Arlington, Va.: Center for Applied Linguistics, 1970.

*Higgins, L. V. Approaching usage in the classroom. *English Journal*, 1960, *49*, 181–185.

*Hill, A. A. Correctness and style in English Composition. *College English*, 1951, *12*, 280–285.

Ires, S. Linguistics in the classroom. *College English*, 1955, *17*, 165–172.

Isenberger, J. & Smith, V. How would you feel if you had to change your dialect? *English Journal*, 1973, *62*, 994–997.

Morse, J. M. *The irrelevant English teacher*. Philadelphia: Temple University Press, 1972.

*Pooley, R. C. Dare schools set a standard in English usage. *English Journal*, 1960, *49*, 176–181.

Stewart, W. A. Foreign language methods in quasi-foreign language situations. In R. W. Fasold & R. W. Shuy (Eds.), *Teaching standard English in the city*. Arlington, Va.: Center for Applied Linguistics, 1970.

Wolfram, W. The role of dialect interference in composition. *ERIC* Document ED 045971, 1971.

Wolfram, W. & Fasold, R. W. A black English translation of John 31–21. *ERIC* Document, ED 025741, 1968.

Appendix G:
A Linguistic Description of
Social Dialects*

In this Appendix, we shall present an abbreviated inventory of some of the descriptive characteristics of several different nonstandard dialects of American English. We have opted to present these in terms of an inventory of features rather than a lengthy discursive account. This means that many of the finer details have been omitted. More elaborate accounts of these features can be found in Labov (1972), Wolfram and Fasold (1974), and Wolfram and Christian (1976).

The following description of various nonstandard American dialects clearly demonstrates their systematic nature. Like all languages, these dialects are governed by regular pronunciation and grammatical rules. In short, what is distinctive about nonstandard dialects is that they are held in low esteem by the speakers of standard dialects and usually by their speakers as well. Nonstandard dialects are not any less a language or any

*The material in this appendix was prepared by Ronald Williams, of the Federal City College (Washington, D.C.), and Walt Wolfram, of the Federal City College and the Center for Applied Linguistics (Arlington, Virginia), for the Committee on Communication Problems in the Urban and Ethnic Populations, the American Speech and Hearing Association (ASHA), in 1974 and then revised in June 1976. A major portion of it was published in 1977 by ASHA as *Social Dialects: Differences in Disorders*. It is reprinted here by permission of the authors and ASHA.

less capable of performing all of the tasks of a language than a standard dialect. It is important to note that many of these features occur variably. That is, a particular dialect may be characterized by the frequency with which certain variants occur rather than their categorical occurrence.

Within the broad category of nonstandard dialects, there are variations which are regional and ethnic. The following code is used here to designate some major varieties of nonstandard dialects and to indicate in which of these dialects certain features are most often found:

NS   Used in all nonstandard varieties of American English, including Northern White, Southern White, Appalachian English, and Black English.

SWNS   Southern White Nonstandard

S   Southern White Standard (possibly considered nonstandard in some Northern contexts).

BE   Black English

AE   Appalachian English

PRONUNCIATION

Consonant Cluster Reduction

(BE/some SWNS)   1. Word-final consonant clusters ending in a stop can be reduced when both members belong to a base word: *tes'* (test), *des'* (desk), *han'* (hand), and *buil'* (build).

Reduction also occurs when grammatical suffix *-ed* is added to produce such words as *rubbed, rained, messed, looked*. Reduced: *rub', rain', mess'*, and *look'*.

When both members of a cluster are either voiced or voiceless, then the rule operates (as above), but when one member is voiced and the other voiceless (e.g., *jump, rent, belt, gulp*, etc.), the rule does not operate.

In standard English (SE), final member of a cluster may be absent if following word begins with a consonant *(bes' kind, tol' Jim, col' cuts*, and *fas' back* are acceptable in SE).

(BE/some SWNS)	Reduction takes place when consonant cluster is followed by a vowel or a pause as well as a consonant: *wes' en'* (west end), *bes' apple* (best apple). The type of clusters affected by this rule are given in Table F–1 at the end of this Appendix.
(BE/some SWNS)	2. *Plural Formations:* words ending in *-sp, -st,* and *-sk,* add the *-es,* instead of *-s* plural. Plural formations follow consonant reduction rule in which words such as *desk, test, ghost,* and *wasp* become *desses, tesses, ghosses,* and *wasses.*
(AE/some BE)	Words ending in *-sp, -st,* and *-sk* add the *-es* plural while retaining the cluster intact, giving *deskes, testes, ghostes,* and *waspes.*
(BE)	3. *Underlying Structure of Consonant Cluster:* clusters present in *testing, scolding, tester, coldest.* When suffix begins with vowel the cluster is present. Some dialects having *tessing, scolling,* etc., may not have underlying cluster.

The *th* Sounds

(NS)	1. *Word intial: d/th* as in *dey* for *they, t/th* as in *taught* for *thought* (Special kind of *t*-unaspirated, lenis).
(BE)	2. *Within a word: f/th* as in *nofin* for *nothing, aufuh* for *author*.
(some BE dialects)	*v/th* as in *bruvah* for *brother, ravah* for *rather, bavin* for *bathing*.
(NS)	*th* contiguous to a nasal is produced as *at,* as in *arithmetic* ('ritmetic), *monthly* (montly), *nothing* (not'n).
(NS)	*d/th* as in *oder* for *other, bruder* for *brother*.
(SWNS/AE/BE)	3. *Voiced fricatives before nasals: th, z, v* become stops before a nasal as in *idn't* for *isn't, sebm* for *seven*.
(some BE/SWNS)	4. *Word final: f/th* predominant production as in *Ruf* (Ruth), *toof* (Tooth), and *souf* (South).

(BE)   *t/th* occasionally (mostly in Southern BE) as in
                                        sout' for *south.*

The r and l

(S)   1. *After a vowel:* The *l* becomes *uh,* as in *steal*
                           (steauh), *sister* (sistuh).

(S)   2. *Preceding a consonant:* the *r* and *l* are absent,
                           as in *help* (hep), *guard* (gua'd). Typically, *l* is
                           completely absent before labial consonants.

(SWNS/BE)   In some areas of the South *r* absent following *o*
                           and *u* with a change in the vowel as well, *four*
                           (foe), *door* (doe).

(SWNS/BE)   3. *Between vowels:* The *r* or *l* may be absent
                           between vowels *(Ca'ol, sto'y,* or *Ma'y,* for
                           Carol, story or *Mary).*

(BE)   4. *Effect on vocabulary and grammar:* Consistent
                           loss of *r* at end of word has caused merging of
                           two words. The change caused by the absence
                           of *r* in *they* and *their* or in *you* and *your* brings
                           them phonetically closer together, producing *It
                           is they book* or *It is you book.*

(BE/SWNS)   Loss of *l* may affect contrasted forms, such as
                           in future modal *will. Tomorrow I bring the
                           thing* for *Tomorrow I'll bring the thing.* This
                           pronunciation may account for the use of *be* to
                           indicate future time. *He be here in a few
                           minutes.* This typically takes place when the
                           following word begins with *b, m,* or *w* (labial
                           sounds).

(SWNS/BE)   5. *r following a consonant:* The *r* may be absent
                           when it follows a consonant in unstressed
                           syllables, giving *p'otect* for *protect* or *p'ofessor*
                           or when following vowel is either an *o* or *u,*
                           giving *th'ow* for *throw* and *th'ough* for *through.*

                        6. *Social stigma:* Absence of *r* and *l* not as socially

stigmatized as other nonstandard pronunciation rules because certain types of *r* and *l* absences are standard for some standard Southern and Northern dialects.

Final b, d, and g

(BE/ some AE)

1. *Devoicing:* At end of syllable voiced stops, , *d,* and *g* are pronounced as the corresponding voiceless stops *p, t,* and *k.* This does not mean that *pig* and *pick, bud* and *butt,* and *cab* and *cap* sound alike in BE, for they are still distinguished by length of vowel. English vowels are held slightly longer when following sound is voiced. For example the *u* in *bud* is held longer than the *u* in *butt,* although the *d* in *bud* is pronounced as a *t.*

   In unstressed syllables rule can operate for all nonstandard dialects, as in *stupit* for *stupid* or *salat* for *salad.*

(BE)

2. *Deletion of d:* In some varieties of BE *d* is absent more frequently when followed by a consonant, such as *ba' man, goo' soldier,* etc. The addition of an *-s* (Realized phonetically as *z)* suffix produces *kiz* for *kids* for *boahz* for *boards.*

(NS)

3. Glottal for *t, d* before syllabic *l* or *n.* This results in pronunciations of *couldn't* something like *coutn* and *bottle* with a glottal for the *tt.*

Nasalization

(NS)

1. *The* -ing *suffix:* The use of *-in'* for *-ing,* such as in *singin', buyin',* and *runnin'* is a feature characteristic of American English. It occurs when the *-ing* is in an unstressed syllable.

(BE)

2. *Nasalized vowels:* A nasalized vowel instead of nasal consonant is most often found at end of syllable, for example, final consonant is

dropped in *man, bun,* and *run.* The final vowel is then nasalized giving *ma', bu',* and *ru'.* This usually found in unstressed syllables, e.g., *mailman.*

(S)   3. *The influence of nasals on* i *and* e: Before a nasal consonant *i* and *e* do not contrast, making words such as *pin* and *pen* or *tin* and *ten* sound identical.

(NS)   4. *Articles:* The differnce between *a* and *an* is neutralized so that *a* occurs before words beginning with vowels as well as consonants, e.g., *a apple, a orange, a pear.*

Unstressed Initial Syllables

In casual spoken SE, initial unstressed syllables of prepositions and adverbs may be deleted, giving *'bout* for *about* or *'cause* for *because.* This tends to be more frequent when preceding word ends in a vowel as opposed to a consonant, so that items like *go 'bout* are more frequent than *went 'bout.*

Final Unstressed ow

(AE)   In word-final position, the *ow* of SE may be produced as *er,* giving *holler* for *hollow, swaller* for *swallow,* or *winder* for *window.* It may also occur when the plural *-s* is added, giving *potatoes* for *'taters* or *winders* for *windows.*

ire Sequences

(AE)   In many varieties of SE, *ire* sequences are pronounced as two syllables, so that *fire* or *tire* is pronounced something like *fayer* or *tayer.* This may be reduced to one syllable which includes the reduction of a glide. Items like *tire* and *fire* may therefore be pronounced much *tar* and *far.*

Other

(BE/SWNS)	*Str-* words *(string, street)* may become *skr-* words *(skring, skreet).*
(BE)	*Ask* may be pronounced *aks,* retaining an earlier English pronunciation.

GRAMMAR

Verbs

Past forms

(BE)

1. *Regular:* The *-ed* suffixes which mark past tense, past participial forms, and derived adjectives are not pronounced because of consonant reduction rule, where *finished, cashed, forged, cracked,* and *named* are pronounced in SE as *finisht, cast, forgd, crackt,* and *namd* and in BE as *finish, cash, forge, crack,* and *name.*

Irregular verbs

(NS)

1. *Regularized forms:* Some verbs with irregular past forms can instead have the regular past tense suffix, *-ed,* added, such as *knowed* for *knew, heared* for *heard, drinked* for *drank.*

2. *Uninflected forms:* Some verbs can have the past tense forms represented by the same form found for the present, giving *come* for *came, run* for *ran, begin* for *begun.*

3. *Different irregular forms:* A small set of verbs have irregular past forms that are different from the SE ones, such as *brung* for *brought, hearn* for *heard* in AE.

4. *Past participle for simple past:* For some verbs which have two different past forms in SE, the

past participle form can be used for the simple
past, such as *seen* for *saw, done* for *did, drunk*
for *drank.*

Perfective constructions

1. *General:* The perfective constructions in NS
and SE:

	NS	SE
Present	I have walked.	I have walked.
Perfect	I('ve) walked.	I've walked.
Past	I had walked.	I had walked.
Perfect		I'd walked.
Completive	I done walked. (SWNS/BE)	
Remote Time	I been walked. (BE)	

2. *Omission of forms of have:* in SE present tense
forms of auxiliary *have* can be contracted to *'ve*
and *'s:*

SE	NS
I've been here for hours.	I been here for hours.
He's gone home.	He gone home.

(BE/SWNS/AE)   3. *Completive aspects with done: done* plus a past
form *I done tried.* This form denotes an action
started and completed at a specific time in the
past.

(BE)   4. *Remote time construction with been: been*
construction indicates speaker thinks of action
having taken place in the distant past. Unlike
done, the *been* construction is used solely in
BE.

*I been had it there for about three years. You
won't get your dues that you been paid.*

Third-person singular
Present tense marker

1. *General:* The suffix *-s* (or *-es)* is used to mark the third person singular in the present tense:

Singular	Plural
I walk	we walk
you walk	you walk
he walks,	they walk,
the man walks	the men walk

(BE)   The *-s* suffix is absent; it is not part of the grammar; *he walk, the man walk, they walk, the men walk.*

(NS)   2. The verb *do* used as an auxiliary in negative constructions. *He doesn't go* becomes *He don't go.*

(BE)   3. *Have and do: d-person forms (has* and *does)* are absent, giving *He have a bike* and *He always do silly things.*

(BE)   4. *Hypercorrect forms:* The absence of *-s* suffix in BE may cause hypercorrection when BE speakers come into contact with SE. BE speakers observe presence of *-s* suffix in some present tense verbs. Unfamiliar with the restriction of *-s* suffix to third-person singular forms, the speaker uses the feature as a foreign language learner might by marking first, second, third-person forms both singular and plural and the *-s* suffix.

This accounts for sentences such as *I walks, You walks,* and *The children walks.* The *-s* suffix then is an importation of a dialectal feature and overgeneralized to the grammar of the dialect from which it was borrowed.

Future

(SWNS/BE)

1. *Gonna: gonna,* as in other dialects, is a future indicator. *Is* and *are* are frequently deleted when *gonna* is used. *He gonna go. You gonna get into trouble.*

(BE)

SE produces a reduction of *gonna: ngna* as in *I' nga go.* In BE and some SWNS reductions not observed in SE are found: *mana* as in *I' mana go, mon* as in *I' mon go,* and *ma* as in *I' ma go.*

(NS)

2. *Will: will* is used to indicate future time in SE and NS. *Will* can be contracted to *'ll.* This contracted form may be eliminated, especially if the following word begins with a labial consonant (particularly BE). *He miss you tomorrow* for *He' ll miss your tomorrow.* Sometimes it appears that the future is indicated by main verb alone.

Invariant be

1. *General:* The verb *to be* appears in SE in one of the three variant forms *is, are,* or *am.* In BE the form *be* can be used as a main verb *(I be here in the evening* and *Sometime he be busy).*

   The use of invariant *be* in BE has two explanations.

2. *Will be or would be: be* begins with a labial consonant making it likely that *'ll* before *be* will be absent. Application of this rule is fairly common in BE and occurs sometimes in SE, giving sentences like *He be here pretty soon* and *They be gone by evening.*

   The contracted from of *would* is *'d* which can merge with the *b* of *be* or be removed by the final elimination rule. A sentence such as *If you gave him a present, he be happy* is possible both in SE and BE.

(BE)

3. *Distributive or nontense be:* The other source of invariant *be* is possible in BE without tense specification and seems to describe "an object or an event distributed intermittently in time". To say "I'm good" is to assert a permanent quality, while *I be good* means that the speaker is good sometimes. This form of invariant *be* is quite socially stigmatized.

A-*verb*-ing

(AE/some SWNS)

An *a-* can be prefixed to a following verb which has an -*ing* participial form. These verb forms may function as progressives as in *I knew he was a-tellin' the truth* or as certain types of adverbials, as in *I went down there a-huntin' for them, He just kep a-beggin, He woke up a-screamin'*.

These forms do not occur when the form functions as a noun or adjective, as in *The movie was shockin'* or *Laughin' is good for you.* The -*a* prefix is also restricted from occurring with a word beginning with an unstressed syllable or one that begins with a vowel, so that we do not get it on items like *discoverin'* or *askin'*.

Absence of forms to be

1. *General:* When contracted forms of the copula *is* and *are* forms are expected in SE, some nonstandard dialects may delete. When the subject is *I*, the SE form *am* or its contraction '*m* is almost always used.

(BE)

2. *Is: Is* may be absent before *gonna* in some Southern dialects, but in BE *is* may be absent whenever it can be contracted in SE, as in *He a man, He bad,* and *He running to school. Is* and *are* are present in grammar of speakers of BE as evidence in exposed clause *(I know he is)* and in tag question *(He is not home, is he?)*.

(SWNS/BE)   3. *Are:* In all nonstandard dialects of English in
                   which copula absence is found, *are* is used less
                   often than *is.* English contraction rule removes
                   all but final consonant of certain auxiliaries *(are*
                   to *'re, will* to *'ll,* and *have* to *'ve). Are* has no
                   final consonant, i.e., it is pronounced *ah.*
                   Regular pronunciation rules reduce *ah* to *uh.*
                   Contraction rule eliminates *are,* and there is no
                   need to use BE rules. Thus, there are speakers
                   who have *are* absence but not *is* absence. (i.e.,
                   You good for *you're good* or *They're good).*

Copula verb concord

(NS)   *They was there. You was there.* Some speakers do
                   not show person number agreement with *be.* This
                   pertains to both past *(You was there)* and present
                   forms of *to be.* It's use with past tense forms (e.g.,
                   You was there) is much more frequent than with
                   nonpast forms *(They is here).*

Double modals

(SWNS/BE/some AE) Certain modals may co-occur within the same verb
                   phrase, giving forms such as *might could, might
                   should, used couldn't,* and so forth.

                   There is also a different subset of items which
                   accompany a past form of the verb, such as *liketa*
                   or *supposeta* as in *It liketa scared me to death* or *It
                   was supposeta been here. Liketa* indicates that the
                   activity in the sentence came close to happening
                   but didn't. *Supposeta* (or *'posta)* is closely related
                   to its SE counterpart, *(be) supposed to have.*

Adverbs

Comparatives and superlatives

(NS)   The *-er* and *-est* suffixes may be extended to words
                   of two or more syllables that end in a consonant
                   where the standard pattern uses the adverbs *more*
                   and *most (awfulest, beautifulest).* In some cases

the comparative adverb and the suffix are both used, as in *more older, most stupidest*. There is also a regularization of some of the irregular comparatives, where the suffix is added to the base word or to the irregular form, as in *baddest, worser, mostest*.

Intensifying adverbs

(SWNS/AE/BE) The intensifier *right* can be used in a wider set of contexts than it can in its standard distribution. These include before adjectives *(right large, right amusing)*, with an expanded group of adverbs *(right loud, right quick)* and in construction with *smart (a right smart while)*. Another intensifier, *plumb*, occurs with adverbs, verbs, and some adjectives and refers to completness *(burn plumb down, scare you plumb to death, plumb foolish)*.

-ly Absence

(NS) For some of the adverbs which require the *-ly* suffix according to the standard pattern, the suffix may be optional, giving *original* for *originally*, *terrible* for *terribly, sincere* for *sincerely*. It is usually more extensive in nonstandard dialects of Southern origin, particularly AE.

Negation

(NS) 1. *The use of ain't for have/has and am/are/is:* A series of phonetic changes in the history of English produced *ain't* for the negative forms of *is, are, am* and auxiliary *have* and *has*, e.g., *I ain't gonna do it* or *He ain't done it*.

(BE) 2. In some varieties of BE *ain't* corresponds to SE *didn't* as in *He ain't go home*.

Multiple negation

(NS) 1. *Negative concord: He didn't do anything.* Negative is attached to main verb and all indefinites following the main verb (e.g. *He didn't do nothing*).

(SWNS/BE)

2. *Preposed negative auxiliary: Couldn't nobody do it.* A sentence with indefinite noun phrase having a negative marker before the main verb may have a negativized form of the verbal auxiliary placed at the beginning of the sentence, such as *can't, wasn't* and *didn't*.

(BE)

3. *Negative auxiliary: Nobody didn't do it.* The negative marker is placed in the noun phrase with the indefinite element, providing the NP comes before the main verb. In BE, both this rule and one which attaches a negative marker to the main verb are used.

(NS)

4. *With negative adverbs: He never hardly does it.* The adverb is used to express negation in addition to negative placement on another adverb, an auxiliary or a negativized indefinite (e.g., *He never hardly does it, He don't hardly do it,* and *Hardly nobody is good*).

(BE/some SWNS)

5. *Negative concord across clause boundaries.* Occasionally, negative concord takes place across clauses. This results in sentences like *There wasn't much I couldn't do* with the meaning "There wasn't much I *could* do" or *Ain't no cat can't get in no coop* meaning that "no cat can get into any coop."

Possessive Construction

(BE)

1. *With common nouns:* Where *'s* possessive is found in SE, BE indicates possessives by the order of words. *The boy's hat* becomes *The boy hat*. BE speakers in Northern urban areas alternate between *'s* and its absence.

2. *With personal names: 's* is used with first name in compound noun forms as in *John's Dawson Car*. This is an example of hypercorrection, resulting from some familiarity with the need to

add possessive -*s* without knowledge of the SE rules for its placement in compound nouns.

(AE)   3. When a possessive pronoun does not modify a following noun phrase, -*n* may be added to it, resulting in forms like *your' n, his' n,* and *our' n.* This form tends to be more characteristic of older speakers.

Plural Suffix

(BE)   1. *Absence of the plural suffix:* Plural suffixes of SE *(-s* or *-es)* are occasionally absent in BE. This results in *He took five book* and *The other teacher, they' ll yell at you.* Most speakers of BE have the predominant use of plural markers in their grammar.

(SWNS/AE)   For nouns that refer to weights and measures, the plural suffix may be absent. Most typically, this occurs when the noun is preceded by a numeral as in *two pound, three foot, twenty year ago.*

(SWNS/BE)   2. *Regular plurals and irregular nouns:* Some nouns in SE form plurals by vowel change, *one foot, two feet,* or with no suffix at all *(one deer, two deer).* For some speakers, these nouns take the regular -*s* suffix *(two foots, two deers).*

Pronominal Apposition

(NS)   Pronominal apposition is the construction in which a pronoun is used in apposition to the noun subject of the sentence, as in *My brother, he bigger than you* or *That teacher, she yell at the kids all the time.*

Relative Clauses

(BE/SWNS/AE)   1. *Relative pronoun deletion:* In most SE dialects a relative pronoun is obligatory if the relative pronoun represents the subject of the subordinate clause. In some NS dialects this relative can be deleted, giving sentences like *That's the dog bit me* or *There's a man comes down the road* for "That's the dog *that* bit me" and "There's a man *who* comes down the road" respectively.

(NS)

2. *Associative use of* which: In SE *which* is generally used to replace nonanimate nouns. In some NS dialects (and also some SE ones) *which* can be used without this antecedent, appearing to be used as a type of associative or conjunction. This is found in sentences like *He gave me this cigar which he knows I don't smoke cigars* or *His daughter is marrying Robert Jenks which he doesn't approve of her marrying a divorced man.*

(NS)

3. *Other relative pronoun forms:* There are speakers of nonstandard English who use forms other than *who, whom, which* and *that* as relative pronouns. These speakers seem largely to be of White rural varieties of English. Examples appear in *A car what runs is good to have* and *There's those as can do it.*

Questions

In SE direct questions the auxiliary is moved to the beginning of the sentence. Thus, *He was walking to the store* becomes *Was he walking to the store* or *He was going somewhere* is *Where was he going?* In an indirect sentence such as *I wonder if he was walking* or *I wonder where he was going,* the forward movement does not occur, and the conjunction *if* or *whether* may be introduced in yes/no questions.

(SWNS/AE/BE)

The same pattern used in the direct question may apply to the indirect question in some dialects, giving *I wonder was he walking* or *I wonder where was he going.* The conjunction *if* introducing indirect yes/no question is eliminated in this process since the question form can be derived from the question word order.

Existential *it*

(SWNS/BE)   *It* is used in place of the standard English *there,* which serves as existential or expletive function as in *It's a store on the corner* or *Is it a show in town?*

(AE/some SWNS)   *They* may also be used as a correspondece for SE *there,* in sentences such as *If they's a lotta wooly worms, it'll be a bad winter* or *They's cooperheads around here.*

Demonstratives

(NS)   1. Them *for* those: Sentences like *I want some of them candies* use the demonstrative *them* where SE would have *those.*

     2. *Use of* here *and* there *as demonstratives:* here and *there* may be added to the demonstratives *these* and *them* to produce sentences like *I like these here pants better than them there ones.*

Pronouns

(BE)   1. *Nominative/objective neutralization:* Occasionally, the forms used in SE as objectives may be used as subjects, as in *Him ain't playing.* This is mostly found to be strictly age-graded so that it is typically found only among preadolescents.

(NS)   2. *Coordinate nominative/objective neutralization:* In coordinate subject noun phrases objective forms are much more common in all nonstandard varieties, giving *Me and her will do it* or *Him and me work together.*

(BE)   3. *Nonpossessive case for possessives:*

Occasionally, nominative of objective case of personal pronouns may be used, giving *James got him book* or *She want she mother*.

(NS)

4. *Absolute possessive forms:* In SE the absolute possessive form of personal pronouns patterns according to the following paradigm:

Singular	*Plural*
mine	ours
yours	yours
his, hers, its	theirs

Except for *mine*, all the forms end in *s*. Some NS dialects regularize the pattern by adding *-s* to *mine* as well, giving *mines*.

(NS)

5. *Reflexives:* The form *-self* may be added to all personal pronouns. The possessive form used in reflexives for first and second persons *(myself, yourself)* can be extended to the third person, resulting in *hisself* and *theirself*.

(S)

6. *Personal Dative:* It is possible to use a nonreflexive pronoun when a direct object is also present, as in *I cut me a limb off a tree* or *I shot me a pheasant*. It is typically restricted to subjects in its reference.

7. *Plural forms of* you: In SE *you* is used for both the singular and plural second-person pronoun. In many varieties of Southern origin, the plural form is differentiated as *y' all*. Other varieties may differentiate plural by different forms, such as *youse* as in *Youse mad at each other* or *you' uns* as found in some rural dialects.

Table 1

Consonant Clusters in which the Final Member of the
Cluster May be Absent

Phonetic Cluster	Examples* Type I	Type II
[st]	test, post, list	missed, messed, dressed
[sp]	wasp, clasp, grasp	
[sk]	desk, risk, mask	
[t]		finished, latched, cashed
[zd]		raised, composed, amazed
[d]		judged, charged, forged
[ft]	left, craft, cleft	laughed, stuffed, roughed
[vd]		loved, lived, moved
[nd]	mind, find, mound	rained, fanned, canned
[md]		named, foamed, rammed
[ld]	cold, wild, old	called, smelled, killed
[pt]	apt, adept, inept	mapped, stopped, clapped
[kt]	act, contact, expect	looked, cooked, cracked

*Where there are no examples under Type I and Type II the cluster does not occur under that category.

REFERENCES

Labov, W. *Language in the inner city*. Philadelphia: University of Pennsylvania Press, 1972.

Wolfram, W., & Christian, D. *Appalachian speech*. Arlington, VA.: Center for Applied Linguistics 1976.

Wolfram, W., & Fasold, R. W. *The study of social dialects in American English*. Englewood Cliffs, N.J.: Prentice-Hall, 1974.

Index